A Real Nobody a Fake Somebody and Me

ENDORSEMENTS

'Reading *A Real Nobody a Fake Somebody and Me*, is like reading a letter you can't put down from a best friend, one who is both sharing her story and encouraging you to tell yours as the tale unfolds.' – **Anne Heffron, author of *You Don't Look Adopted* and *To Be Real***

'A compelling, tell-all account of the extraordinary events this young brave woman endured, exposing the truth behind her identity and existence to heal and inspire all.' – **Fiona White, author of *The Wise Woman's Way through Divorce and Beyond***

'Sherry Bridgette is a powerful and much-needed voice for adoptees under the Forced and Closed Adoption laws. Her story is enlightening, thought-provoking, and heart-wrenchingly real.' – **Amy Islip, Psychotherapist and relationship counsellor**

'This truly captivating and powerful memoir encapsulates an inspiring journey to demonstrate that even those who endure the deepest trauma from their past need not be a victim but an empowered creator of their future.' – **Rochelle Weir, conscious creator coach**

'What a pleasure it has been to meet Sherry Bridgette and her personality parts at our Bali Clinical Resource Therapy Training Program. Sherry Bridgette's story and life journey shine forth in these pages. Her kindness, intelligence, and passion for advocacy in the adoption space with lived experience of the failures in our system are a testament to her resilience and intelligence. I have no doubt Sherry will make a difference in many people's lives, on so many levels: personal, professional, and in the wider legislative space globally. Her hard-earned knowledge will inspire transformation. As a therapist I for one learned of the inadequacies of the system and the desperate need for more compassionate care and for adoptees to have a voice. Thanks, Sherry Bridgette, for sharing yours with us!' – **Philipa Thornton, President, Resource Therapy International and CEO, Resource Therapy Institute Australia**

'Human adoption disrupts that sense of an unbroken line. It starts with physical disseverance and proceeds by creating a permanent legal fiction, something instinctively and intrinsically outside normal human experience. This poignant work of Sherry's is an important addition to the growing memoir genre written by those with lived experience of adoption.' – **Barbara Sumner, author of *Tree of Strangers***

'Sherry Bridgette Healey has written a raw, honest testimony of life as an adoptee…all readers – and especially fellow adoptees – can learn from her experiences, as well as the compassionate wisdom and advice she shares.' – **Megan Close Zavala, book editor & CEO, Turn the Page Book Coaching & Editorial**

'Sherry's perspective is intense, gripping, compelling, and deeply authentic. She has brought colour into her own backstory while [also] weaving a protective net that will allow others with their own hidden pasts to bring their own unique stories to light. Sherry's book is a must read for adoptees, their families and loved ones.' – **Maryanne Katsidis, entrepreneur and host of** *Heart-Led Changemakers*

'Sherry Bridgette Healey invites you into the most intimate journey of finding herself, Sherry's enthralling story about forced adoption reveals the deep trauma of lacking secure attachment and identity. She's the voice that encourages you to go within, that offers guidance and empowers you to live a life true to yourself.' – **Anja Stroehlein, clinical psychologist and resource therapist**

'A raw and candid reflection of the adoptee experience. The poignant moments of connection will ripple through the adopted and wow the unexposed.' – **Heather Waters, producer at Waters Productions and adoptee**

'I felt such a deep loss in me, a sadness for all mothers' children that walk this journey of adoption and the need for disclosure of the life lived experience. Acknowledgement to Sherry for her impulse of inner truth [and] her purpose – a journey of knowing, healing evolving self, now supporting many. We receive life from our mother, when this is disrupted, saying yes to life can be a continuing challenge.' – **Susan Altschwager, family constellation trainer and facilitator, author of** *New Story for Humanity*

'An unflinchingly honest and courageous exploration of what it means to be adopted. In sharing her own experiences, Sherry also helps guide other adoptees on their path to healing.' – **Abe Maddison, author of** *Crazy Bastard:* **A** *Memoir of Forced Adoption*

'Sherry Bridgette Healey's memoir really showcases the complexity of adoption trauma. And it is so important for the mental health and adoption communities to hear adoptee voices to understand the impact of adoption as trauma.' – **Scott E. Kazarian, MA, LMFT, author, adoptions therapist, and adoptee**

'Sherry Bridgette Healey's memoir powerfully describes the far-reaching impacts of forced and secret adoption. Using contrasting voices to tell not only her story but in some measure, the story of anyone who has experienced adoption, the reader is expertly guided through the complicated maze of constructing a complete and thriving person who knows their place in the world. From the stability of this place, the writer courageously and confidently recounts the journey from the perspectives of different parts of herself. The account includes segments from 'Coach Charlie' who provides gentle, encouraging and insightful reflective questions to the reader. Anyone who has shared a similar experience will benefit greatly from considering these respectful prompts towards self-knowledge. Highly recommended to assist others who walk a similar path. – **Leanne Hyndman, clinical counsellor**

'Sherry Bridgette Healey has written a truly, frank and inspirational account of her courage and tenacity in the face of extreme adversity. Her retelling of the journey she has undertaken to establish her identity is compelling and speaks to her determination to do so, while overcoming a myriad of personal, interpersonal, and societal barriers. This book not only relates to her personal struggles but also shines a light on the important issues facing others who have been subject to the adoption process in which they, like her, were involuntarily involved. I wholeheartedly recommend this book, as a significant contribution to the promotion of awareness of the way in which identity is central to human flourishing, the pitfalls to its establishment and the triumph of the spirit in overcoming those pitfalls.' – **Christian J. Paulin, B.Sc. psych (Hons) M. psychol, consultant psychologist; advanced clinical resource therapist, senior trainer & supervisor**

'In this well written, pacy memoir, Sherry Bridgette shines a fresh light onto the darkness of forced and closed adoption, melding personal experiences in the voice of different personae with the nitty gritty of rupture, loss and repair. There is courage (and humour) at the edge of despair, liberation through internal and external acceptance and connection. The reader is given many "platforms for reflection" about their own particular experience of universal human themes. As well as a gripping narrative, there are opportunities and invitations towards greater awareness and integration.' – **Vas Ajello, clinical psychologist and teacher, University of Auckland, New Zealand**

A Real Nobody a Fake Somebody and Me

A Memoir of Forced and Closed Adoption

Sherry Bridgette Healey

*For my son – the light of my life, I love you beyond eternity.
You taught me how to love, you taught me how to trust,
and you taught me the true value and meaning of 'family.'*

*To all adoptees of the Forced and Closed Adoption era
– I see you, I hear you, I feel you, I love you.*

Publisher, Copyright, and Additional Information

A Real Nobody A Fake Somebody and Me by Sherry Bridgette Healey

Copyright © 2024 by Sherry Bridgette Healey

All rights reserved. No part of this book may be reproduced or transmitted in any form or by any means, electronic or mechanical, including photocopying, recording, or by any information storage and retrieval system without the written permission of the author, except where permitted by law.

ISBN- 9798338176559 (Paperback)

Editing by Megan Close Zavala, book editor & CEO, Turn the Page Book Coaching & Editorial

Cover design and interior design by CoverKitchen

A NOTE FROM THE AUTHOR: This memoir is based on the author's aggregation of memory. All identities have been changed to protect the privacy of individuals. Any resemblance to actual persons, living or dead, is purely coincidental and unintentional. This memoir reflects the author's personal experiences, perspectives, and opinions. While comparisons and conclusions are drawn from research and the author's understanding, they are subjective interpretations and should not be taken as definitive statements of fact.

CONTENTS

ENDORSEMENTS ... 3

PREFACE ... 17

INTRODUCTION ... 29

PART ONE: A REAL NOBODY ... 35

CHAPTER 1: Kaiyah's Birth Recall ... 37

CHAPTER 2: The Living Room for the Non-Living and the Paint-By-Numbers Kid ... 59

CHAPTER 3: That Grade 1 Teacher Who Got Away ... 71

CHAPTER 4: My Guardian Alien ... 79

CHAPTER 5: If I Could Just Pay You for a Cuddle ... 93

CHAPTER 6: What Ever Happened to Little Sammy? ... 99

CHAPTER 7: Amy and Her Voice Save the Day ... 111

CHAPTER 8: Sam Takes the Plunge ... 125

PART TWO: A FAKE SOMEBODY ... 137

CHAPTER 9: Case Files, Unfiled ... 139

CHAPTER 10: The Day I Met My Mother ... 155

CHAPTER 11: Oh, I Remember Those Eyes! ... 173

CHAPTER 12: In the Name of the Father 191

CHAPTER 13:
So Which Mother Did You Come From, Dear? 207

CHAPTER 14: The Undoing 225

CHAPTER 15: 47 and Rather Discombobulated 241

CHAPTER 16: Love and Other Strange Occurrences 261

PART THREE: ME 285

CHAPTER 17: The Nazi Regime and the Forced
and Closed Adoption Act of 1955 287

CHAPTER 18: I've Never Been to Me 305

CHAPTER 19: Snakes and Ladders
and Somewhere in the Middle 321

CHAPTER 20: Completion 341

CONCLUSION 359

RECOMMENDED READING AND RESOURCES 369

SUPPORT SERVICES 365

ACKNOWLEDGEMENTS 371

SOURCES 375

PREFACE

As soon as I arrived on planet Earth, I was ripped apart from my mother. Severed from her body on my very first breath.

My subconscious likely preverbally wired up one question: what had I done for it to be this bad, to be so unworthy of her love, and to be so unwanted by my family?

Three weeks overdue – how remiss of me. She had tried to abort me as soon as she found out she was pregnant, but it was too far along into that first trimester. So, she took a pill to miscarry me, which did not work either.

Facing these failed attempts to get rid of me, the heartache of the sudden break-up and abandonment by her fiancé (my father), and the shame of disgracing her parents and the family name – it all nearly broke her. She was shipped from the north of the country to the south, hidden away and forced to work as a cleaner to support herself financially, without any other option but to carry me to full term. Inevitably, this all led to her having a nervous breakdown in her third trimester, and my grandmother had to stay and spoon-feed her and read her Walt Disney stories until I was finally on my way out of her body, and out of her life.

'Like a piece of rubber,' is how she later described the sensation of my birth.

The plan was in place – signed off months ago – that she would simply leave me at the hospital. The rules were that she was not to look at me, let alone touch me. I never got to breastfeed the colostrum which would have strengthened my immunity.

I wanted to return to the home I had lived in for nine-plus months – even though it wasn't exactly the Comfort Inn. Here, outside of her, it was all wrong. Dangerous. Cold. Alien.

She gave me the name of Bridgette.

Motherless, I cried for hours on my birthday – my 'death day.' More death days went by, and then a whole week. But no matter how hard I cried and screamed for my mother, she never came back. The drugs (barbiturates) that I was given each day calmed me down, silenced me, and deadened my soul, but they didn't numb the feelings of helplessness, never-ending torment, and shock. (This was set into my belief system for life from that time and until now, and I have never fully recovered from that trauma.)

I wonder when I finally knew she wasn't coming back.

After weeks of surviving annihilation, living in drugged-out desperation, and being tortured with a searing hunger for my mother, the unbearable feelings of grief and loss crushed the lifeforce from my heart and squeezed me, with every shaken breath, into a vice-like grip of terror.

Intuitively, I feel that is when I first left my body. Psychologists call it a 'split' – a dissociation, which can be misdiagnosed as dissociative identity disorder. This is what I was 'diagnosed'

PREFACE

with once, and this misdiagnosis is now listed on my psychological medical history records. I do not have any such 'disorder,' and the psychologist who labelled me with this, admitted during our sessions that she had never worked with adoptees before, let alone adoptees who also endured pain and suffering at the hands of their adoptive parents/family. She told me I was her 'muse,' her little guinea pig to experiment and play with, to gain insight into what happens when an adoption 'goes wrong.'

Of course, being the people pleaser that I was, I didn't object. *Me too*

So now I have a medical record branding me with a false diagnosis – call me crazy, but that makes me feel so psychotic!

Upon further research, I realized that it's no wonder professionals in psychology and psychiatry are not equipped with tailored therapeutic education, insights, or resources. Once again, it is expected (and it is the general narrative in the mental health industry) that adoptees have no such thing as primal wounding, and that we do not experience emotional dysregulation, lack of boundaries, low self-worth, depression, feeling like we are defective or don't belong, deep shame, guilt, anxiety, disenfranchised grief, hypervigilance, relinquishment trauma, and pre-traumatic stress disorders – the list goes on for days. They believe we are born as a 'Clean Slate' to be moulded into another person. But we do experience these feelings in the womb and when our mother leaves us - and we suffer the consequences of the frustrating inability to attach or bond with anyone, any place or any 'thing,' and we are in constant fight, flight or freeze mode. To this day, this research is still disgracefully incomplete, and consequently these injuries are excluded from the DSMV-5 as a psychological injury from such 'lived experience' – which is why the causes for our behaviours are grossly misdiagnosed and consequently left untreated.

Do you know how many serial killers were abandoned as infants and raised in trauma? Most of them. Especially females.

But why would this industry invest in specific training in assisting adoptees when the global cultural narrative is that we should be grateful that we were chosen at all? Why would anyone need to train to assist adoptees if the general understanding is that our adoptive parents saved us, and that we lived happily ever after in our forever home? These are the lies that have blinded everyone to the truth.

Often, we were told to never speak to anyone about the truth, of how we came into 'that' family or how we feel about being adopted. This silencing has been designed to uphold the illusion of the narrative that we are all happy little adoptees! Often, we grow up not ever knowing we were adopted, or we find out much later in our lives.

Governments around the world are still applauding the success of the millions of humans that were adopted out over the past 50 years, still believing – or perhaps convincing themselves – that it was a highly successful social experiment. No need to be accountable for all the mass destruction, suicides, mental health issues, incarcerations, murders, and trauma that ensued. (Yes, in Australia one of the prime ministers apologized to our birth mothers, birth fathers and to us, but I feel it was more of an apology to the birth mothers.)

While writing my book, I have discovered many shocking truths about the entire adoption industry. For example, I found out that less than two percent of the general psychology degree curriculum is dedicated to the exploration of separation trauma/non-attachment, specifically with adoptees in any given psychology degree. The world is also blinded by global cultural ignorance, and misinformation about the impacts of adoption on the adoptee.

The consequences of working with a psychologist uneducated in the myriad ramifications of forced and closed adoptions, meant that me stating that I had experienced several 'personality parts' and could identify who they were – their names, their roles in my life, their characteristics and looks – suddenly meant that I had dissociative identity disorder. All because my therapist was untrained as an expert in the field of adoption wounding AND untrained in resource therapy.

So, as I introduced her to the 'parts' of me, she misdiagnosed me, looked at me wide-eyed and sideways too many times, leaving me believing that indeed I was crazy and making me want to jump out of her so-called therapeutic window. She never recommended any psychiatry or medications; she just labelled me, and it stuck – until I realized what was really going on, and that these were my personality parts and clever resources! I later went on to study resource therapy professionally to gain a deeper insight and to gain the skillset required to assist others to understand their own resourceful parts. If only I had done that sooner, but resource therapy was still a fairly new modality of psychotherapy in psychology around this time of my misdiagnosis in 2016.

Anyway, let's meet these parts of me, my inner family system, my resourceful personality parts – the ones that spun my therapist's head upside down, shall we?

Amy – She is the bubbly cheerleader, the positive, cute, bouncy, girly-girl whom everyone adores. She knows how to cheer people on, and makes excuses for their bad behaviour, and she constantly dehumanizes herself, putting others' feelings first – in an effort to ensure that everybody loves her, she is a total people pleaser. She cheers me, encouraging me to stay in the shallow end and to just keep going when the going gets tough.

Definitely

She is pretty, but not *too* sexy, because she knows women hate that, but she also just can't help being a little sexy. Her mother hated her sexiness and was jealous of the way her adoptive father paid particular attention to Amy as a teenager.

Amy tried so hard to appease her adoptive mother, putting up with her narcissistic, bullying behaviour, and Amy ended up with the same type of boyfriend, friend, partner and employer – just to prove that she could handle it. She helped me to diffuse conflict and avoid pain with my adoptive mother, and she also gave me the resilience I needed to endure workplace bullying and harassment and to focus on the money and status, which obviously was not a great idea. She and Georgiana (whom you will meet next up) are similar – leaving toxic people was extremely difficult for me, as both of them wanted to keep me stuck there.

Amy just wants to belong and to be accepted. She often feels unlovable and unaccepted, and her superpower is the ability to do anything to belong. She can 'read,' anticipating which behaviour to display to fit the mould that others expect of her, no matter the consequences. She doesn't swallow her pain; she simply doesn't register it – and if she does, she immediately runs away from it. Her goal in life is to win people over and make

<u>them love her</u>, especially the toxic, bullying narcissistic ones.

Georgiana – She is the corporate chick, suited and booted and perfectly made up. She makes herself look as best as she possibly can – hair extensions, Botox, nails, and <u>makeup done just to go get groceries.</u> Due to her constant need to be perfect and to look perfect, it is exhausting being Georgiana. Constantly dieting, finding new gyms to join, and incessant online shopping – always buying more shoes. She is afraid of aging and will do anything she can to look younger and skinnier. She watches her calories and starves herself – she hates her body and face.

She is highly accomplished, but she feels she needs to constantly uplevel and upskill, even though she is way over-qualified for what it is that she wants to do. <u>She is spiritual but has a closed heart</u>, which makes others in the spiritual world wary of her. She just wants to be the best and to be perfect. In order to be accepted and to gain approval, her superpower is 'I need to be capable and prepared, and to show no cracks or defaults.' She is, as I mentioned before, similar to Amy, but she is even more focused on her appearance and how she comes across to others. She wants to appear intelligent, well-studied, articulate, well-mannered, graceful, and accomplished and this is because she doesn't feel capable enough.

She hopes to attract the perfect man, and she will do anything to ensure she is ready for him when he crosses her path. It is all about planning, prepping, and perfection for the future.

She ignores the past as she doesn't want anyone to know about her past experiences or her weaknesses and faults. Her energy is often powerful – you know when she is in the room.

This intimidates people sometimes, which is not Georgiana's intention at all. Maintaining this high-voltage energy is extremely exhausting, so she does splurge on things like retreats, massages, and travel. She isolates to replenish herself before she heads out to blow the world away again.

Sam – She is the protector/guardian of us all. Sam is tough and very angry at the world, and if you hurt any of us look out, because Sam is coming for you. To say she holds a grudge is an understatement. She swallows her pain with alcohol and smokes to dissipate her anger, secretly waiting for the right moment to pounce in revenge. She is often described as 'a mean bitch' when she drinks too much, and we all agree – she can be vile. She acts out the hatred spilled onto her and conditioned into her from her adoptive mother's self-hatred. She will push you away. Sometimes she even puts herself in danger – she has been known to walk barefoot through busy traffic and not give a fuck. (Sorry, that's Sam speaking, not me.) If you ever cross her – she will come for you. She can forgive, but only after she attacks you – and even then, she will never forget what you did.

She is a butch, heavy-set lesbian type but isn't a lesbian; she just looks that way, and she likes both men and women. She has the patience of an oak seed growing into an oak tree, and she is highly intuitive, courageous, brave, calculating, and physically strong. She has high levels of resilience, and she does not suffer fools like Amy and Georgiana do, but they can overpower her when it's two against one.

She has the confidence, self-esteem, and courage of a whole village. She doesn't care if you don't like her – she loves herself just the way she is, and she doesn't need your approval. She really doesn't like people in general, except for her son and a few friends – in fact, she prefers animals.

Sam has saved my life when I have been in potentially dangerous situations. Her superpower is 'I am not safe, and it is not safe to be here, so I will protect and be on guard.' She has a suit of armour on and her sword at the ready. A true Warrior. She is so happy I am writing this book, and she gives me wine to cope with the difficult parts of my recount. I really love Sam – she just needs to feel that love and to be open to it, to know that it is safe to be loved and to feel what it is like to love someone. Her scars – from the womb and birth and life in the 'dysfunctional adoption house' – run so deep. I doubt she will ever fully recover and be completely open to love, but I do know that writing this book is helping her heal.

Kaiyah – Talk about a change of character here! Kaiyah is the peaceful, spiritual, warrior woman and Shaman. Botox- and make-up-free, she only uses natural products. She is a vegetarian, and very slim, toned, and tanned. She wears hemp clothing and crystals and has feathers in her hair – you get the picture.

She sponsors charities and not-for-profit organizations. She offers free coaching and readings wherever and whenever possible, which really pisses Georgiana off, of course, because Georgiana loves to make money and invest. Kaiyah earns an income as a Reiki Healer, workshop facilitator, psychic intuitive, and coach to support herself and her donations.

She is all about the heart, and she is more into giving than receiving. She has so much love to offer to others, and she loves to facilitate workshops on anything to do with enlightenment, past lives, numerology, sacred laws, and spiritual development. She is highly intuitive, and she loves to do readings and coach others to reach their highest potentials.

She tends to suffer from bouts of anxiety and depression, and she is very insecure about herself. She needs to feel she is in control of her environment, and she avoids stepping out of her comfort zone. She doesn't discuss her adoption openly, as she prefers to keep this part of herself safe, protected, and silent. It is a part of her that she feels will not be understood or accepted as it is not the perfect persona she prefers to project to the world and those around her. Nevertheless, Kaiyah loves to look as if she is a free spirit, and she would just love to live in a caravan by a peaceful river, preferably in a commune, so she could do yoga and reiki self-healing, meditate on a rock, and live off the land.

Kaiyah views her adoption as a gift to balance the scales of her karmic past, as if the adoption wounding is clearing her karmic debts of many, many lifetimes. She sees herself and other adoptees as enlightened little buddhas – even stronger than the Buddha, because we have come in without attachment right from the start without the 'mother bonding'!

What we like about her is that she is very healthy and loves massages, meditation, and relaxation – she is so calm and stress-free that she floats through life; she is not really 'in the body and of this world.'

Kaiyah's superpower is that she can forgive what has happened to her and that she is focused on healing any karmic ties and learning her karmic lessons in this lifetime. She really doesn't need to feel she belongs here in order to happily co-exist on planet Earth. She has an affinity with the spirit world and has the ability to bring this understanding of the soul level realms back down to us. She also yearns to return to the life beyond and would prefer to never have to incarnate back here again so she ensures she is not creating further karma for herself.

Ultimately, she is focused on being good and perfect, but she never feels good or perfect enough. She makes sure to act in kindness, spreading the love wherever she goes. She wants to be a good person and make a difference in people's lives whilst she is here.

Coach Charlie – The Superconscious Creator, and another Shaman as well! He is the only one who understands us all – he knows where our belief systems come from, where they lead us, and why. He understands each of our identity dysfunctional tendencies, and he simply reminds us of our greatness, guiding us back into our bubble of genius. He teaches us all about becoming superconscious, living as a magnetically-aligned creator – to have the lives we love, and to have health and vitality. He teaches us that to integrate so we can live as our true nature, find our true purpose, and to be the predominant creator in our lives, we need to be a whole person.

Coach Charlie has a balanced life – he likes a drink, to work out, to look as best as he can, and to muck about, and he has such a huge heart and is quite the eccentric. He makes people laugh and cry with his love and awareness. He has so many books inside of him to write, and this is the first of many. He showed us that to write this book will finally give us the closure we are ready to receive from our past, finally allowing us to integrate all our parts into the whole circle of us, and to become the person we were born to be.

Coach Charlie has guided us to finally tell our stories. We all love Coach Charlie; he is knowledgeable, wise, intelligent, and intuitive, while also being funny, silly, and playful like a child. Coach Charlie is helping us help you, through sharing his insights and coaching after each chapter. He is also helping me to launch my new business as an author, a transformational coach, resource therapist, writing mentor, intuitive reader, and teacher.

And I am Bridgette – I am the sum of my parts, the whole person forged from the fragments of my personality. An authentic, sovereign being, forced by government decree to adopt an identity that was completely fake because my original identity was mandated to die. I am the little baby girl, stripped of her life, existing only as a ghost to weave within these fractured parts. Coach Charlie resurrected me, bringing me back to my own skin, but I felt like a real nobody, living as a fake somebody.

I had yet to meet the wise woman, the shaman within, who is Sherry Bridgette Healey. She is my true self, the essence of who I am. The collective soul identity of us all. The one who remembered us, and who took the time to listen to the stories of our past and found the courage to write them down.

INTRODUCTION

Gabor Mate says trauma – from the Greek word for 'wound' – is not what happens to you; it is what happens *inside you as a result of what happens to you*. As I mentioned earlier, it wasn't until I was writing this book that I discovered that I wasn't split – I had parts of me that were resources I have developed to help me cope with trauma; they have helped me to survive. I realized that my five personality parts retained information on pivotal events from my past and had specific ways of coping with that stress – you will see what I mean as you read each chapter.

We all have our personality parts, and I believe that it is rather genius of us to create these parts to deal with trauma we have experienced along our lifetime. They help us to avoid any further damage by recognizing the signposts. As Coach Charlie says, 'Our parts are our dysfunctional belief systems of what we think is our identity. They are just strategies – not our greatness.' Studies have shown these parts are created from our unconscious conditioning, starting from the womb, and evolving until around the age of eight. They become strategies for coping and avoiding further pain/fear/hurt. They are hypervigilant in their protectiveness and guardianship to ensure that we survive better the *next time* we are experiencing this. For example, Sam's role was to protect me from feeling bullied and hurt, because she believed early on that if you are vulnerable and needy, you will be harmed. Sam must protect and fight back, and Amy's role has been to avoid pain and pretend that everything is wonderful on the outside, running away from herself when the wheels started to fall off. She believes that it is safer to not feel anything but positivity, and then all will be well in her world.

As I, Bridgette, had suffered the serious trauma of abandonment as well as non-attachment and non-bonding with my mother at birth, I was suffering from pre-trauma. It was pre-trauma – not PTSD – as there was nothing for me to return to, unlike post-traumatic stress, which happens later in life. I was stuck there. Nancy Verrier, in her book, *Primal Wound*, implies that this type of torture is more traumatic than being a war veteran – I can only comment from my personal experience as an adoptee raised in a toxic adopted family.

These parts of me took over, to help me to cope with the fact that my mother didn't want me. That I was unwanted, that I didn't exist, that she didn't love me and was never coming back for me. As I was handed around to strangers until being placed as a 'ward of the state' in a stranger's home, to be rebranded and raised as if I were their own, and to be abused by my adoptive mother - these parts helped me to survive. I had to live as if I was epigenetically enmeshed in my new family's DNA – which is obviously impossible – and these parts helped me cope with that, as well as the future family dysfunctions and entanglements I was subjected to, both in my adoptive family and my birth families.

I was a motherless child whose natural-born life was literally wiped off the face of the earth. What I mean by that is that when we go through a forced and closed adoption, our real identity – who we are at birth, our birth name and birth parents – are wiped clean, and our original birth certificate is locked in a vault, often never to be seen again. <u>We are then issued with a new birth certificate, with a new name and new parents</u>. We go from being a 'Real Nobody' to becoming a 'Fake Somebody,' and we <u>spend the rest of our lives trying to find out who the 'me' part really is</u> – hence the name of the book!

✳ ✳ ✳

So, I lived as a ghost inside of my body, with a fake name purchased by a fake family and rebranded as if I were their own biological child. One day, many years later, 'they' – my famous five parts – all found me. These five parts of me discovered the truth of who 'we' really were on my 18th birthday, when they found me inside of a manilla folder that had been locked away in my parents' study all that time, finally handed to me by my adoptive mother. I remember sensing that it was both an act of generosity and a burden lifted off of her at the same time – it was always about her, of course.

Each personality part I created will recount parts of my life to you, and Coach Charlie will interject at the end of the chapters with coaching, guidance, resources, self-reflection questions, and healing messages.

You have now already met each of them, but you will get to know them further as they share their specific memories and events. **Kaiyah** will speak of events from when she stepped into the womb, her pivotal spiritual experiences and beliefs and her search for her family. In Chapters 1, 10 and 11, she talks about her rebirthing experience, how she met her birth mother and maternal grandparents. She also shares her views on her spiritual beliefs around the karma of being adopted.

Then in Chapters 2, 3, 4, 5 and 9, **Georgiana** will share her experiences of her resilience and her need to be perfect in order to be loved. She also discusses her insatiable need to feel more capable in all areas of her life, a way of living she stepped into from around three years of age. Georgiana talks about when she was first told she was adopted, the abuse by her adoptive mother, teacher and aliens, and how this played out in her adult life.

Next, **Sam** will share from the time she stepped in – at around seven years of age – to intimidate and derail others from ever getting close enough to hurt her and the consequences that ensued. In Chapters 6, 8, 14 and 15, Sam reveals when she shut her feelings down, her plan to murder her adoptive mother, and a voice in her head that controlled and moulded her. She discusses the times she felt she could 'be real,' and her natural gravitation toward being the protector and guardian, and her compulsion to never let others in, mainly for their own safety.

Amy stepped in around the age of 10, and she will speak about her people-pleasing patterns and the self-sacrifices she made to be accepted and to keep herself safe. You will hear her perspective in Chapters 7, 12, 13 and 16, in which she will detail how she always looks for the silver lining in any challenge, and how she steps into her genius self to seek out a solution when life becomes too difficult. She shares about finding her birth father and their subsequent dysfunctional relationship, as well as how she handled his sexualization towards her. She speaks about genetic sexual attraction and the implications on her life, as well as her preference to live in the shallow end of all relationships, in the interest of self-preservation.

Coach Charlie stepped in when I was around 10, and he 'came out' in my early 50s to help me blossom fully into life in order to write this book and give me the superconscious edge I was searching for all my life. Coach Charlie shares insights, research, coaching, fun transformational exercises, and loving guidance at the end of each chapter.

And, finally, **Bridgette** – yours truly, born as Bridgette, then forced to disappear by her family and the Government of New Zealand. Living beyond the grave, I was called back into the scene at 18 years of age, when 'we' saw my name on my original birth certificate. The wise one, aware and introspective, I share my voice in Chapters 2, 9, 17, 18, 19 and 20. I talk about living a life trapped inside a fake family, with a fake name, on a fake family tree, and the impacts and insights of not belonging anywhere as my true self. I speak about the damage my adoption has created, and its implications on my neurological development, as well as how it compromised my ability to trust and love myself and others. I will bare my soul with you and share the truth of my adoption – the good, the bad and the ugly. I also relay my research on the history of adoption and the connections to the

Nazi regime. I will share my elixir for self-healing and growth from not belonging – of not having a sense of self, or an identity – and how this impacts everybody, not just adoptees.

In conclusion, we all collaborate for the final chapter where we further explore the wonderful world of resource therapy and how it enabled me to appreciate how my personality parts were an ingenious resource I created to deal with life's challenges – conflicted with each other and, at times, becoming pathological.

I identify as Sherry Bridgette Healey – the narrator, the author, and the girl on that piece of paper. I am the whole of all the personality parts, the main personality. They are me, in all their glorious dysfunction and function. I am Sherry Bridgette Healey – the sum of all my parts.

I had already been through so much by the age of 18, when the parts of me finally met the girl who was stolen and kept as a secret – locked away in a cupboard but buried beneath all life. And my parts still help me out, each playing their support role until I take over in the still rare times when I feel safe and strong enough to do so. Together, we will share with you the experience of abandonment, adoption, survival, and the victory of reclaiming a life lost.

PART ONE

A REAL NOBODY

CHAPTER 1

Kaiyah's Birth Recall

(Kaiyah)

'Push! Push! That's it. Push! Goooooooooood.'

As I was being pushed through a tight but stretchy, slippery tube of rainbow colours, I was suddenly blinded by white light. I flew out over the edge and landed into cold, rubber-gloved hands. I don't know why but my body felt like a piece of rubber.

'Noooooooooooo! No. No. NO!' I cried. 'Put me back immediately!'

The air was so cold, stinging my lungs. The room was too bright, too noisy. It is so cold. Wait – where's my mother? Why do I smell chlorine and not her skin? Who are you, and where are you taking me? Stop! Ouch!

The blanket made my skin itch. I couldn't move. I felt too hot. I felt sick. I was hungry. I was scared.

I screamed hysterically for my mother to comfort me, but she wasn't there. This isn't right – don't touch me, stranger! I want my mummy. Where is she? Help!

I felt my blood pumping through me then. Warmth. Blurred vision. Noise softly muted. I suddenly felt sleepy, warm, and buzzy and fuzzy. I slept. I woke up. In a plastic container. Alone. There were many babies, lined up and wrapped up. Different people wiped me, fed me, changed me, and hugged me. I cried again for HER. I miss her heartbeat, her smell, her - everything. Surely, she is coming back for me?

Medicine time. Sleep time. Sobbed hysterically, wailed until I knew she wasn't coming back. I was numb. Give me more of those drugs. I need help here. Help me!

'Help! I WANT MY MOTHER!' *I screamed, which was a little disruptive for the rebirthers in the cozy classroom, on day two of a weekend rebirthing workshop.*

But I wasn't in that room – I was in the nursery room for orphans. I spiralled back down fast along the umbilical cord and landed back into the room in the arms of my rebirther person – rebirth over.

'Fuck – I am NEVER doing that again.' *I said to myself.*

'Fuck, this girl is mental.' *Said my rebirthing partner, accidentally out loud.*

✳ ✳ ✳

That was fifteen years ago, when I was running my own coaching, intuitive reading and energetic healing practice, and had just finished training to be a Reiki Master. One day, I offered to give an introductory healing and counselling session to a new client, Geoff, who told me he was a rebirthing therapist, specialising in healing the primal pain and trauma of birth. He had come to see me for help in dealing with his divorce acceptance and closure.

After completing my session with Geoff, I was curious to find out more about rebirthing as it sounded intriguing.

'Well, why don't you come along this weekend and find out?' he asked.

Being the spontaneous type, and always up for learning, I didn't even check my calendar – I was all in. Afterall, it was the Universe telling me I must now be ready for something big because a new teacher had appeared!

Let's return to my memory of when I returned into the reluctant arms of my rebirther...

The sunlit, overly warm workshop room was filled with people still in their pairs; one was crying, even howling, and the other was soothing them. Multiply this by 12 pairs of people, and it was just so terrifyingly noisy. You could even smell the adrenaline pulsating around the room. I thanked my partner awkwardly, grabbed my water bottle, and hastily slipped out the door – I really needed some air. And a stiff drink.

Breathe. Be still now. You are safe. Breathe in the sunshine, the Warmth. Look at the pale blue skies. Listen to the quiet of the leaves bristling in the trees. Feel the warm air swirling around your face. Feel your feet on the ground. Say: 'I am calm, calmer; I am calm. Grounding, grounding, I am grounded in my body. I am calm and I am safe. I am here in my body. I am safe.'

After working through this little mindfulness self-guided meditation, I decided I'd better get back in there. *I can do this*, I told myself. I peeked through the door window. It seemed like they were having a debriefing – gingerly, I snuck back in and found my cushion patiently waiting for me in the group circle.

Soon it was my time to share. *I hate this. I cannot do this; I am not ready to do this, to share. Their mothers probably kept them.* To stay safe, perfect, and silent, I just focused on speaking about what I observed. I didn't share about the rubber body thing, or that my mother left me straight away. *The talking stick can get stuffed.*

'Yeah, so overall, it was quite the cathartic experience, right? Just, wow! Wow! Thanks so much, Geoff!' I handed the talking stick over like a hot potato, and then I phased out from the group. I was lost in space, floating, and detached. *So much for my mindfulness practice...*

I heard Geoff's voice in the distance, finally wrapping up the weekend. 'OK guys, thank you all so much for coming and for showing up for your birth. Again!'

People seemed to want to leave on time today – the energy in the room felt thick and heavy, and the comforts of home or the pub were calling.

Unfortunately, I caught Geoff's eye as I darted for the door.

'Geoff, I thank you for this experience,' I said again. 'It really was just sooooo great. Let's catch up for a coffee soon, OK? Namaste!' *Isn't that what we all say for such farewells?*

Two days of this and now I desperately needed to reach the bottom of a bottle or two. I was exhausted; Sam was stepping in, and I was happy for her to take over for a bit. I was worn out – not from the course itself, but from all the people around me, all the pretending to care, all the deep sharing, and of course from all the noises of adults being 'birthed' in that room today. I'd had enough; I just had to go. Right then. I turned to go. *Headache. Panic attack. Wine. Needed. Now.* I didn't really connect it all to the

CHAPTER 1

fact that I was just 'there' at my birth.

'Bridgette, wait!' Geoff gently turned me to face him. 'Hey, Bridgette, how are you doing? I mean, how are you, really? You seemed to have released something from what you shared today, but I can see something bigger is still going on behind those eyes.'

Oh Geoff, you bloody insightful thing, you. I conjured up the sweetest smile and lunged in for a quick farewell hug, hoping to distract him enough so that I could just escape.

He held me halfway and locked my eyes with his. 'Whoa, hold on there. I...I can see it. I wondered what it was.' He was now looking directly into my soul – and I didn't let anyone go there. 'Bridgette, yesterday you were a distant mountain of solid rock and up close I see you are now like an angry, seething volcano. I can't let you go out the door yet because I fear that you may well erupt! Please stay. I need to make sure you are OK. *Really* OK.'

I AM OK! I wanted to yell at him. *Piss off and mind your own bloody business, Geoff.*

'Honestly, hun, I am fine.' *And we all know what that really means...*

Geoff looked worried; I had never seen his frown lines run so deep before. *What was I thinking, coming here?* Sam was in my head. 'Of course, this would expose everything I've worked so hard to cover up, from everyone, including myself. I am better than this – how could I have been so stupid and completely vulnerable like this? My hard work and my whole cover – blown!'

You, Bridgette, are meant to be the enlightened one, the coach who has healed her own pain in order to heal others. You are not supposed to have any cracks in your demureness and overall demeanour.

41

Your own little witness protection program has been obliterated in one weekend. Well, that's just great! See what happens when Kaiyah takes the wheel?'

Geoff gestured for me to sit with him, bringing me back, and then he continued with saying: 'Most people complete this weekend and leave with a little more light in their aura from the massive realizations and shifts of clearing the unconscious egoic agendas. This naturally happens through the birth recall and birth release.'

He took a deep breath and shook his head whilst he said, 'But you – you seem to be surrounded with dark clouds of...of doom and heaviness and...and now I see even more of that seething, raging fire in you right now! I feel very worried about you. Do you have someone you can see professionally tomorrow...or to talk to now? God, Bridgette, I am just really concerned.' He scratched the back of his head, looked out the window, 'Shit, what have I done...I am sorry about this.' Looking forlorn, he lamented now, softening his gaze.

Who was he looking at? Goodness, I felt for him; this isn't his fault, and I could see that he truly cared! My thoughts were racing – *should I just tell him I was adopted, and that revisiting my day of birth and the pain I had endured was probably not the best idea and this is probably why I felt totally triggered?* He deserves to know. I would have to break my vow of silence about my adoption and that is a big deal for me. He would then be the second therapist to know what happened to me.

I reasoned that I could tell him to help him understand what he was intuiting. I could then reassure him that I would line up specific help for myself this week with my spiritual counsellor.

CHAPTER 1

<u>I wanted him to feel better</u> – <u>the rescuer in me, always.</u>

Take a breath, Bridgette. We are already in too deep. Here goes nothing. Just take it nice and slow...

'Geoff it's not your fault. I had an amazing weekend but there's something you need to know. When I was born, I was immediately and permanently separated from my mother, right at birth. Forever. I was an orphan, then I was placed into foster care with a married couple and then they legally adopted me when I was nine months old. I was raised to never tell anyone I wasn't theirs.'

'This family was nuts,' I blurted. 'I was subjected to psychological abuse. I had to obey or suffer, and, in hindsight, I did both. I can deal with it, and I have a counsellor if the wheels go wobbly, but I don't talk about it to anyone else. And I have concluded why all of that happened to me, from my soul's perspective: I believe I chose this for my own soul's evolution, and that gives me peace. That is my theory.'

His face said it all – he seemed relieved to know that it wasn't his fault I seemed...well... a little screwed up.

'What you see now are remnants of my egoic pained self – the one that *isn't* so enlightened. The one who forgets and gets caught up in the drama of it all. I just need to come back to my theory – and book up my calendar with clients next week to distract myself – and then all this pain disappears. I will share more of this theory with you, so you know that I am OK, if you like?' I hoped I had conveyed an air of calm, but little did Geoff know, my palms were as sweaty as a fat man in a sauna and the contents of my lunch were now stuck in my throat.

'Oh Bridgette! I am so sorry! I didn't know you were *ad-*

opted!' He portrayed that it was something he felt responsible for or that I should have told him up front – it is very common to receive this reaction from others, like I am an imposter or something to feel sorry for. I didn't share this, but I've always felt that way in my soul.

He went on to tell me he really did want to know about my spiritual views on adoption – he had never talked openly like this with someone who had been adopted, and he wanted to learn. He thanked me for opening up like this to him.

I explained that even though I had great comfort from my spiritual insight, the mountain he could see was obviously still there. To live invisibly on the outside of myself, I had grown up lost inside of it; it was a part of me. Now he had seen the two of me, the stoic or erupting mountain of me and the peaceful detached me. I had grown to live as both, and I had done a lot of work on myself (so I thought), and I told him that I may have been triggered from this weekend (you think?). The noise, the intensity, the deep conversations about myself, being in a strange environment – just a few of the things I preferred to avoid at all costs.

And I *really* needed a drink. 'Ah, shall we head off to the pub to talk?' I asked, hoping he would say yes. But there was no need – he had a stash of booze in the cupboard that he was going to offer to the class, to celebrate the workshop wins, but everyone had scurried away too fast. So, he cracked open a bottle of red wine and we made a toast. I gratefully sipped away, savouring the familiar warmth of it, trying not to gulp it down.

Pen and paper in his hand, he looked more than ready for me to begin. And the dammed-up words started to flow...it

CHAPTER 1

feels like a surge of bolting wild horses had been set free when I am presented with such a rare opportunity like this. Only my spiritual counsellor had given me that opportunity before. Kaiyah was just warming up here – she loves to talk about her thoughts on the matter...

'There is an inner peace I can usually anchor to, whenever I get lost at sea from being triggered about my adoption,' I began. 'I just consciously remind myself of my belief and theory that all abandoned babies are really 'Enlightened Beings,' we, the abandoned and adopted ones, are old and advanced souls.

We are just like the Buddha; except he, Prince Gautama, was 29 years old when he electively removed himself from his family and the comforts of his palace and sat under the Bodhi Tree until he reached enlightenment. He *chose* to be completely separated and removed from his family, detached from his possessions and the luxurious world he was born into. He went on a spiritual quest to begin and sustain an ascetic life with the aim of achieving enlightenment, to which he did. Buddha teaches us that to find enlightenment, we are to detach from people, worldly possessions, from any desires and emotional attachments. In non-attachment, we will find unity and we will become a spiritual master like Buddha - free of attachment.'

Geoff was either extremely engrossed in his handwriting skills or he was avoiding all eye contact; I couldn't tell. I noticed the whirring of the air conditioner as it had kicked in and felt a slight relief in knowing that it must just be the room temperature that was making the back of my neck sweat. Filled with trepidation, I continued.

'We adoptees were detached immediately from our family

at birth, separated from our mother and detached from our birthright and cut off from our family tree. *Detached forcefully – not electively like the Buddha.* We are to be like lone wolf cubs, surviving in a world full of strangers and predators. Even if we wanted to attach, we only would be able to connect to others from our wounded selves, leading to destructive relationships. And this is because of the unbearable loss of the forced and permanent detachment from our mother at birth.

Detachment from her was like a death without a funeral, without the grieving of permanent loss. Loss for us both. Total disenfranchised grief. But we were merely babies, already buried but alive in our lives to survive in our forever wounded, broken-hearted, bleeding, and dying soul, ultimately unable to attach to anyone or anything. Buddha *chose* to detach; he had his birth mother, his birth father, his entire birth family, his wealth, and entire lineage and his inheritance. He had his epigenetic identity. He left everything. We had nothing to begin with.

I caught my breath and snuck in a quick glance at Geoff. He was head down in his notebook, scribbling what appeared to be trees. Maybe this is all a little too much for a non-adoptee to take in. 'You all good over there?' I asked, looking at him sideways, my eyebrows raised along with my voice.

He looked a little embarrassed, 'Yes, yes of course, I am just processing and listening, listening and processing – please keep going.' I was a little miffed that he wasn't taking notes but decided to continue.

'I believe that we adoptees chose to detach, we immediately did so without ever attaching to anything other than our mother's body. Throughout my spiritual searching and reasoning,

CHAPTER 1

the question I have asked myself often has been, 'Why would I choose this? Why? Was I a bad person in a past life? Is this my Karma? Did I do this to my own child in a previous lifetime? You get what I mean, right, Geoff?'

Geoff was now lying down on the cushions, but he sat up and nodded at me as a yes to continue. 'Most of us are left ill-equipped to form healthy attachments to others, due to the lost opportunity to connect and bond with our first true love: our mother. But even in the warmth and security of the womb, being fed and given what we needed whilst there, we were often under attack from the energy of her thoughts and feelings of not ever being wanted by her.

Some of us were subjected to her swallowing poison to kill us off, or suffering her mental breakdowns, chronic depression, and self-loathing, and some even knew of her plans to abort us. The shame was always placed on us, as we were too far gone in the trimester. We were in the way – even before birth we felt completely unloved, unwanted, guilty, ashamed, and unworthy – simply not good enough, like a 'thing' that shouldn't exist.'

I suddenly felt like having a cigarette, even though I had given them up months ago. Was it the wine or the weekend I was having? I am pretty sure it wasn't just either of them – this is why I prefer not to talk about my adoption and my theories. That is Sam coming through to protect me and numb me out; that's what she does.

'All OK, Bridgette?' Geoff enquired. I composed myself and continued.

Kaiyah was now fully charged – and she relishes being in the naked spotlight on the stage in front of a captivated audience speaking about her adoption theories. 'Yes, I am OK, just so much I want to tell you now that the floodgates have opened. So, Nancy Verrier, in her book *Primal Wound*, says we just *know* that we don't belong here, inside of our birth mothers, and we don't belong 'there' – at that place outside of the womb. We don't belong anywhere, and we are forcibly detached before we need to do it to ourselves.'

Detachment. I had pins and needles, reminding me I am in this body. I needed to stretch and move – I did a deep downward dog and exhaled out, slowly. Then I sat back down and reached for my glass. *Sam loves to distract.*

'Geoff, could I have some more, please? Are you still taking notes?' I had the feeling he had been watching me for quite some time – in between his scribbling of trees.

'Well, I hope you don't mind,' he said, 'but I decided to record you on voice memo – easier for me to be present with you and listen. I want to write this all up later to use as a new teaching segment, as a case study in adoption, if that's OK with you?'

I felt bad for being miffed at him before, and nodded an overly enthusiastic 'yes,' then Geoff continued: 'I have been totally remiss not including this in my teachings – I don't think I have ever had any adopted people attend my rebirthing weekends. I never even thought to ask! Is that a complete oversight? Nobody has ever once told me they were adopted!'

He looked hard at me for my response. I was too busy gulping down my wine and getting more comfortable, settling amongst the softness of the cushions whilst I was thinking of telling him the many reasons why we usually don't talk about this. It could be because we are in denial, we took a vow of silence, we were threatened, or we simply don't know that we are adopted, or we don't think it is of any consequence. So many of us are in any of those places. Sometimes I wished I was still there in the not knowingness or 'not giving a stuff about it.' But you can never unlearn once you learn.

'Don't be too hard on yourself Geoff,' I continued. 'Better late than never to incorporate this into your rebirthing weekends! I think it's so important that you do! Shall we continue?'

We both gave each other a deep smile, raised up our glasses and off I went. 'As a fetus, we detach in utero from her – our birth mother – and from our self. Then we detach again, after birth, from the separation of the world of her body. Her skin. Her smell. Her voice. Our everything. We detach even further after we realize that no matter how hard we cry and scream for our mother to come back for us, she never does, and she never will.'

Despair. Detachment. Dissociation. Trauma. Denial. The adoption wrecking ball.

'We often suffer from scoliosis, stomach issues, lung congestion issues, asthma, sinus, compromised immunity and, of course, a multitude of psychological issues.

The nurses give us barbiturates to calm us down, so we detach again, now into a drug-induced state. Deeper and deeper we fall out of the atmosphere, detaching inside our fear when we start to realize that if we were not wanted, then she is never coming back to get us. We deny this – remember, we are grieving. When we wail and scream out our denial, we are sedated until we are exhausted, and then we disappear from ourselves. Just like everyone else wants us to do – to just disappear.'

Geoff exclaimed excitedly but with sincerity, 'Oh wow! This

explanation is so similar with certain clients of mine who were prem babies or who suffered complications during their mother's pregnancy and then after being born – left in an incubator! They have recalled similar issues! I am finally understanding this phenomenon!'

'Yes, I would imagine they do,' I said, 'and this is just as important to address. But for us adoptees or for babies whose mother has died during childbirth – we are motherless.

One day, and it may be weeks later, we finally realize the cold hard truth: she is literally *never* coming back. We have no choice then but to detach even further – now from our own wants and needs. Now we are in a state of learned helplessness. We are full of cortisol, because we have never experienced the joy of endorphins as loved babies do. We are also in separation trauma, and studies also show that this affects us psychologically, and that there is also physiological organic damage to the brain. We have now learned another detachment, doing so to 'control and protect' what remains left of our sanity. Now we only have one goal: to survive this hell, or to get out.' *Detachment. To the maximum!*

'If we believe we chose this path of detachment for ourselves *before* we were born, then we believe we created this situation – our soul chose this for us. More wine, Geoffrey, please!'

He filled our glasses, and we sat in silence for a bit. 'But what if people aren't as spiritually inclined like you are?' he asked. 'What would you say to those particular adopted people as to why this happened to them and not to somebody else?'

'Well, yes, good question. I would say that alternatively, if we don't believe in any such nonsense, then we can put it all down

CHAPTER 1

to a rather very unfortunate event! Our separation from our mother, our entire family of origin, and our legal birthright – severed from our entire sovereignty – was just due to a random circumstance that happened to us. It happened for no other reason than that – two people had sex, got pregnant, and didn't want us. Or perhaps they were forced to give us away.' I went on to share with Geoff that in my case, my parents were engaged, got pregnant, broke up before realizing they were pregnant with me and then my mother was forced by my grandparents to give me away. My father had offered no support whatsoever and my mother couldn't afford to keep me.

'Bridgette, people are going to ask why the hell they would choose this, let alone how they created this choice in the first place? They would feel that to imply such a thing, that they had a hand in it – would seem ludicrous!'

Geoff was bang on there – it did seem ludicrous alright. So, I went in with the big guns next: 'Totally. But what if we really *did* choose this? Before my 'enlightenment aha,' I asked myself time and time again, *why in the hell would we plan such an undertaking to undo ourselves in the very beginning of life, let alone right to the end?* There must be some big payoff for us in the end – like winning the lotto or something, surely! Or was it instead, some kind of evil curse from a...a...warlock? A curse found in the black book of 'forced detachment' spells for humans?' I got the giggles. 'Wine please!'

As he filled my glass, he looked at me sideways like I had seriously gone bonkers. 'Or shall we just put it down to bad karma? Or maybe, just maybe, could it be that because we are so enlightened, we wanted to ensure we stay free of attachment right from the beginning of this lifetime, unto the end? Wouldn't life inevitably be easier to get through that way, Geoff?'

He was staring out the window, as if in a trance. 'Geoff?'

He finally replied: 'Yeah, yeah. You've really got me thinking.' He stood up and stretched slowly. Then started to clean his reading glasses. I waited for him to top up our wine.

I was just getting to the juicy bits now. 'In any case, Geoff, the adopted people of the 'forced and closed adoption' era between 1940 and 1985 were separated right at birth from their mother and cut off from their families. It happened to over 200,000 babies in Australia and over 100,000 in New Zealand. One in 15 people in Australia are affected by this legacy adoption left behind! One in 15!

What if we could help adoptees find some inner peace about what happened? What if we could make our own choices now around what happened to us? We don't belong to any family tree, but what if we could choose to belong to Buddha's Bodhi Tree if we wanted to? Make up our own tree. What if we could choose the 'higher path' and not give ourselves any permission to be a victim anymore!'

Geoff's eyes looked glazed over – was it me, or was it the wine? *Me and my 'what ifs' again...* He was back to his notebook, but this time he was frantically making notes. Not a time for questions.

I persevered: 'OK. Maybe, we could just choose to feel empowered for once. The enlightened ones would say yes, we chose this, to stop pointing the finger at everyone else! They would say we chose this to balance the scales of karma, because maybe you did this to your own baby. Or your birth mother was once the child that you abandoned in a previous lifetime!'

'Gosh, that's a bit harsh.' Geoff's look told me he wasn't convinced.

I pushed on. 'Yes, it is very harsh. But that's what some people believe about reincarnation. Maybe they would say that we are just born enlightened, but you can be sure that they would say 'it' wasn't a random event that was 'done' to us. They would say every soul makes a choice before incarnating here, returning to ultimately reach ascension in this lifetime. If I look at it another way, my soul chose not to be loved by my biological parents, not to be loved by my adoptive parents, and to feel unloved in general. Why? So, I could learn self-love, self-worth, and self-respect. To learn to love myself without being loved by anyone else. That is honestly what I choose to believe – it diffuses my anger, makes me feel better about the whole thing after walking blindly in thick fog for most of my life. Maybe it is my way of finding acceptance.'

I had finished glass number three and prayed he had more wine here. I stood up and did a walk around the room with some deep breaths in and out. I was feeling very centred within myself and my craving for a cigarette had dissipated, thank God.

'Inner peace,' said Geoff. Yes, inner peace exactly. I shot a glance up at him as he opened another bottle – good to meet another booze hound. Let's hear it for addictive personality types, huh?

I settled back into the lovely, soft nest of cushions. I suddenly felt a little worn out. As if sensing I needed a rest, Geoff asked if he could interject for a bit. 'Gladly,' I sighed and sipped on.

He concluded that my unconscious beliefs of not feeling

loved, worthy, or good enough actually helped me to develop coping skills to survive my childhood – and now adulthood. This gave me resilience, but the problem was that I didn't have an off switch, even when things were good, I wouldn't allow myself to feel good or to let love in from the outside. This would explain why I kept recreating the same circumstances, <u>oscillating between being abandoned or abandoning people.</u> He called it the 'unconscious egoic agenda,' a set of beliefs that made security and stability feel unsafe. How bizarre! My mountain of safety had, in the end, become my prison. I had not coded up any other reality – I wasn't safe outside of the mountain – and I wasn't safe inside it.

He described what he calls an 'internal representation of reality,' a frame of reference that is created in the womb and which subconsciously sets up invisible structures. This internal representation of rules and belief systems codes up our entire perception of reality as we grow. And because it's invisible and because of repetitive neurological looping, it sets up an internal structure that only strengthens the older we get. We act out this same behaviour unconsciously, until it is no longer invisible to us. We suddenly start seeing 'it' as it shows up in our lives, through negative repetitive events or maybe through therapy, and we often misinterpret it as our 'rock bottom' – or, more positively, as our 'breakthrough.'

Some may call it their awakening or their spiritual epiphany – to finally be able to see our struggles, our failures, our escapism, and our learned helplessness for what it is – playing itself out. Like the glitch with the black cat in the matrix, we suddenly see through the illusion!

CHAPTER 1

Geoff was visibly inspired by his wisdom – he looked quite chuffed when he stated, '… and then, after all that struggle and resistance, we now begin to take the correct action to flip it! To change it, to let it go. To choose a better 'end result' and not settle for the halfway mark anymore.' He stretched out across the cushions with a big Cheshire grin on his face.

'OK, so if that is the case, then maybe it is our entire soul's purpose to reach the tipping point to bring the 'in-visible to the outer-visible' so we can begin to love it consciously,' I concluded. 'Consciously living and co-creating! That truly is our superpower, I reckon!' I was equally enthusiastic and impressed with my inner genius self.

'Well, damn!' Geoff said. 'I reckon we both sound pretty awesome right now! Thank God I've recorded us! Cheers to us, Bridgette!'

He joked about what our superpowers would look like if they showed up right now. His was a lion in a red cape and mine was an Amazonian woman – one who looked like Wonder Woman but with feathers in her hair and gemstones everywhere. Well of course!

Coach Charlie:

As we grow, we are at the mercy of not one, but two competing structures. These are really our agendas, or we can call them our 'structures.' These two compete against each other, and whoever screams the loudest wins.

Ultimately, they both lose, however. The self-conscious agenda says, 'I am this' and 'I want to be that.'

The unconscious egoic agenda says, 'Yeah, you want to be that, but I won't ever let you be, because it isn't safe to change yourself. It would mean that 'we' would no longer exist, and we would have to die!'

So, as soon as we move towards 'it,' suddenly, something happens to stop us from going for what we want. In other words, the self-conscious agenda wants this, but then we are tripped up by the unconscious egoic belief agenda that says 'STOP! We are getting too far out of our safety zone, and I need to pull you back!'

Like a rubber band it stretches, and its resistance gets stronger and stronger and simply bounces us back. Success and failure are essentially structural. Not personal. Bridgette is oscillating between the two agendas – on the one hand, she protects her feelings inside her mountain, as it is a container for them, and on the other hand, she wants to feel the freedom of total acceptance, joy, and inner peace in her theory of enlightenment. But both are forms of escapism from feelings of detachment.

Remember, this detachment all started at the perinatal stage – feeling unwanted and unsafe in the womb. Everything is coded up unconsciously in our genes before the age of three – by the age of seven, we realize that we are an individual, separate from others, and more importantly, we begin to feel totally separated from the unified field of consciousness. These feelings of insignificance – not being good enough, not perfect enough, not belonging, feeling unwanted – all formed Bridgette's belief system by the time she was seven; the ego created a genius system to keep her feeling safe from rejection and abandonment, ultimately, 'to belong' and to not be cast out again.

CHAPTER 1

This is why she created the five parts of her personality, her genius created resources to cope with her timeline of events and to prepare her to cope with future events.

Thinking of you,
Coach Charlie X

CHAPTER 2

The Living Room for the Non-Living and the Paint-By-Numbers Kid

(Georgiana and Bridgette)

Georgiana:

I am sitting in a shadowy corner of the living room. As I look up from my paint-by-numbers kit, I see the sun reflecting on the glasses worn by my mother and my sister, cozied up together, sitting across the room from me. It is as if I am alerted to their gazing upon me by some mysterious force – and when I do focus more on them, my mother's voice suddenly rings shrill, like a whip cracking in the air. Immediately the room seems to darken, the temperature drops, and my vision begins to swirl.

Today is my fifth birthday, and my mother is now telling me that I am old enough to know something very important, something a little sad – but as I am a big girl now, I am not to cry. *Good God, what had I done this time?*

I was always getting into trouble with her, even though I tried so hard to be good. Now she looks rather solemn, however, as if she is the one who is in trouble with me.

She pulls her youngest closer into her and just lets her words spill out, without holding back. I hear her say that am not 'their' daughter. *I am sad my father isn't there, but she said she is speaking on his behalf - she always did. I really do quite like him; he seems like a very nice American man whom I see once a year, and when he comes to stay it is always the best time of my year because she is finally happy.*

She continues to tell me that I was 'chosen' because I was special and needed a home. I was given to them – which means I was what is called 'adopted.' *I was adopted. What is that?* Immediately, I am not invited to ask any questions, and I am told that I can never speak about this ever again, to never even *think* about telling somebody. I am not allowed to talk about my adoption at all with her after this announcement. As you can well imagine, it is quite a lot to take in as a five-year-old – let alone how it would be for someone who finds this information out when they are 50 (which is happening more and more these days.)

I sit there as if I am being reprimanded, being delivered a speech by a woman who uses the right words but conveys zero emotion or love towards me. It sounds like a very well-rehearsed speech, laced with the sweet saccharine that hides its secret poison to place me into a state of immediate confusion and fear.

I spin her words around in my head whilst *her* daughter cuddles into her, both now bathing back in that golden sunlight and somehow, I know what she means even though I am too young to understand. In the years to come, when I begin to comprehend that she isn't my biological/natural/first/real mother, and that Erica is not my blood sister, I do experience a little feeling that I am by now *very* unfamiliar with – a feeling of *happiness*. Erica is theirs and I am not. Thank God, because she is such an obnoxious twat, and that lady is worse than the meanest witch.

At her words I feel relief; I don't feel safe around her, and I dream of her being scalped by Indians, just like in the cowboy movies I see on TV. My 'sister' is only 13 months younger than me, but we never play together, and we have nothing in common. I don't seem to have many memories of her at all growing up together. She is her favourite, which makes sense, as she came from her blood and bone. I wouldn't mind being the daughter of that nice American man who visits once a year though...and he seems sad, like me.

So now what? I am not their daughter, and I am not her sister, and I am to live in this family forever and pretend that this conversation never happened? I am never to talk about this with anyone because it is our family secret, and if I don't obey my adoptive mother's orders, I will be punished. Severely no doubt – God knows when she's lit – she can certainly smack hard, when she isn't swallowing me up in her dark mood swings, bullying and intimidating me with her anger, or causing me to fear for my life. Talk about coercive control and narcissism.

Deep, deep down inside myself, I had already known I didn't belong here, and I desperately wanted to escape from her control. I knew she wasn't my mother, I just did, but this day splits me further into pieces. Before today, I felt cut in half, and numb from my heart to my head. Now, on my fifth sojourn around the sun, I feel a strange feeling – maybe it really *is* happiness. (In retrospect, I now know that I was *ecstatic* that I wasn't her child, and I am so proud that I had somehow already intuited that I wasn't hers.)

At this moment, however, by default - I am forced and doomed to live as an imposter going forward – to live a lie and pretend I am this 'other' person. I am forced to pretend that I am in fact her child, and that Erica is my sister. Worse still, I am forced to live in this house with them.

I find peace in my daydreams about who my real mother is, however – where she might be, when she might come and find me and take me away from here – even though I believe that it was all my fault and that I must be very bad and unworthy of her love. I am stuck in a living lie that I have been ordained to uphold, and my daydreams cannot take that away.

My newly branded 'adoptive' mother goes on to tell me that my 'real' mother loved me so much that she gave me away to them – what kind of a belief system did that ultimately create? Well, let's just say that if I thought you loved me, I was fairly confident that you would soon be leaving me. You can imagine what my chances were like of having any semblance of a healthy relationship with anyone in the near future – that's correct: zero.

By the age of seven, I feel as if I am living someone else's life. I am living outside myself, and although I feel heavy carrying my body around with me, I keep my head above water in a life that isn't my own. I exist in this way because I don't want to feel anything – and this gives me my escape. Feelings are not acknowledged by my adoptive mother and then one day there just isn't any urge to express them; nothing phases me at all. Always sick with bronchitis, sinus, ear infections, hay fever, or the flu, I am medicated with antihistamines, antibiotics and an assortment of pills that make me high. I am floating above myself now – those pills just make me sneeze less.

At that time, I don't know what I look like – isn't that weird? I observe myself in the mirror or in photographs, but I don't really *look* at myself. I feel as if I am not inside this body, but my body still manages to successfully accomplish things like performing at piano and ballet recitals, competing in netball matches and in swimming tournaments. I only have Sundays off. I am always performing, competing, and people-pleasing for my adoptive mother to get some positive attention from her for doing something good so I can exhale.

This is all before the age of seven.

The only attention I get from my adoptive mum is when she is either pissed off at me or showing me off as her other trophy daughter. Regardless, I am the one who ignites her anger, and she certainly lets me know it every day, sucking the oxygen right out of the room and making the blue skies grey; dark thunderstorms, whirlwind tornadoes and volcanic eruptions are her moods. My tears are certainly unacceptable, and I am praised by her for not crying about things kids should be allowed to cry about – like being told you are adopted. The house is one big cesspool of emotional deprivation, and I am in emotional lockdown. I no longer feel sad enough to cry anyway.

It is safer this way, however. I had learned this as a newborn already when I was abandoned, drugged and fed by nurses and then issued to strangers, and now, after living with a mother who rejects me, I have mastered the art of detachment completely – even if it means always abandoning even myself.

***

Bridgette:

In that living room for the non-living, the ghost of me became a paint-by-numbers kid! I loved painting from these kits. They were easy – as long as you never paint outside the lines and you use the right colours, the painting came out great. Easy. I prefer to paint this way, instead of creating my own art, expressing the inner me. Doing that is too risky; it's best to just duplicate, to do what is required. Then I can be perfect for everybody else. Safe: existing between the lines, all perfect, pleasing, and well-behaved. This way I am not 'bad' or 'defunct,' and I won't be 'returned' – or, God forbid, be 'disowned' again.

Recently during an inner child meditation, my five-year-old self shared this with me. I also remain intrigued by the fact that I already felt I didn't belong before I was even told that my adoptive parents weren't my real parents – but I realize that it was my intuition telling me the truth and it continues to do so.

I remember the scene in the living room a little differently than Georgiana does:

Here I am at five years old, sitting in the lounge opposite my mother, listening to her telling me that I am 'adopted', that they 'chose' me. That my 'real' mother couldn't keep me and loved me so much, she gave me away. I am special; I am just so, so special. Because out of all the pretty babies lined up in a row ready for sale behind a window, they chose me. My future career could well have led me to Amsterdam to dance naked behind a bigger glass window.

CHAPTER 2

The hot sun that was illuminating my painting kit now shines on me, but my blood runs ice-cold. My thoughts drown her out – all I can hear is *my real mummy loved me so much that she gave me away.*

'You *must* keep this a secret,' threatens my mother who is now in fact, my 'adoptive mother.' 'You must never tell anybody about this, and please do not ever talk about this with me again. If you do, there will be consequences; you will be punished. I am your mother now and we do not need to discuss any more of this. Do you understand?' Her voice shrilled at the end of her sentence.

My heart was set to below freezing from that day and it never melted until recently [until I had my kids]. Only my son could ever fix that problem. Until I was his mum, I had never been able to allow myself to feel truly loved, or to let anybody really love me. If I did, that meant I would be tossed away again. That's why my mother left, after all – because *she loved me so much.*

I became the one to leave first every time – I was coded up in this. Plus, I consequently became the greatest keeper of secrets, especially the ones I kept from myself.

My inner child was right; when it comes to my feelings, my inner child is my navigator. If I don't listen to her, she will literally drive the car at high speed right off the cliff. I agree with her: yes, I am a 'paint-by-numbers kid/kit.'

My adoptive parents were given a kit, the 'Perfect Child' kit. It had the genetic preferences and likenesses to the picture of the child they wanted to emerge so that I could birth them into parenthood – it's never the other way around, is it?

The kit had a list of possible attributes of epigenetic predispositions to expect. The list had just a few dot points of my birth parents' looks, education, vocation, talents, and hobbies, but back then adoptive parents were told by social workers not to worry if there is something about us that is not quite what they want. Prospective adoptive parents would be told, 'Remember, the baby is a blank canvas; a 'clean slate' - just consider it as if it were your own.'

In other words, the fake parents had the magic marker to change any pre-printed picture on the canvas to suit them. They were told, *'Don't worry; bonding will be easy because they are only a baby – a blank canvas, a clean slate with no memories or personality.'* These social workers were the ones who also told my parents not to issue me with this 'list' of who I 'was' before, until I was 18 years old. They were also advised they could just bury the file for good.

My entire destiny after being adopted was kitted out and re-purposed – a new name, new parents, new family, a fake branch stuck onto a new family tree. I had to lie to the world; I had to pretend that I was one of their own. I had to match into their design, a paint-by-numbers kid. It puts a new twist on throwing the baby out with the bath water!

What did this mean for me? Inevitably, my original canvas had to change to suit the customer's needs, these strangers who were my new parents. But research has shown that babies are not born as a blank canvas, so, there was a lot of work to do. The grey lines needed to be erased and then redesigned structurally to suit where and what they wanted to paint 'me' into. This was also according to the numbers they chose for the paint; they also chose the colours they wanted for each number and there

CHAPTER 2

was to be no mixing – that wouldn't match, and besides, it's tedious. They were to just paint a new me – '*as if she were your own*', said the Adoption agency.

Also, apparently ANYBODY back in the day could adopt a baby; the only pre-requisite was that you were a straight married couple. The typical reason for adopting was that you were infertile or had lost a child. None of the so-called professionals in the industry were educated or experienced in adoption, let alone the soon to be adoptive parents. It was all a secret affair to save the 'illegitimate baby' and to label it as your own and place it on your tree, like a decoration. Save the 'reject baby' and turn it into your own by giving it a new label!

No experience required; the baby was yours to colour match to your own. Bonus alert: you also got to choose a new label AND you got to give it a new birth certificate listing you as their parent. It has already been labelled by its first mother, but now you get to rebrand the baby.

Congratulations! What would you like to call 'it' for 'it' to really feel like it's your own DNA?

Wait a minute – my existence, which was beautiful and perfect in its own unique way, was now to be painted over? Was I destined to forever pretend as if I were their own child? To look, act, think, feel, see, hear, speak as if I was an entirely different canvas? Was I to have no say in the matter because I was just a baby, and everyone thought my feelings didn't exist?

Because I couldn't yet speak, no one thought I could feel anything – but I DID FEEL EVERYTHING.

But it wasn't long until I could not feel anything, which is how I was raised. A double hit: feelings were whitewashed away, along with my true identity.

That is why I created these magical personality parts; I really had no other choice in the matter.

Or did I?

Coach Charlie:

How has this chapter impacted you? Do you also identify feeling this way? Or perhaps you have a loved one who is experiencing similar beliefs and feelings? The roadblocks will tell you, and so will your behaviours. Your behaviour is the highest form of communication – to yourself, to others and to the world.

Georgiana and Bridgette have shared where their identity dysfunction – their 'ego state' – stemmed from and how this impacted their identity. Right from conception, from the womb, through awareness and observation, our ego is already trying to understand how to best function and survive. We create our identity belief systems here, and then we use these fundamental beliefs to navigate our way out into the world after we are born.

These conditions are developed and coded up into our sub-consciousness, right up until around eight years of age. Our period of accelerated learning installs belief systems that are on a structure of unconscious neurological looping, dictating how we must think, feel, act – behave – to get what we want and to avoid pain.

When we were in utero, or when we were an infant or child, our life was completely different to what it is now. So how different is the way you think, feel, act, and behave now - to the way you were then? You will be surprised to know that without awareness, without discovering what your unconscious ego agenda (belief systems) are, and without working on how to step out of them and into your magical greatness, you will be still stuck inside that matrix of responding to life as if you are still that child!

That matrix, as demonstrated in the movie by the same name, is an array of definitions, algorithms, and meanings, coded up within you as a baby, infant, and child that you have brought into your present life, and that perpetuates your future outcomes. These thoughts and feelings are not real, and your actual reality is being bypassed by the illusion of the past.

==You became so used to the identity of not feeling capable enough, not good enough, not worthy enough to be able to go for what you want – that is because most of us needed to perform and be a certain way, to change our original identity in order to have it.== What did you need to do as a child to get what you wanted? How is this still being projected out into the world so you can get what you want as an adult? How are these infantile decisions working for you right now?

What if you could be the magician, and step into a new reality, with the ability to focus on your end results – creating a life you want – that lives outside of this matrix and *inside* of your pure potential self? How about we redefine who you really are by stepping you out of your past identity through the alchemy of redefinition?

Your focus on your past creates your reality, which creates a chain of events to keep you stuck in the past forever. Whenever you go for anything – a choice, a goal, a desire – you activate your ego from the past. This doesn't look at the current moment, it draws upon the conditioned beliefs of the past and THEN attempts to go for it, but this orientation perpetuates the same reality based upon your identity as an infant – and that infant is preventing you from having it now!

You need to learn and practice and to stop identifying with your past self, to experience little steppingstones and build up your muscle of a new identity. Perhaps today you could just start with having the awareness and some self-talk, telling yourself, 'Yes, I am aware I am feeling like this – I know where I first believed that was real and where it came from – but I am choosing to feel safe/loved/worthy/happy/good enough/beautiful/etc.' Ask yourself: 'What is my reality that I choose from my true nature and purpose as I am now? My old reality of self is an illusion, so I replace this with a definition of a higher, magical reality within a new structure.' Structure has integrity – change your reality and you change the structure and your integrity with yourself.

You are a beautiful genius! Stand in your greatness and change the structure of your past. The past is over; stand in your power and create a life you want – just because you want it!

With love,
Coach Charlie X

CHAPTER 3

That Grade 1 Teacher Who Got Away

(Georgiana)

I knew I was a good kid. But life appeared to be intent on kicking it out of me.

I was now into my first few weeks of school, aching for some reprieve from my suffocating, unpleasant home life. But instead, I felt scared and trapped at school as well, everything I did was misinterpreted as being purposefully wrong. For example, I couldn't help writing left-handed, so I got scolded for it each day for disobeying the school rules of 'thou shalt not be a lefthanded child,' and I was even threatened with the leather strap! My persistence won – but that was to cost me dearly.

Were all the adults in my life replicas of the most terrifying of encounters? Judging by the line-up, I concluded that yes, aside from my grandfather (and that nice American man who visited now and then, whom was now my adoptive father called 'Dad') - all adults were deemed scary, cruel, and angry people who were never to be trusted. The females were the real culprits, and the scary witch award was a tiebreaker between my adoptive mum and nana. 'You are the Devil's Spawn', is what my nana would say to me – I had no idea what 'spawn' was, but judging by her coldness and disapproval towards me, I guessed I wasn't exactly her favourite.

My first-grade teacher was no exception to my philosophy on the adults in my world. A wiry, white-haired, witchy old man, he wore black suits and a white shirt and black tie every day. He looked like a lean, mean old undertaker, and he had black, squinty eyes that would stab through you, making you definitely not want to put your hand up. I'm sure he saw us all – not just me – as very small, stupid, and annoying. Mostly, he just ignored me – except when he yelled at me for talking too much or threatened to punish me for my left handedness. If only I could tell him what I know now. That lefthanders are always in their *right* mind. That would have sent him 'right off!'

I tried my best to blot him out of my head at night, like I did with the rest of them. If only somebody would have loved me, then maybe I would have felt safe to talk about all of this. But I was so unloved and uncared for, and I interpreted this to mean that I was insignificant AND unlovable. I heard my adoptive mother's words repeatedly in my mind: 'Your mother loved you so much, she gave you up.'

Maybe it was safer to stay unloved after all.

One day, the school principal visited our classroom. It was a big deal, and I made sure I had on my best smile and looked down to check that my shoes were polished enough. We were all lined up as he was making the rounds, and when it was my turn to meet him, I almost wanted to curtsy. I attempted to squeak a hello, but I was distracted by his fixation on my blue cardigan – I had missed a button! He moved in closer and slowly re-buttoned it. I felt so stupid.

Still, was it okay to feel his warm hand lingering a little too long on my chest like that?

I had already missed part of the school year due to illness (I just think I was allergic to my adoptive mother), and I couldn't wait to be out of the house to finally join my class about three months later. My classmates had already established little sub-groups and there wasn't room for me, just like at home.

Was I always to feel I didn't belong?

My teacher asked the boys to sit in a circle for reading time on the mat; the girls were supposed to remain seated at their desks to continue with their assigned writing task. This felt like it was the routine drill, but I didn't understand why I couldn't join the boys. The room filled with gasps from the girls, as I pirouetted across the room to find my own place in the circle. But none of the boys would let me in, however, and the teacher was sitting in the middle of the circle, which I thought was odd.

And then I saw something that should've never been seen: the boys each had their penises out in their hand. I knew what penises were – I had baths with my little cousins – and now, I was looking at about 15 of the little blighters.

'Bridgette! What do you think you are doing?' my teacher screeched, his voice at high volume.

He stood up, marched over to me and yanked me up by my arm, forcing me to my feet – ouch, that really hurt. Dragging me into a corner by the locker bay, he pushed me down to the floor, hard. All eyes were on me.

'Turn your head and face outward toward the windows NOW!' he bellowed. 'Further...further...turn it more. Stay like that. If I catch you turning your head an inch looking back into this class, even a centimetre, you will get the ruler.' How far was a centimetre? I had no idea, but I did know that a ruler was usually only used to hit the boys.

Whatever he said under his breath to me in addition to that threat, was hideous and I can't recall but I froze in that position, as instructed.

It wasn't until the school bell rang, hours later, that he let me move. My neck was so pained, and my body was sore from his pulling and pushing.

Whatever he threatened me with – it worked. I had blocked the whole traumatic event out. I didn't even remember the actual event until decades later, when I was talking to a friend about memories of our past primary school teachers.

The two people a little child should have been able to trust – a parent and a teacher – had hurt me and then threatened me regarding ever talking about their emotionally-abusive, sexualized behaviour. I was conditioned by the age of five to just let people walk all over me and to never stand up for myself or to ask anyone for help. This played out so predictively throughout my life, as I kept attracting the many narcissistic bullies like flies and letting them suffocate me. After the incident at school, my self-respect – which was already virtually non-existent – was going to take another four decades to start to find it again.

I don't remember much about the rest of that school year, or much about any time of my life between five and 10 years of age. I wasn't important to anyone else, so I made myself just as unimportant to myself.

Recently, I did try to track down who that teacher was and make a complaint – but of course, there was never any police record, and no other complaints were recorded.

He was just another teacher that got away.

Coach Charlie:

Learned helplessness...coercion...control...abuse...silencing...unworthiness...insignificance...fear. These are some of the events and feelings adoptees are forced to deal with as soon as they are born. Some researchers believe that these feelings are also potentially transmitted in utero, from the mother to their soon-to-be-relinquished child.

In her article, 'Relinquishment Trauma: The Forgotten Trauma' Marie Dolfi writes: 'Research has shown that babies in utero learn their mother's characteristics...the newborn child may become frightened and overwhelmed when the caretaker is not their first mother. The greater discrepancies between the adoptee's prenatal and early life (sound of mother's heartbeat, language, sounds, facial features, smells, their gait of walking, level of activity) - the greater stress on the infant. When an infant is not with their first mother day after day, the infant can become anxious and confused, causing the infant's body to release stress hormones.

Even newborns that are placed with the adoptive parent within days of their birth, can feel the terror of their mother missing. Babies know their mother is missing and they are being cared for by strangers. Common sentiments expressed by adoptees are that they feel like something is missing, they have a hole inside of them, or their connections feel fragile and insecure. The newborn's trauma is multiplied when there are numerous caregivers and placements before the child joins their adoptive family...can increase the likelihood of an adoptee experiencing anxiety, depression, attachment issues, post-traumatic stress disorder, or complex PTSD.'

I highly recommend that you read Marie's article and also spend some time reviewing the project she is working on, the Adverse Relinquishment & Adoption Experiences (ARAEs) Assessment Project. That, along with Nancy Verrier, Betty Jean Lifton, and Paul Sunderland's videos on adoption and addiction, speak out on the truth of what is slowly coming to be recognized as 'relinquishment trauma' and development trauma disorder.

Many adoptees internalize that they are to blame for being abandoned; this is especially if their adoptive families do not give them opportunities to explore their true feelings, or to share their fears and beliefs around their adoption – let alone ask questions about their family of origin. Being told – or threatened – to never speak about their adoption causes the adoptee to detach and to dehumanize their true feelings. Consequently, this creates belief systems early on, such as: 'I am not allowed to have any feelings,' 'my feelings are unimportant,' 'it isn't safe to speak up for myself,' and 'if I am good and quiet, I will not be punished.' And remember, this is in addition to what the general narrative was from our adoptive parents: 'Your mother gave you away, because she loved you so much.'

So, we can't ever trust in the power and healing of being loved. This all inhibits the natural development of the brain, because adoptees need to accelerate self-management skills in a very unnatural way. This has several consequences, including 'normalizing' the internalization of a lack of self-worth, shame, and trauma, which leads to bypassing building empathy for self and for others, creating isolation, secrecy, and insignificance of self.

Can you see how the experience with my adoptive mother and nana, that School Principal and the first-grade teacher would have further cemented such belief systems?

Were there specific events that happened in your life before the age of eight, that could have created limiting belief systems in your unconscious brain? How are they still being played out? Your behaviour is the highest form of communication, so take a look at that closely and you will find the answer.

We must understand that adoption is not a one-time event – it is a lifelong journey that impacts adoptees, their first parents, their adoptive parents and siblings, adoptees' own children, past and future generations, and extended family members. In Australia alone, studies have shown that 1 in 15 people will be affected by adoption; therefore, adoptees are not the only ones suffering the consequences of adoption.

Hugs to you,
Coach Charlie X

CHAPTER 4

My Guardian Alien

(Georgiana)

I had always spoken freely about my 'guardian angel'; my adoptive mother must have planted that name and concept into my head very early on – I wonder why? I knew how to say the name perfectly by the age of three. I always had a sense of her, my angel; I felt her around me, right from the start. It was a warm and loving energy, in such contrast to the world I was stuck inside of, initially from the 'womb room' and now from the view of the world I had observed around me. I dreaded venturing out from both vistas.

    I felt my guardian angel watching me, protecting me. It was later in my life, when I was shown clearer visions of her – once, for example, I saw when she first revealed herself to me in a dream in which I was laying in the bassinet. She was standing over me, a beautiful lady clothed in blue, cloaked like a nun with warm eyes full of love. My bedroom in the dream appeared hazy, misty from the floor up, as if we were outside after the rain fell on the hot pavement. She was gently rocking the bassinet and humming sweetly to me. I watched her closely in my dream state, and I felt this deep sense of comfort that she loved me so much. The feeling was easy to distinguish from my current reality, which was filled with constant aloneness, and the isolation of lovelessness from the grief of missing my birth mother and dealing with my disruptive adoptive one.

I was shown another vision of my guardian angel when I was five years old, after I was told by the woman whom I thought was my mother that she was indeed *not* my 'real' mother. My guardian angel entered my dreams again, but this time it felt so real. She called to me softly, enticingly, literally awakening me from my sleep. It was dark in my bedroom, but I could see her aura surrounded by a soft warm glow. Instinctively, I reached out for her hand, and she gently guided me down the hallway and out of the door into the backyard.

I remember feeling the cool air swirling around me, and standing in the soft, velvety grass that was wet under my bare feet as we looked up into the milky way sky that twinkled above us.

I heard a whirling deep low noise, like a big street generator. Suddenly, but ever so slowly, we were floating upwards together, towards a magnificent bright blue and white light that had suddenly appeared in the sky.

She said, 'Do not be afraid; you are safe with me. I love you.' Without moving her lips, she spoke to me, 'mind to mind.' I eagerly absorbed every word I received, and she and I continued to communicate this way. Her eyes were so bright, so big and blue, and as she held my gaze, they brought me to tears. It astounded me, and even though I was conditioned by my adoptive mother that crying was weak and forbidden, I just couldn't help myself. Just like when I heard beautiful music playing from the lounge late at night through my bedroom wall, I couldn't help crying into my pillow from the sheer beauty and magic of that music. It moved me so deeply beyond my years.

This beautiful angel's warmth, her welcoming embrace, made me feel the freedom to let go of the tears built up from all the pain of my short life, and I felt the sweet release, more so than when I would weep into my pillow feeling so alone.

With her, I didn't need to conceal the fear, and I was no longer uncared for. She conveyed that she loved my realness, my vulnerability with her. Together, we shared what seemed like an eternal timeline of my five years of feelings, and even beyond that lifetime, and we kept floating up, higher and higher, entering further into the milky, starry sky.

We floated closer to what looked like a rounded, circular spaceship with aqua blue lights around the middle section. As we approached, I felt that somehow, I had arrived at a 'place of home.' I immediately liked it here. Everyone – the beings – were very tall and dressed in long, velvety, blue hooded cloaks. They seemed to float instead of walk, and their energy felt so nice, and music seemed to constantly play, like a tranquil harp echoing dreamily through a waterfall. As I looked around, I was aware that there were many children lying down on soft, white, lit-up beds. The children's eyes were closed, and they all looked very comfortable and peaceful.

I was soon taken over to one of those beds. My guardian angel asked me to lie down when I was ready, and to relax and close my eyes. I did as she asked; I felt so safe there. It was so relaxing, and yet exciting at the same time!

I woke up in my own bed at my house. I could see it was still dark outside because my bed was right beside the window – I had even lifted the curtains to check.

I knew this wasn't just a dream, but I didn't really recall much about what had happened. I remembered everything up to the part where I lay down on the soft bed, gazing into my beautiful angel's eyes.

I don't know why, but I immediately wanted to run into my adoptive mother's bedroom and wake her up to tell her all about it. But I talked myself out of it, for fear of angering her and getting a smack for my silly, silly childishness. I finally decided to tell her later, after the household awoke. I told her a little of my adventures, and she said that if what I said really happened, then I would have woken her up in the night. She reasoned that therefore, it was something I made up completely in my imagination, or I was a liar. Then she just decided that I was a complete liar and taunted me about it for the rest of the week, labelling me a liar.

I didn't know what to do with what had happened to me, or where to go with it. So, just like when I learned about being adopted, and just like I had learned from the incident with my teacher, I locked myself away, even further. I was starting to shut myself down – and I am only five years old at this time.

I was simply too scared to tell my adoptive mother the truth as to why I didn't want to wake her that night. I didn't want to deal with her anger or ridicule – or, what she loved to do the most –luring me in under false pretenses and then later using whatever I shared to shame, ridicule, and punish me later when

CHAPTER 4

she felt like it. She thrived on this power over me. She knew a little of my story (as I kept most of it to myself,) but that was enough to brand me a liar, forever.

Years later, I still was able to remember the long green blades of grass blowing sideways in the backyard, the momentum of lifting up into the starry night sky, and the whirring sounds of the big lights above – and of course my guardian angel's voice in my head and how wonderful I felt. But who would believe me?

Let me fast-track you to 37 years later, when I attended an Inner Child Practitioner Training course, which took place over ten days in the middle of the desert in Uluru, Ayers Rock, Australia.

Yup, here I go again, doing another course in my adult years, because I just didn't feel capable enough or *whatever* enough to be able to do what I wanted to do – which was to coach people out of their identity blocks and limited belief systems and into their true potential. I'd had successful results working with clients in this field for several years, but I sensed that I was missing something within myself that I kept tripping over.

Here I was, seated in a circle, one of 20 students looking across the outdoor classroom in anticipation, watching the dragonflies in the distance, waiting for the teacher to kick off the next day of training.

We were seated on large mats, surrounded by the deep, red earth of the desert, underneath a huge white tarpaulin erected to protect us from the mid-winter sun. The grass on the walk over was dewy, and our shoes squeaked from the condensation as we tried to position ourselves gracefully upon the colourful cushions on waterproof mats. Today was already proving to be particularly eerie, with many eagles soaring and squawking as they circled above us. We had been briefed on the drill: we would each take our turn with the talking stick, to share about yesterday's learnings. Boring – I just wanted to get right into the day's lessons. I watched a huge black ant linger on my big toe a little too long for my liking. I'd heard their bites were disarming and that was right, but that was nothing compared to the sting I was about to receive at today's session.

'Alien Implant Retrieval,' our teacher said. 'Yes, you heard me correctly. Today we are going to diagnose which of you has been abducted by aliens and has been contaminated with implants. This is not a joke; this is real. They are pesky little devices that are placed energetically inside of you, designed to give aliens information and energy – but they will mess you up, emotionally and physically. Implants in your body can block your meridians and chakras.' The teacher, adorned in her billowing silk tie-dyed scarf and her moonstone crystal regalia, stared intently at each one of us, lasering us one by one with her lizard-like green eyes. She was getting an intuitive 'read' on us – was *she* an alien?

I wondered who the victim of such an alien implanting perpetrator had been – how terrible! With her jingling bracelets and sparkling earrings, she went on to ask us the following question:

'Who here has had a traumatic childhood? You know what, I already know the answer. Most of you will *think* that you have. Psychics, healers, and counsellors have usually experienced quite the traumatic childhood, and that is why they work professionally in this field. But trauma happens to each of us at

CHAPTER 4

some point, at any point, when we are children. It can stem from even the silliest of things. We take EVERYTHING so personally and we feel the slightest of slights as a personal trauma. Psychologists and psychiatrists secure their property investment portfolios off people like us throwing money at them by the hour. Trauma is a guaranteed money spinner.'

I looked around at the group. I always love to observe and get a read on people; it's good to tune in. Most of them were staring into space processing what she was saying or thinking of when the next flight out would be.

'What I am talking about when I ask if you have had childhood trauma, let me clarify,' she said. 'I am asking about the particular kind of trauma where you didn't feel like you were loved by your mother, the kind of trauma where you felt you were in the way, or you felt or knew that you didn't belong or were unwanted by your mother. Adoptees and foster children especially – was your mother cold or dismissive to your needs and wants? Did you feel unloved, insignificant, unworthy? Some of you may have felt very depressed or anxious in her presence. So, in reframing my question, again, I ask you – who here has had such a traumatic childhood?'

I instantly went into freeze mode. Or maybe flight mode. Whatever the mode was, I was not in the mood to be a volunteer. But I had to be honest with her, as she already knew I was adopted.

Because of the new specification, out of 20, only three of us put up our hand – tentatively, however, as we just knew we were headed for the chopping board. Off with our heads! This lady was tough and yet strangely sincere, once you admitted to such a thing, you would be trapped, and our old belief systems would be annihilated and then potentially reborn with her. She wanted us to think that our terror was soon to be our finest victory.

On the first day, we had taken a vow of honesty and congruency as part of the 'course treaty.' However, now it felt more like a vow of submission – she was going to pick us apart, bone by bone, in all our dysfunction, for the world to see, and her 'threat of karmic intervention' – should we choose to not 'submit' to the moment here – scared the bejeezus out of us. No backing out now.

She started the session by beckoning Simon up to the front. The cool guy – shaved head, muscle shirt and ripped shorts, rugged face with tatts on his neck. Didn't sleep in the cabins like the rest of us softies; he camped under the stars with the dingoes. I couldn't figure him out – I thought he had a thing for me, but then found out he was gay, and he was only being friendly. Maybe I was the one with a 'thing' for him? It was unsettling to me, as there was something about him, but I just didn't know what it was. I didn't feel it was just a physical attraction.

✱✱✱

We had become fast friends from the first time we spoke, as we were boarding the plane.

'First time in Alice Springs?' he asked, looking like he had hiked all the way here. He held out his hand to me. 'Hi, I'm Simon.'

His eyes were a mix of green and blue. Beautiful. Although they did look a little red for the colour of the sea in the midst of them – I could smell sweet, dank alcohol on his breath. He offered me his flask. 'Want a shot? I hate flying so I need a little help.'

I thanked him for the offer and whilst still shaking his hand I said, 'Hi Simon, my name is Bridgette. Nice to meet you!'

I looked more intently at him and our eyes locked, deepening our handshake, and I immediately felt the electricity running through me. 'Have we met before?' his eyes asked me before he had said the words. To deter my obvious faltering, I asked for a shot of whatever the hell was in that flask.

I wish this could be the bit where I say we then built up a monumental chemistry of lust and then acted out our desires and fell in love and got married and so on, but you know me enough already to know that kind of dreamy life wasn't destined for the likes of me. I'd never had much luck turning guys who like guys either.

I fumbled and said, 'Thank God we have cabins with air conditioning in the middle of the desert with dingoes and tarantulas and snakes.'

Flippantly, he said he preferred to 'camp under the stars.'

Now, as intriguing as it sounds, have you ever been to Ayers Rock? Think snakes, spiders, bull ants, mosquitos, dingoes – hey, whatever your flavour is, that's who your animal friends are in the desert.

It's not for me, but for Simon, it was no problem whatsoever. 'This is an adventure,' he said, 'to lay underneath a blanket of stars lined up below the Milky Way and then catch the full moon beams all night tonight. I can't wait to get there!' I adored that he was such a romantic!

We landed safely and had our first group dinner together at

the local pub, then an early night for a fresh start in the morning.

* * *

Let us return to that morning when Simon is being summoned to the healing table – he really seemed delighted to assist. There were four healers, including the teacher who conducted the retreat. As she started to speak about the processes for intuitively feeling for implants energetically, the healers began locating 'devices' in his body and proceeding to lift them out of him. Watching them work was both fascinating and terrifying, and it didn't help that Simon was grimacing and writhing in pain on the healing table at times.

Suddenly, I started to notice that I was feeling extremely uncomfortable in my body, and I felt very teary and emotional. I couldn't really watch anymore because I felt I was going to literally lose it – I never cried, and yet my throat ached with tears welling up to be released. I was really starting to feel traumatized by witnessing all of this when I became aware of my body rocking on its own volition, as I was seated on the ground. I felt that I had left my body and was now right beside Simon.

Wait a minute – I actually saw my five-year-old self lying down on that spacecraft, in a healing bed, *right beside him*. I looked up and saw the same group of children, lying in such beds in a circular, lit-up room. I was transported back in time by watching Simon being worked upon by the healers as they removed his alien implants. It seemed to have triggered some kind of cellular memory in me.

Before I knew it, the healers had finished with Simon and

were now guiding *me* over to the healing table to do some work on me. I was completely out of my body, as if I was hypnotized. They took off my silver jewellery and started pulling out what I could see in my mind as long wires and devices from my head and my face. Then they located what they were calling 'the motherboard' in my left thigh. It took a lot of force from two of them to pull this out from my leg; I could feel it lodged deeply in there.

I know this all sounds like a whole heap of poococky, but trust me, it was as real as real gets. I don't remember how long this all went on for, but when they asked me to stand up from the table, I literally struggled to walk. My legs were so heavy, and my body felt so dense and bruised and I just wanted to be carried to my room and then to sleep for days. I somehow managed to make it to my room with some help, and the teachers knew to just let me rest.

I slept for about 12 hours, but when I awoke before sunrise the next day, I realized I hadn't forgotten a thing. I saw that the teachers had cleansed my jewellery and left it all on my bedside table – how kind and thoughtful of them. As I put the rings, bracelets, and necklace back on, I noticed they were much lighter and brighter – unlike how I was feeling. I was also extremely thirsty.

I drank about a litre of water and I headed to Simon's campsite, stumbling through the desert still lit up under the Milky Way skies. I had zero energy, and terrible body aches slowed me down and attracted some unwanted attention from the dingoes, but I needed to tell him about the vision I saw when the healing was taking place yesterday.

'Simon!' I called as I approached. 'Wake up! It's me! I need to tell you – I saw you! You were there! With me! On the ship! In 1975 – I had just turned five and you would have only been three! Simon!'

When I found him, I grabbed him by the shoulders like a hysterical banshee, but he was already lying there awake. He told me he had been waiting for me to come to him. He hadn't slept a wink, filled with anticipation for the right time to talk together. He already knew what I was going to say: 'Bridge. I know, I know. It's all okay – I had the same vision, too. It all makes sense to me now, my reaction upon seeing you at the airport. Like we had met before. But it was so much deeper than that – you made a promise to me when we were on that ship that you would find me again. Do you remember saying that? And wow! You found me!'

His bright green-blue eyes lit up as the morning sunrise sparkled in their hue, and his smile was dazzling. Suddenly, I saw him again, as a three-year-old little boy. I reached for his hand, and we just sat there together, watching the sunrise light up the red desert dirt, basking in the wonderful wonder of what we had discovered. I had no recall of any promise to find him, yet here we are! I had found him and I also 'found him' incredibly intriguing but, unfortunately, he was definitely unavailable – story of my life!

We remained good friends for years to come, until cancer took him away far too early. But at least we met again – and again, we shall meet.

CHAPTER 4

Coach Charlie:

I really do not have too much to say here regarding any link between the likelihood of alien abductions and childhood trauma. Maybe, do the research for yourself on the connection between the two…it is something that I am not fully convinced about… however, I can't deny the truth of this happening to us/me/Bridgette. In fact, when she was around twenty-three years of age a strange visitation occurred – which can only be described as 'other worldly.' It was as if 'they' were caught in the act of observing her and were not prepared for her to see them doing so.

I also can't deny that alien abductions happen – there are so many people who have shared their own experiences. Maybe it is an unconscious creation to feel a sense of belonging somewhere else, if you can't feel you belong here on earth? Maybe it is our imagination taking over, or our dream state showing us that life exists beyond the earthly realms? Or maybe aliens do abduct us – if we feel like an outcast here, we are more willing or more vulnerable for such an event to occur.

What do you think about the possibility of this? Have you encountered aliens too?

With kindness,
Coach Charlie X

CHAPTER 5

If I Could Just Pay You for a Cuddle

(Georgiana)

'Who do you know that walks over the bridge to school?'

My adoptive mother asked me this question randomly one school morning. In between scoffing down my Vegemite on toast with gulps of warmed milk, I relayed off the names of the kids that I knew who walked over that bridge – wrong. No, still wrong. She was prompting me to dig deeper, to name more and more kids, as if I was in some kind of Spanish inquisition. I didn't realize the ramifications of not answering her question correctly until later that day – I thought it was just another one of the mind games she liked to play with me to prove that she was right, and I was wrong.

Off to school I went. When I got there, I was greeted by my friends, but not with their usual smiles of happiness – instead, with an explosion of tears. My peers were hugging me, then each other, then hugging teachers. Teachers were sobbing and hugging each other, hugging parents who were crying. The school grounds were flooding with tears – I was literally the only person with a dry eye. Barely seven years of age, I was not used to anyone crying like this – I had certainly never witnessed adults crying at all, ever. I had no idea what was wrong because nobody could speak from all the tears!

I went to look for my friends James and Vaughan. They were my classmates, and we often hung out before and after school. They would tell me bluntly what was up, as boys were straighter to the point like that. Especially James.

Suddenly, my friend, Jane, came running up to me in tears (of course).

'Jane, what's happened?' I asked. 'What's wrong with everybody?' She looked at me in a way that told me I wasn't going to like this at all, but also her eyes were asking why the hell I didn't know? What she went on to tell me was something that no other seven-year-old should have to speak about to another.

'James is dead,' she said. 'His little sister and brother are also. They were murdered.' She stood there holding my shoulders, shaking, with red rimmed eyes.

'What? No! Stop it, Jane. Why are you saying this to me? If that were true, my mother would have told me! No way! I don't believe you!' I searched her eyes for reprieve, but they were locked in the depths of pain.

'Bridgey, it's true. On Friday after school last week, when they got home, well, their mother killed each of them.' She was barely able to get the words out. I didn't believe her – no way!

My self-talk was on a fast-tracking loop. Why would Jane lie like this? She was not the kind of person to lie, but surely if it were true, my adoptive mother would have told me. What was

CHAPTER 5

happening here? I didn't like this. I felt out of control. Nobody was in control; they were a mess, even the teachers!

James and I had been in the same class since grade one, and he was also my dear friend. I knew his little siblings and his mother. In fact, it was only a weekend earlier that my adoptive mother and I were talking with them at the big community fair as we lined up at the Ferris wheel ride. There was no way I was going to accept this. My mother would have told me if it were true, surely!

'Come on Jane, you are coming with me,' I said.

I lived across the road from the southern school field, and I was not taking 'no' for an answer. In minutes, we were standing in my living room.

'You tell my mum what you've just said, and she will tell us it isn't true!' I commanded her.

As we stood in front of my adoptive mother, waiting for Jane to speak, she suddenly interjected, 'Bridgette, if this is about James and his siblings and what his mother did, I tried to tell you this morning, but you wouldn't get your answer right – you didn't guess his name! It's your fault that I didn't get the chance to tell you! What Jane is going to say is correct. Their mother killed them on Friday after school. Bridgette, I tried to tell you!' She finished up in a voice that portrayed that it was she, who was the victim.

I felt swallowed up; I thought I was going crazy, but I wasn't sure if it was from the stupid mind games of my adoptive mother or the fact that I had just found out my friend had been murdered. Why didn't my mother just tell me? Either way, whatever good feelings I had left about myself, my adoptive mother, and the world – had spiralled downward for the worse.

In addition to this, she even went on to apologize to Jane about *me* – for being so at fault and for forcing Jane to our house. *What?* I couldn't deal with any of this; I really needed a nurturing loving mother right then – perhaps even a hug would have been nice – but all she did was blame me and shame me, ridiculing me in front of my friend.

It scared me to think of the motive behind a mother killing their child. Maybe James's mother didn't like him? Maybe that is why she murdered him, his little sister and brother – why else would she kill them?

So now the big elephant in the room for me was this: what if my adoptive mother was going to soon kill *me?* She didn't seem to like me being around, wanting her attention, wanting her to acknowledge me. As I began to grieve the loss of my friend, I wanted her to hug me so much, and boy, did I already have a mountain of grief to shed about this entire 'adoption' thing. I didn't understand what I was feeling; I just really needed some affection. Any affection, really – doing so would greatly reassure me that she wasn't thinking of doing the same thing to me. How could I get her to love me without annoying her, so that she wouldn't kill me?

Maybe I could pay her for a cuddle, maybe she would like that. It might be a great solution for us both; she gets the money, and I get the hug. She starts to like me, and I get to live! Right then would be a good time to feel loved by both of my 'new' parents. Just a warm hug like the other kids get from their mothers – I've seen it happen; I know hugs from parents is a real *'thing'*. I can't remember the last time I even saw my adoptive father...

So just maybe, if I could find that big, shiny, 50-cent piece,

I could just offer to pay her to hold me? But I never found that coin, so I never got the hugs.

I don't feel I ever felt loved by her. I just resigned myself to detaching from the yearning and the fear, being strong and resilient, and never wanting such natural, self-developmentally healthy experiences that a child needs to receive from their parents. I just stepped it right up with the people-pleasing and with being 'the good girl.' I learned how to behave to survive.

I am thankful she never killed me, but inside myself, I felt like she had extinguished whatever was left alive.

Coach Charlie:

I would love for you to take some time for yourself to reflect on the following questions:

Have you hugged someone today? A pet? A tree? Have you asked for a hug this week?

How do you internalize your adoption? How do you internalize not getting your needs met? How do you cope with loss? Whom have you grieved? How do you use self-care when you need a hug but there's nobody there? How are you resilient in your life? Is it to protect yourself from feeling pain or is it to persevere when the tough times prevail? What is the difference?

What is your understanding of disenfranchised grief? Would you want to explore that?

How has your childhood shaped you? Are you still a people pleaser, or a 'yes' person when you need to be saying no?

How open are you to love without fear of rejection or abandonment?

What beliefs do you want to let go of?

If you love yourself first – how is that going to create healthy boundaries? How will that change your existing relationships?

How has your adoption created conditioned belief systems? What are they? What patterns do you keep seeing play out in your life, in your relationships with partners, friends, colleagues, bosses, etc.?

The past really is over – how much of it still exists now? What kind of future do you want for yourself?

Now choose the four following orientations to have as a focus for your life, right now. Just say them aloud to yourself as you sit uninterrupted, with your hand over your heart if you like, breathing in what you see and what you feel after you say each of these powerful life choices aloud:

1. I choose the end result of living a life I love.
2. I choose the end result of health and vitality.
3. I choose the end result of living in my true nature and purpose.
4. I choose the end result of being the predominant creative force in my life.

Breathe it in. See it; be it. Create whatever each of the four core choices are and step into them – just act and feel as if you have it already. Create from this present moment the 'future you'. Do this every day as your sacred meditation and mantra and focus on the end result – WHAT you want, not HOW you are going to get it. Take the next obvious action step and really start to live the life you love! Go for it! And give yourself a hug today!

With peace and love,
Coach Charlie X

CHAPTER 6

What Ever Happened to Little Sammy?

(Sam)

When I was a child, I loved to climb. You could usually find me scaling up the back of the big garden shed to climb across the branches of the large plum tree next door. Being up high, above the world and looking down was the greatest escape, aside from a good book.

I would push myself to climb up the plum tree higher, further along the branches to snatch a juicy purple plum or two. The sun on my closed eyes would flicker like strobe lights between the leaves that fluttered in the soft breeze, and I would lie back on a big branch and anticipate that first juicy bite, right before my teeth pierced the tight skin of the plum. As I passed the monotonous ebb of time in between classes, eating, and sleep time, and mainly avoiding my adoptive mother, the dribble of the purple juice would bake on my chin. I loved to nestle into the tree and create angels in the clouds.

It would have been nice to have shared this tree with a friend, but they were all too busy enjoying their big swimming pools with their nice shiny families, having fun together on warm days. My friend James would have liked it up here, but he was now up somewhere else, somewhere in heaven.

My adoptive grandfather built a playhouse out of a ten-by-ten-foot wooden storage crate for my little sister Erica and me. He painted it brown and cut out windows and even made a door. Our little brown house was all kitted out, with a kitchen, a table, and chairs, and all of the related paraphernalia. Plastic teacups and saucers, colouring books and pens were strewn everywhere, muffin trays overflowing with cracked, dry, colourful playdough.

Our little house was tucked away in the corner of the far end of our huge open-air garage, close to the vegetable garden, runner bean wall and creek. It was south facing, so it was always very cold and dark, especially in the early winter afternoons. I appreciated the feeling of solitude it gifted me – when I was inside the playhouse, I was always alone.

Erica and I didn't 'hang out' together at all. She especially loved keeping to herself and staying indoors, baking playdough muffins or being in the main house with her mother. I preferred the fresh air and any sunshine I could get – either up the plum tree, riding my bike around the neighbourhood, or leaning up against my favourite willow tree, reading.

The yard was so big, and we had willow and birch trees that ran along the side of the creek bed, and it was here that our grandfather built us our very own handmade merry-go-round! Ropes wound around old car tires that I would sit inside of,

CHAPTER 6

which were then attached to a big Hills Rotary Hoist clothes line, and then he would spin it and I would fly around.

Still, things were not happy on the home front, and I had planned to run away, to escape 'her' by following down along the grassy sides of the creek bed. Until one day, my grandfather built a fence up along the length of it. How did he know? Did my adoptive mother tell him of my sinister thoughts of running away one day? How did she read my mind like that? Another dream dashed because of her – was she to always stand on my dreams? Was she ever going to stop tormenting me, making my life miserable? Why was she so mean and nasty to me?

Like the day I thought I could save a little bird.

My cat Nicky had trapped a sparrow underneath the car in the driveway. I crawled under the car on the shingle driveway, scraping the skin off my knees in an attempt to grab the bird, but Nicky was just too fast for me. I will never forget the crunch of the bird's neck as its head disappeared in her mouth. I felt so guilty that I had not been able to save its little life; I had been so close.

I would have never usually cried – there was no place for tears in this household. But that afternoon by the car, my guilt over not saving that bird crushed me in a way that threw my defences off-kilter. The dam burst, and a torrent river of tears just wouldn't stop pouring out of me.

I tried to move my body, but I was frozen to the spot. I couldn't run and cover this moment up; I couldn't even breathe properly. The tears were heaving through my lungs, bouncing off the grey shingled stones of the driveway, making them blotchy. I was trying so hard to stop, holding my breath when I could, but the uncontrollable monster of pain inside of me was too big today. I felt done for, and I had no other choice than to allow myself to just give into the weakness of my sadness.

Suddenly, I was aware of a figure looming over me, a big, dark, scary shadow blocking out the sunlight. The skies darkened, and the air chilled – she had caught me out; I had broken the 'no crying' rule.

My adoptive mother stood smirking over me. 'Oh, look at the little baby crying,' she said with a sneer. 'What's happened this time to make the cry-baby cry?'

The ridicule in her voice was too much – by now I was sobbing in great heaving gusts. I really needed soothing and calming, a mother's loving hug to comfort me and to tell me that everything was going to be alright. I really, really needed her to take my guilt away over not saving the bird, but I was also experiencing a deep sense of overwhelming unhappiness that had been long ago locked away – it wasn't just about the bird.

'What have I told you about crying?' she continued. 'You are a big girl now and big girls don't cry. Are you always going to act like a baby?' Taunting me and with jest she demanded, 'Tell me why you are crying, little baby?'

She was actually laughing at me now. I couldn't stand her ridicule, and at the same time I couldn't stand her disappointment in me. I felt so ashamed. If I could just tell her *why* I was crying, then maybe today she might be kind to me, but I knew I was kidding myself with my hopefulness. The contrast between my yearning to be held and loved, versus the stark reality that she was never going to give me anything but bullying and punishment, was really killing me off. I sucked up whatever I could fathom to run past her, into the house, and into the bathroom. I bolted the door, letting myself cry into masses of toilet paper until I could quickly mask my feelings.

She started banging on the door seconds later, but I was ready for her. I had somehow managed to flick a switch and self-regulate, and I was back to the stoic, steel robot of a child that she approved of.

I opened the door to her, and I said in a voice – that didn't seem to be mine, and years beyond my age – that I had been sneezing from a sudden bout of hay fever, and that I needed some more of the pills her doctor had prescribed for me. I said I was sorry for running to the toilet.

With a business-like look, she nodded. 'That's right,' she said. 'Apologize. You were being so pathetic. It is unacceptable; you must always do as I say. Now go take a pill.'

She was so right – and at this point in my life, I believed her. There was no point in being anything other than what she wanted. There was no way out; I was here to please and obey her, to take care of her every need. She could dump her self-hatred onto me and blame me for it all, and she did. I would own it as if it were my own shit, and I thought I could take it. After all, her mother treated her in the same way, and my adoptive grandmother treated me with nothing but contempt – calling me 'the devil's spawn.' At least the pills helped me cope.

Those women in the female family line – both my first, original family and now my adoptive family – all hated me for being born. I was in the way, and I wasn't worthy of their love. I wasn't worthy of anything.

I was the only one – in the house, or in the family, or in the community – that knew of my adoptive mother this way. My adoptive mother and I had our special little secret – a toxic, co-dependent, wretched relationship that nobody else could see or know about.

My sister had no idea; she thought she was a saint. The neighbours, the people at the supermarket, her few friends that dropped by – they all thought she was an angel, such a great mother. They would say that we were the luckiest kids to have her as our mum. She was generous, affectionate, gregarious, bubbly – who wouldn't love her? She charmed everyone who crossed her path. And don't even get me started on Christmases and birthdays – she was the 'Queen of Celebrations', and she lavished me with gifts galore, especially if there were people around. But it really confused me – half of the time I didn't know anybody who attended my birthday parties, as it was all a part of her charade to impress others. And why all the gifts if she didn't like me?

When the show was over for the world, I could set a stopwatch for the time when the devil in her would be aching to be let loose, like he had been left starving and restrained and would suddenly need to explode – suffocating the room and taking away my oxygen to feed on me once again.

Whilst devouring me, the angelic part of her would still be there for Erica – at the same time! She left her alone, instead she showered her with affection, adoration, cuddles, love, and respect. Maybe it was because she was her biological daughter. She could be split in two – the disgruntled adoptive mother for me, and the loving, nurturing mother for her.

The doorbell would ring, and she would tuck herself back in, all neat and tidy-like, put on that charming smile, and ooze out love and warmth in her voice to whomever was at the door. That spell would last until she would 'turn' or become bored with herself. She craved my innocence and my light, and her hunger was never satiated. When I was reading a book, enjoying my own time, she would suddenly accuse me of doing something that I hadn't done. She thoroughly enjoyed breaking me when she saw I was strong, but she especially enjoyed destroying me when I was feeling weak and defenceless. Keeping me weak was her strength and snapping me into pieces with her words or by hitting me or sexualizing me had become her daily meditation and medication.

At this young stage of my life, I haven't mentioned it to anyone, as I thought that it was a 'normal' thing mothers do. To inflict pain and complete humiliation. Like smacking my bare bottom so hard it stung and left red marks for hours. Or, when she would force me to run around the yard naked whilst she was talking to the neighbours, who had full view of me over the fence. She even forced me to bike ride around in a skin-coloured bikini, which was so embarrassing – I looked completely naked, for the whole world to see! I thought it was also 'normal' for mothers to force their children to undress in front of them, or 'normal' for mothers to walk around the house in their underwear or see-through nightgowns all morning. I also thought it was 'normal' for our mothers to invite strange men over for dinner, whilst our fathers (their husbands), were living across the other side of the world. Normal, is what I thought because it was all I knew.

I filled her with the power she needed to get through her day, and I became that part of her that she could beat up on when she felt bad about herself. In time, I learned how to flatter and placate her when it got too intense. I could calm her; I was the demon whisperer. But that was only after she attacked again.

If I knew we had the option to kill ourselves, I would have done it. But I had no concept of it – I guess I wasn't meant to know of such an easy escape. I escaped a different way, one which was pretty genius for an eight-year-old. It happened the day when I shook hands with myself and made myself a promise to never feel anything, or to want anything, or to need anything for myself, ever again. It proved to be a good decision – you can escape internally if you are not able to externally. It was around this moment when Sam – not Samantha, not Sammy – really stepped in and hardened any of the softness that was left in me. To protect and shield me. That's what happened to little Sammy.

Nothing fazed me after my decision to cut myself off from ever feeling happy or sad again. After I made my secret pact with myself, her mission to break me – with her cruel words, her gaslighting, her hitting me hard on my bare backside, her yelling, her blaming me for her tears and her misery, her obvious hatred and anger towards me, or her evil wrath – nothing like that could never hurt me again.

It took the birth of my son when I was 25 years old, for me to begin to feel anything again. I really had no idea of the power she had over me and what she had taken from my life or the lengths I was forced to go to in order to get by. Her bullying had only intensified across my adult years, growing more insidious, deceitful, and strategic. She turned my father and their friends against me, then Erica, other relatives, and even some of my friends. She painted me into someone I wasn't, gaslighting the world to see through her eyes.

It was to be another 20 years later, when the weight of her suffocation was finally lifted off my chest. I no longer felt buried under the world of her misery, the misery of the world that I thought was real.

That was the day I found out she had died, and that was the day I started to live.

Coach Charlie:

In my opinion, Bridgette's adoptive mother was an undiagnosed narcissist with borderline personality disorder and depression. This is my conclusion, from years of research and training in this field and from introspection and discussions with other professionals. Being raised by a mother like that will only damage a child, especially when there isn't a father or other guardian around to potentially be a protector. Sam stepped in when Bridgette could no longer cope with it all, and then Sam took over as her guardian and protector. Sam didn't need to connect. She didn't need to belong. This literally saved my sanity.

The question I have been searching for the answer to is this: 'How could an unhappily married couple, with such obvious disregard for each other, and a lack of empathy and understanding for the responsibilities of raising an already severely traumatized child, be able to adopt?'

The obvious oversight in New Zealand, in my opinion, was in the vetting process from the Social Welfare Department – right from my parents' initial application to adopt, to them being foster parents, to them finally being granted the authority to legally adopt. It is important for you to know that this couple not only conceived their own child four months after adopting Bridgette, but they also split up two years later, leaving an angry, overwhelmed, psychotic, mentally ill woman to raise two children under the age of two, favouring her biological child and letting their father only visit once or twice a year!

Because of the specific skills, understanding, commitment, and special nurturing required for traumatized babies, in my opinion, prospective parents should have been vetted properly by at least examining and gaining awareness of their own abandonment issues, their issues concerning their infertility, their reasons for wanting to adopt, and the depth of their commitment to each other. They should have been vetted for their willingness to acknowledge the differences between biological and adoptive families and be examined regarding their own expectations for providing the best possible relationship for the child's highest welfare. They should have had some kind of psychological testing concerning how it might feel for them to raise a biological stranger, who, due to different epigenetics and DNA, is totally different from them. They should have been tested on whether they are adopting the child to give the child the love it needs, for the child's best interests – or, because they wanted the child for their *own* best interests – to fix the marriage, to fix the infertility, to fix the shame. In our case, this couple used Bridgette to 'fix' them.

This is my opinion.

Prospective adoptive parents should be screened to ensure that they have no prejudices. Treating an adopted child who is growing up in their family unit as if they were their own biological child, is a kind of racism and discrimination, because it denies the child the right to be who they were born to be, who they really are.

Once again, this is my opinion.

Look at the ramifications Bridgette had to deal with already, just because she was merely being herself. She had to change and bend her natural tendencies to accommodate and fit in, just like you may have had to. Are you still doing this now? How are you accommodating others? What are you going to do to address this and to take better care of your true self? How are you going to step into living as your true nature and be the predominant creative force in your life? Keep reading chapter by chapter for further insights and encouragement.

Lots of love,
Coach Charlie X

CHAPTER 7

Amy and Her Voice Save the Day

(Amy)

'You suck.'

'Why do you pretend to sound like the Queen?'

'You aren't one of us.'

'What are you doing here, British girl?'

Every day at my new school in Hawaii, many other derogatory comments were made about how my accent was just plain 'wrong' – something about it really offended these stupid kids! One day right after the lunch bell, a group of five students or so fenced me off in the corridor. Then I heard a familiar voice: 'Hey, Miss Australia! How about you just fly back there on your emu today, huh? How 'bout you just fuck off out of where you don't belong!'

Wait – is that Lainey? I thought that she was my friend! I thought I could count on her, at least.

Our parents were friends – we had all had dinner together on the previous Sunday evening. My dad was in the Navy and

Lainey's stepfather was in the Army, and we both lived in beautiful houses along the same street. The neighbours would often have BBQs and watch the Super Bowl together, while we would play kick ball or skateboard down the paved crater.

Plus, I had already told her that emus don't fly.

We had moved here from New Zealand when I was 10 years old, after my adoptive parents decided to give the marriage a go following an eight-year separation. I had only met my adoptive father once a year since I was two, so, to me, he was just a nice American man in his Navy whites who gave me cool dolls from around the world, purchased wherever he was based. My adoptive mother had certainly calmed down a lot since they got back together – she even seemed happy. Which meant that I could be happy, though not at school. There seemed to always be a debt I incurred for me being allowed to be happy somewhere in my life.

'But L...Lain..Lainey!' I stuttered, 'you know I am from New Zealand, just like I know that you are from Texas – neither one of us comes from Hawaii. You have an accent, too! Why are you being like this? I thought we were friends?'

The group all turned their glaring eyes from me to Lainey. Her eyes turned dark, and I held my breath. Launching at me and pinning me hard against the corridor wall, she said, 'Listen to me: I am NOT your friend.' When she yelled, I caught a waft of her breath, which smelt like tuna. She glanced around at the group with a smirk, and I could see she had a little piece of lettuce caught in her right front tooth, but I still bowed my head out of despair. I tried hard to fight back the tears.

I was so gutted; I truly thought she was my ally. She had confided in me and had shared so much about her feelings she had

CHAPTER 7

about her stepfather, and how she felt he was a creep because of the way he perved at her and her big sister sometimes. She had shown me friendship, but now suddenly, she had nothing but hatred in her eyes and disgust spitting out in her words. I couldn't understand the sudden change in her.

'Listen hard, Bridgette. I only pretended to be nice to you during summer break in front of my parents because they told me you needed a friend as you were new to the neighbourhood. They promised to buy me a new pair of Calvin Klein jeans if I was nice to you. Well, I have my jeans now, so my job is done!'

With that, she tore off my schoolbag while also managing to rip my front pocket off my favourite shirt. Then she threw my bag over the balcony which caught me off guard – giving her the opportunity to suddenly punch me in the face. Crack – a right hook to the side of my jaw.

I fell to the ground, stunned, holding my jaw. Everyone laughed at this and cheered her on further, but she must have thought that was enough. For that, I was grateful.

Another kid stood on my left leg and said, 'If you don't start talking and acting like the rest of us, we are going to do this to you every day. Is that what you want, you chubby, stuck-up Londoner princess? And if we catch you not putting your hand over your heart or not singing our national anthem at the top of your lungs, things are going to get very bad for you here.'

I looked up at all of them surrounding me, a tall wall of tin-faced enemies. *Where were the teachers?*

'OK, OK, just leave me alone,' I said. 'And don't worry, I won't tell the teachers about this, OK?'

One of the boys in the group responded: 'Don't worry?

We're not worried! The teachers hate you too! They would never believe you, or even care!' His southern drawl was so thick – we all sounded so different from each other, but why did they have to pick on *me*?

With that, they all walked away, and I was suddenly aware of the pain throbbing in my jaw and the fact that I had to rescue my school bag. I stood up and winced with the pain – things were quickly going from bad to worse, and it was only the beginning of the first semester here.

I collected up my bag and checked that my lunch box had survived the fall. I was looking forward to comforting myself with my food. At lunch I would sit alone or with the other rejects, swallowing my feelings along with the contents of my lunch.

✷ ✷ ✷

I could never tell my adoptive parents anything that they wouldn't want to believe or deal with – like about being attacked at school. If bad things had happened that I needed help with, they just thought I made them up, and if there were things I felt stressed about, my well-being was just not important to them. They only wanted to know about the good stuff, like how many A's I got that day or how well I recited my English essay. They just told me to 'rise above it and think positively', sighing at my woes and telling me to 'change my attitude' and to forgive anyone who trespasses against me. They especially loved to make me believe that anything bad was all my fault; they were experts in gaslighting me.

CHAPTER 7

I only ever wanted to be good and perfect for them, so they wouldn't drop me at the orphanage. Plus, being at home wasn't so bad now they were back together, as my adoptive mother was being so...nice. When I was younger, she had threatened to leave me at an orphanage one day, and that scared me so much. I had nobody to turn to for help when I was scared. Nowhere to place my worries, no one to talk to, nobody there for me – so again I buried all my pain down deeper inside of me. I could control my feelings if I visualized locking them all in a vault under the sea. I did this nearly every day to cope.

It was only when I forgot to lock it, that 'The Voice' would take over me. Being stressed and tired gave it power, and sometimes, it made me do terrible things, things I would never think of doing, nor have the capacity to actually carry out. The voice spoke to me over my Lucky Charms cereal the next morning after the bullying at school, telling me what I should do that day – to survive. The voice was a teenage male around 17 years old. 'He' had a low, velvety tenor sound, which could get quite melodical at times. I named him after Cain from the Bible, and he really was my Cain. I knew that biblical Cain was angry from being rejected by God in preference of his brother Abel, and then ended up killing Abel out of jealousy and rage. It felt that way between us, like he could easily kill me if I didn't obey him. Sam deals with him often, she is quite the match.

It wasn't all bad, though – sometimes he would sing to me, and I would have to decipher the message from the lyrics as to what he wanted me to do next. I learned quickly that there was no point in blocking him out – trying to do so would only make him more demanding and ferocious.

One day, however, I was pleasantly surprised by Cain's gentleness, and I felt a sense of calm. He told me he was going to sort out those stupid school bullies once and for all. He had a plan, and it was my job to execute it today.

* * *

It was lunch time again, and I was standing alone in the corner of the huge, sprawling schoolyard, eating my egg sandwich, and looking across at the view. The school was built high up on a huge span of land, on top of an old volcano crater and it had views overlooking Ala Moana. Some days I wished it wasn't dormant. In the distance, on a clear day, you could see parts of Waikiki Beach. A warm, light breeze was blowing, and I was purposefully wearing my lucky t-shirt and favourite faded jeans. I looked down at the red dirt, happy with my choice to wear my new cool Nike sneakers that my parents had bought me to cheer me up – they showed love through gifts – my love language was beyond incompatible with theirs. Anyway, it was important that I dressed to impress today so I was happy with the gift.

Cain permitted me to finish up the last crumb of my lunch before sternly stating that it was now or never to follow his instructions – he was in a no-nonsense mood with me today.

I had been learning to play the recorder since I was five years old, and I could play 'by ear' and sight read, too. Through these abilities, I had developed a very cool party trick that I used for my friends and family back home – I could play songs off the radio, any song really. I listened to the radio a lot here in Hawaii, and thank-

CHAPTER 7

fully, the same music that was cool here was cool in New Zealand.

Cain thought I could win this battle by playing a few songs. I drew in a breath and put the recorder to my lips. There were a few kids playing nearby and I knew I was in earshot. I began to play.

'Hey, what's that new British girl doing? Can you hear that? Is she playing 'I Love Rock n Roll' on the recorder?'

They stopped what they were doing and walked over to me. I faltered; Cain yelled at me to keep it up.

'No don't stop, please. Go on, keep playing.' I glanced around the group and saw the cutest guy, whom I hoped had said those words. Feeling wobbly, I continued.

'Hey, I know that song! It IS 'I Love Rock n Roll!' Wow! It's cool!'

I stopped midway through the chorus – hooking them in – and asked them if they had any requests. By now, I had attracted an audience of about 10 more kids.

'Mmmm...do you know 'Open Arms' by Journey?'

That was one of my favourites; of course, I knew it. I shut my eyes to play, and after I had finished the entire song, I opened my eyes. The audience had doubled in size – younger kids, older kids, even teachers. Wow!

'How do you DO that? Are you a professional? Is that what you did in Australia? What else have you got?' asked Eddy, one of the popular boys and usually a first-class bully to me.

'Well...first of all, Eddy,' I said. 'I just love to play. Secondly, let's get this straight before I play any further – I am from a beautiful country called New Zealand, a little country near Australia. Across the ditch, we like to say! I am NOT British either. And, hey, I am just a normal kid like you - not a princess.

But yeah, I can play. I work best if I am asked a request. If I don't know it, you will need to just give me another song.'

I was standing strong but feeling a little out of my depth here with all of the attention, so each time I played a request, I just closed my eyes and pretended that I was back home playing to my friends and cousins. By the time the lunch bell had rung for classes to recommence, I must have played about 10 songs to my receptive little group of fans.

The questions poured all over me on the walk back to class, and a little light was beginning to shine inside.

'Hey, what is your name?'

'Where is New Zealand again?'

'You do sound British, but some of us think you are Australian like Sandy off the movie *Grease*. You sort of even look like her if she were a kid too.'

'Where did you learn to play like that? Can you teach me? I have a recorder at home, can I bring it tomorrow and meet you here and you can teach me?'

I was stunned.

Walking back from the field to the classroom was about a five-minute journey, and it was the best five minutes of my life. I tackled a whole bunch of questions at a time and ended it with saying whoever has a recorder to bring it tomorrow and meet me at the same place at lunchtime and that we would go from there. That little light inside grew even brighter. I was watching myself from the outside with Cain, and we saw a happy Bridgette. Suddenly I wasn't walking back to the classroom with the usual feeling of doom and dread; I was chatting and laughing with my newfound 'followers' – even some of the bullies were befriending me. I felt like some kind of Pied Piper. *Maybe my life could change here for the better now? And wait until they hear me sing – that is really what I do best!*

Later that week, a teacher asked me to join the school orchestra, and I became the lead recorder soloist! Nobody ever bullied me at that school again. Cain, we smashed it!

Coach Charlie:

More about 'The Voice' later, I promise. It gets pretty hairy, that's for sure!

I want to speak with you about the common recurring theme as shared by the child personality parts of Bridgette from whom we've met so far, Georgiana, Sam and Amy: the incessant bullying and harassment. The experience in Bridgette's new school in Hawaii was no exception; Bridgette was conditioned to be a victim of bullying at an early age from her adoptive mother. She was groomed to enable the narcissist, the bully. She learned how to survive and was in continual survival mode. This modus operandi created a structure within Bridgette to keep on attracting bullies, to prove she could still survive. She couldn't help it; it was her programming that was embedded into her subconscious, initially from her birth mother and then consequently from her adoptive mother – from the womb to around eight years of age.

When we are raised in narcissistic family systems, we seek connection *more* than we seek truth with every single person we 'let in' going forward. This is on repeat play until we wake up from its curse – and doing so is a miracle in and of itself.

In my research and training as a magnetic mind coach, I came across the concept of 'Family Entanglements' and 'Family Constellations' – we as children are conditioned to suffer what is called the 'Obligations of Love.' The child unconsciously acts out of love to resolve a family wound or family system issue, and the result is that the child becomes 'entangled', acting out the subconscious design or the fate of other family members. This is mainly from the parents, but science has demonstrated that family entanglements and constellations (patterns and behaviours) can go back seven generations in the family lineage.

The only way to resolve it is to 'give it back' to that person (living or dying) to whom it belongs.

I find this very interesting, in that adoptees are removed from their natural family entanglements, family constellations and systems, and entire epigenetics, and then have to cope with resolving how to take on the healing of a 'stranger' family system – a foreign family ecology – even dealing with their original family systems.

Burt Hellinger (1925 - 2019), was one of Germany's most visible and controversial authors and psychotherapists who developed 'Family Constellations' Therapy back in 1980. Some of his books include *Love's Hidden Symmetry*, *Love's Own Truths*, and *Orders of Love* – I recommend you read them. Weaving throughout all of Burt Hellinger's work, he defines some 'family rules' as being three main rules that are unspoken and are a part of the subconscious, passed down from the seven generations of 'mother and father' in every family system:

1. Nobody in this family is going to have a better experience of me than I have of me.

2. Nobody in this family is going to have a better experience of life than I have had or am having.
3. Nobody is going to have a better experience of themselves than I have of me.

When we unconsciously/subconsciously create such 'suffering contracts', we suffer these obligations of love. Our access to unconditional love, freedom, acceptance, self-worth, empowerment, self-esteem, self-love – all are compromised.

Some of the most common Suffering Obligations of Love are:

'Mum, I will be your victim, so you won't have to be the victim of perpetrators.'

'Dad, I will be a perpetrator like you so you will feel less guilty.'

'Mum, I will be a victim like you so it will seem like you had no other choice.'

This is how physical, mental, sexual, and emotional abuse is passed down through generations – as 'Suffering Obligations of Love.' The healthier the family, the weaker the system of rules are. The weaker the family, the stronger the enforcement of these systems of rules are.

Hellinger teaches that children have an obligation to honour their family of origin and that is enforced neurologically across and up to seven generations. He goes on to say that this is not dependent or subject to any kind of override, which I think is especially interesting for adoptees. We are neurologically wired to honour our family of origin, which we have not been raised in, and have to therefore adapt to a foreign generational wiring of neurological family systems. No wonder life is such a challenge for us adoptees – we are removed from our natural environment and our family of ecology, plonked into a different foreign family system, and expected to operate and behave in a way that *allows us to belong*. We never feel we truly belong – we know we are not with our birth family from the moment we are conscious enough to be aware that we have been abandoned.

There is a very interesting quote from Hellinger which highlights this: 'In a family of thieves, the child who will not steal has a guilty conscience.'

When a child cannot heal the family, the child takes on the pain in order to help the family, to honour and belong to them. I guess I wanted to share this with you because once I realized how much pain I was carrying around inside of me for wanting to heal my biological family *and* my adoptive family, I stopped attracting narcissistic bullies and bullying situations into my life, and I also stopped attracting people who didn't love me for who I was. I stopped attracting in rejection and abandonment. It took me up until the age of 50, where I finally reached rock bottom with being bullied. (More on that later.)

Once I gave those systems back to each of my *four* parents, I was free from the systematic obligation that was ruining my life. I also realized how each parent was simply honouring the conditioning of their own parental family systems, and I was able to forgive and release this energetically from my own internal system. My adoptive mother was bullied terribly by her mother, for example. According to Hellinger, this could be backed up by seven generations in her family system. My first mother (my biological mother) was shamed and controlled by her mother – and once again, my grandmother was probably shamed and controlled by my great grandmother and so on. I have been to many therapeutic family constellation sessions to address the subconscious behaviours I absorbed from each of my four parents. I was seeking help so that I could finally understand the patterns that were at play, and how these were killing my life force and happiness, with false belief systems that I'd inherited and was raised within and believed in.

Awareness is power and taking the right action step is life-changing.

What insights have you gained from my coaching today? I sincerely hope you have had some 'a-ha awakening' moments from reading this chapter.

Thinking of you,
Coach Charlie X

CHAPTER 8

Sam Takes the Plunge

(Sam)

Firstly, let me be clear here for you: my teenage fantasy of killing my adoptive mother is not *completely* due to the irrefutable damage of being separated at birth from my first mother. Not all of us are natural born killers, though adoption was a crime done to me – the same crime that has happened to the majority of imprisoned adoptees serving a sentence for murder. In those cases, I say the government has the wrong original criminals in jail – they should have arrested whoever was responsible for the Forced and Closed Adoption Act, the lack of screening/vetting of prospective parents, and the overall failure of the system, as well as anyone else who coerced our birth mothers into giving us away. In my opinion, we should turn our attention to those in the Hague Convention prior to 1988 and hold them accountable for adoptees sentenced to murder. The seriousness of the adverse effects of adoption is not even considered by anyone in the law or courts to explain the reasons behind adoptees who murder.

Secondly, I know *emphatically* that had I felt loved, protected, and nurtured by my adoptive mother, I would have wanted to keep her around, instead of wanting to end her life. But unfortunately for me, she was a grown-ass woman with the mind of a child. Like 'skinny fat' syndrome – where you look skinny, but your insides are fat – she looked like an adult but was really a pathetic, immature, moody, poorly-behaved child. How can a child raise a baby? How can a child go on to raise two children *and* on her own? It was a terrible situation.

Thirdly, my fantasies of killing my mother honestly started way before my teenage years. I was around six when I used to repeatedly daydream of American Indians scalping her and slicing her throat. I would see them on TV, and I would imagine them just leaping through the windowpanes and marching over to her, holding her down and killing her in cold blood.

Brutal. Satisfying. Hopeful. I think you know my story well enough by now not to be shocked about this.

I never had any desire to kill my adoptive father. We didn't have much history together, but after we started living with him in Hawaii when I was 10, I just felt sorry for him. Though he had a beautiful smile, sadness darkened in his pale blue eyes. I knew he drank – I am pretty sure he hid it in his coffee cup, and he used to down quite a few coffees a day. We would work out at the gym together a few weeknights when I was a teenager, so perhaps it was just coffee some days. When I was 16, he would come to listen to me perform on stage and then drive me home afterwards.

He was kind and gentle and he never laid a hand on me. He would restrict me to my room, but only at the mercy of my adoptive mother telling him to do that. She liked to use him as her chess piece, a little pawn in her game of power over me. He was absent from my life from the age of two to ten, leaving me to cope with that insane bully of a woman, but I didn't dislike him – I just didn't forgive him for it. Later, in my forties, he told me that she used to hit and bully him. I said, 'Well, who do you think she hit and bullied when you weren't around for all those years, let alone into my adult life?'

He always seemed to be very melancholy. He used to make grandiose family announcements at the dinner table, saying that we would all be better off when he was 'in the ground pushing up daisies' – I hated it when he'd say that. I loved him, but not as deeply as I wanted to or needed to – I simply couldn't 'love' like that. I didn't know how to.

He did apologize to me before he died. It took me years to be able to forgive him for not protecting me from her or their daughter.

* * *

I was around 16 when she finally pushed me to the edge.

Yelling at me in the kitchen after school again, making up her sordid lies, and threatening to tell my father – whatever it was about – it was on that day and in that moment that I had to decide if she would live or die. Her back turned, I leapt across the kitchen to the knife stand, wanting to grab the biggest, sharpest knife. I envisioned stabbing her torso, liver, kidneys, and heart, over and over and over, until she gasped her last breath.

At the same time, however, I was shown a vision of me in

orange overalls in prison, and, well, I got spooked. Though at that point, I really wished I'd known about all of the perks I could have received from spending my time locked away. I like to think that I would have delved right into my studies, finishing my schooling first to get into university. And when I turned 18, I would have applied to obtain a bachelor's degree in psychology and then would also have completed a Bachelor of Law undergraduate degree and a Juris Doctor postgraduate degree. Then I would have gone on to get a PhD in psychology. Professionally I would have specialized in adoptee pre-trauma and ongoing PTSD for victims of a forced and closed adoption, researching the effects of being abandoned and then placed into toxic adoptive families. I would have my own lived experience to draw upon, and adoptees are over-represented in prison, so I would have been able to conduct plenty of case studies for my PhD. I would also have become the lawyer to represent them, and the lawyer that would take class action suits against the New Zealand government on behalf of adoptees who wanted to sue for damages.

This is what I would have done. I think about this a lot.

I would also have become friends with a few of the adoptees there in prison. Perhaps I would have met a woman who would tell me all about her adoption…let's call her Debbie. Debbie would have the same reservations that I did, and perhaps that you may have too, about sharing her adoption experience. Maybe this is how the conversation would have gone:

'Thank you, Debbie, for entrusting me with your story and for contributing to my case study, which will eventually be a compilation of stories from adoptees and then adapted into a novel.'

A look of deep concern might register on her face. She might say, 'But I would need to remain anonymous. I wouldn't want anyone to know it was me.'

I would assure her with, 'Your identity will not be revealed in the novel – some people may read it and connect the dots, but then again, they might not. If you encourage your adoptive or birth family to read it, then we could assume they will read your story, but you can protect yourself and change all names, places, etc. to avoid any potential legal issues. Do you understand what I mean?'

Debbie would nod. 'Yes...I think so. You mean that it won't be easy for the reader to connect my story to me? Or even not at all?'

I would share with her that this is a very common concern, as it also was for me, even thinking of creating such a book. She might say, 'Because, if they did, it could be incriminating for my birth and adoptive families!'

I would need to reassure her but, also, earn her complete trust first. I would hope she would give me the go ahead by saying something like, 'I feel safe with you, and I am not going to withhold anything from you. This really is my turn to finally tell my story. You have given me permission to finally speak and be heard. Bridgette, I am ready for this to be opened, for myself, and for others who need to hear my story and for its eventual closure.'

Debbie would probably be looking at me with an intensity in her eyes – perhaps they would begin to fill with tears. I would hold her hand gently, reassuring her with my words: 'Debbie, we can create a different country, different names, different genders – we can have fun getting really creative with this.

Nobody in your story will be identified by name or place, and that includes you! If someone reads it and thinks it is written about them and tries to accuse you of defaming them litigiously, there is no direct evidence in the book. In fact, most writers who write fiction have also thought that family and friends would easily identify the characters – but it goes completely under the radar. So, how do you feel about what I just said?'

I would hold her gaze, still holding her hand. Debbie would draw in a deep breath and would probably say, 'It's my turn to be able to finally tell the truth about what happened to me, and according to you, why I am just so…so…angry! I know that my anger fuelled my drunken rage to murder my husband in cold blood; I know I had some sort of blackout, too. But I never knew how much I was carrying this around inside of me until that moment where it just exploded into a terrifying monster that seemed to completely possess me. I was overpowered by an evil force that wanted to attack him so violently, to kill him and make everything bad about my life go away. But it hasn't of course – he is dead, but the monster inside of me is just asleep. If anyone triggers me again like he did, I am so scared that the monster will awaken, and I will do it to somebody else.'

Trembling now, she would really start to sob and release. Then I would call in Coach Charlie. And then Bridgette and my fabulous editor, Megan, would help her write her book.

That's what would have happened.

Being in prison, locked up in a cell at night but given free rein to watch TV, work out, study, save my allowance, be fed three meals a day, and hang out with some pretty interesting people, would have been a dream for me. Instead, I put my adoptive mother's life first and let her live on, continuing to vilify and gaslight me, and defame and bully me – and this would go on well into my forties, before I cut her out.

I am not going to lie to you. I really wish I had killed that bitch.

Coach Charlie:

Often adoptees unconsciously transfer their pain onto the people they love. They act out from the fear of being abandoned by those closest to them, which leads to them creating what they fear. They hurt those whom they love, sometimes killing them. People often leave relationships with adoptees due to such deeply disturbing behaviour. People have been killed by adoptees, due to being a target of certain behaviour from others, that then released trauma trigger points buried within them. Maybe it didn't take much at all to reactivate their subconscious memory of feeling unwanted, unloved, overpowered, controlled, left alone, and abandoned, not to mention the experiences of often being manipulated or rejected again by their adoptive family.

Bridgette and Debbie might have lost control from the deep-seated pain of pre-trauma and adoption placement trauma, for example. That triggered a violent rage upon her adoptive mother from Bridgette which was obviously exacerbated by her adoptive mother's unruly taunts. Likewise for our imaginary Debbie and her husband.

This happens more than you know. But this isn't recognized in court, is it? Not as evidence in most cases, in my opinion.

Bridgette's pain and anger stemmed from her birth trauma,

re-living itself in a neurological looping system. This would be her pain of the death experience she had from losing her mother at birth and essentially losing herself. In Nancy Verrier's profound book *The Primal Wound*, she talks about the need to acknowledge the impacts of this pain of separation, and the impact of being silenced when adoptees are told to never talk about their adoption.

How can we ever have the chance to deal with it? To get the help that we need? How do we heal? We need to have the right resources of course, but before that, we need to be able to identify with the parts that want to receive the help to change and heal.

Denying and internalising this pain and being told to be grateful for the fact that their identity was completely erased by the government, can really screw someone up. Being handed over to strangers after surviving the trauma of being separated from their mothers for hours, weeks, and now forever – well, this is going to *really* fuck you up.

With the prolonged separation, and eventual permanent separation from their mothers, babies lose all sense of self-integration, as well as the healthy development of the ego that some authors refer to as the 'ideal state of the self.' This interference of the wound that happens – before the baby has processed separating their own individuation or ego from the mother – will often create a feeling of 'disappearance,' resulting in 'dissociation' where the false self and not the true self takes charge. This is referred to by Nancy Verrier as the 'primal wound.'

Please note that I am speaking specifically with regards to the 'Forced and Closed' Adoption era (1930s - 1980s).

After being relinquished at the primal phase of separation

from the womb, and not being given any contact ever from their mother, they are then placed into a home. In this home they must be the compliant child who knows they are different, and even when they are told they are adopted (which confirms their feelings of being so 'different') then often they are told not to speak about it ever again. They become indifferent to themselves, and they are forced to dehumanize it all.

Being the compliant child who is afraid of being abandoned again by their 'new' set of parents, they must comply – but that will cost them, others, and the world dearly. Even if you think you are dealing with your adoption – have you ever considered what it has cost you? How has it impacted you? Or how your adoption will impact your future generations to come?

Eventually, some adoptees act out our psychological pain of separation from our mother and our true selves. There is no escaping that. We have never been given the opportunity to mourn both of our losses, let alone speak about them to anyone. So of course, we often act out through various addictions, and our actions lead to being misdiagnosed by therapists and inevitably being placed into psychiatric wards – or worse, our 'infant rage' explodes into a violent, subconsciously-driven episode, and sometimes, we end up in prison.

I am truly fascinated that, aside from research on inmates who are victims of adoption in American prisons, there are no actual statistics recorded on how many inmates are victims of adoption in New Zealand or Australia. Being incarcerated is often the result of this unique and misdiagnosed suppressed rage, this lack of healing of our guilt and shame for being born, this shame for being adopted that we carry into our future.

Where is the transparency and the help that is desperately needed? How are we ever to move on?

To illustrate this with an example, I was at a 'family' gathering in my 40s with my extended adopted family (cousins) and I told one of them that she was so lucky to have my 'name.'

'What are you talking about?' she exclaimed. 'But your name isn't Bridgette!'

'But it *was* – and it *is*. Surely you know that I was adopted by now?'

She recoiled. 'What? I had *no idea* that you were adopted! I am so sorry. Please don't be mad at me for having your real name; I obviously had no say in the matter. My parents gave me your birth name? That's so terrible! I don't know what else to say.'

Of course, it would be ridiculous to be mad at her – she had nothing to do with this situation, and I assured her of that. But we didn't discuss it any further, and I was instantly propelled back into my identity of shame and guilt for being the one to tell her the truth about me. We never spoke about it again. I just carried more shame over that incident up until now.

We adoptees internalize what happened to us as if it is our fault. Studies have also shown that we carry the emotions that our mothers felt about the pregnancy – it filters down into us as a live energetic current – all of our mother's feelings of fear, guilt, shame, panic, severe anxiety, and depression, all uploaded into our DNA 'programming.' There are many therapists and healers who work in this field, and I have been to many. Some are good, but most are not so good. Rebirthing was an interesting experience, but the therapist had never considered the experience for an abandoned baby. Awareness is key. It helps to choose to be aware of the effects that adoption has on our psyche. Once again, please remember that I am focusing on the Forced and Closed Adoption Act of 1955, not an open adoption.

Some adoptees of a forced and closed adoption choose not to delve into this because they feel they had a fabulous childhood and are loved by their adoptive families. They feel they would be betraying them if they even started to acknowledge what happened to them and address it, let alone go on a search for their birth family. They are not interested in any therapy around their relinquishment trauma, thinking they somehow magically escaped that damage.

This adoptee subgroup cannot stand my voice; I doubt they will be reading this book. They have totally disregarded any evidence I have shared with them in the past about the ramifications of being relinquished at birth, and of being an orphan who was handed over to strangers and given new birth certificates with fake names and families, their original identities wiped clean. They hate it when I say that we were most probably adopted to 'fix' a problem in a marriage, usually infertility. In my opinion, I think we do sometimes we 'fix' the prospective parents deep-set need to be seen as such wonderful, caring people, going over and above by rescuing a baby from the throes of abandonment. Usually they are the narcissistic type, using the baby to show to the world how 'great' they are, even as they abuse the child. How noble of them. But that is only my opinion.

In solidarity,
Coach Charlie X

PART TWO

A FAKE SOMEBODY

CHAPTER 9

Case Files, Unfiled

(Georgiana & Bridgette)
Georgiana:

It turned out that singing in lonely country pubs and restaurants wasn't exactly fast-tracking my singing career in the way I had hoped for. I couldn't afford to head to Hollywood and try my luck there, so I needed something to become – maybe I could be a psychologist or a sociologist one day? Unfortunately, without the right help, it is impossible to believe in yourself when you've been traumatised since birth, psychologically abused, controlled and told you are worthless and stupid. Thinking you can really make it in the world isn't exactly in the forefront of your mind...

So, I dropped out of high school and decided to study sociology at a local community college. We had to submit an essay on a topic we were passionate about, and I decided to write a paper on adoption law in New Zealand. I wanted to get some kind of understanding of what had happened to me and why I wasn't allowed any information, such as my original birth certificate. I dove right in, discovering the history of adoption law and finding out about this hideous crime against humanity called the Forced and Closed Adoption Act of New Zealand.

What I discovered truly shocked me to the core. Created by the Hague Convention, the Forced and Closed Adoption Act reflects the 'complete break' – or 'clean break' – theory. This theory supports that all children are born a 'blank slate', and any 'shameful' genetic traits of the child can be defeated by a 'nurturing' upbringing. Because of this, the Act required that all contact and knowledge of the child's biological parents was to be severed.

As if that information wasn't disturbing enough, I dug deeper to discover this clean break theory gained widespread acceptance following World War II! The results of Nazi rule in Germany accredited eugenics, with its emphasis on concerns of hereditary characteristics, but experts increasingly claimed that babies were a 'clean slate' to be shaped by their environment. The Nazis believed both theories could work together for their ultimate objective, and therefore and this is in my opinion only, maybe they influenced the rollout of such an unlawful act.

Also, according to my research, it was Sigmund and Anna Freud who believed in forced and closed adoption, promoting early separation of mother and child on this basis. Similarly, the influential British psychologist, psychiatrist, and psychoanalyst John Bowlby argued for prompt separation of the birth mother and baby, so that early experiences would not disrupt personality development. According to these influencers of their times, they stated that forced and closed adoptions also helped the adoptive parents create stronger bonds. I was gob smacked after finding this out!

Back then society considered married couples more able to provide advantages than single mothers. In this way, they argued that the 'complete break' theory gave credence to a widespread policy of removing the babies from these mothers between about 1935 and 1985. To make matters even worse, birth mothers were not given any information about the whereabouts of their children and vice versa, all in the interests of preventing any 'disruption' to the adoptive family.

Under the Forced and Closed Adoption Act, around 90,000 babies were taken from birth mothers between the 1950s and 1980s in New Zealand alone, in a system where many gave birth 'in mother-and-baby' homes. Adoptions peaked in the 1970s with nearly **4,000** children adopted each year on average; most of these adoptees are still alive. And I recently found out that in 2020 there were only 125 adoptions granted by the Family Court in New Zealand.

As I began to dig deeper into my research, I learned that children adopted in New Zealand after 1986 were governed under the Open Adoption Act, which meant that expectant parents and adoptive applicants would have shared their identifying information with each other. When the infant moved to the care of their adoptive family, the contact agreement described the commitments that the parties had made regarding ongoing contact, and it developed their relationship into the future. Contact agreements varied depending on the wishes of the parties involved; some arrangements involved frequent direct contact between the expectant parents and their wider family members, and the adoptive applicants and the child, and other arrangements involved some connection with each other through letters, emails, or phone calls, possibly at pre-arranged times.

As unlucky as my life had been so far, it was not a surprise that my birth had happened before the Open Adoption Act, and I knew the chances of me finding out about my origins, or being given my original birth certificate and birth file was…remote.

Under the Forced and Closed Adoption Act, I was potentially not legally eligible to access any information on my birth parents or my birth records. That shocked me and, I still couldn't get over the link between what had happened to me and the Nazi eugenics rule. I just had to explore more on that later. My paper on the Forced and Closed Adoption Act propelled me further into wanting to reclaim my birth right, in defiance of a corrupt system and the inhumane injustices.

At that particular point in time, my journey to find out what had happened to my roots walked me headlong into a wall. My adoptive parents were really the only help on hand, and they had repeatedly insisted that they had no information about my past – therefore, I didn't have any information to take to the Social Welfare Department. I thought I had to just stop there, giving up any hope of ever finding myself. I had literally given up all hope of ever finding who my 'real' mother was as well.

And then a miracle happened.

On my 18th birthday, my adoptive mother presented me with a manilla folder containing adoption documents they were issued when they adopted me. 'Here you go,' she said. 'You're old enough now to know the truth of your birth. There's not much to go by, but at least it's something. Happy Birthday.'

CHAPTER 9

I stood there, like 20 deer in headlights, as my mother turned on her heels and sashayed down the hallway. Well, what the hell kind of a birthday present is this? When I had dared to ask my adoptive parents if they had any documents about my birth, I had previously been told they had no information. Why did they continually lie to me and berate me all the time?

More lies and more truths about who I was and wasn't.

Bridgette:

The file contained very little information, just a document entitled 'Certified Copy of Entry of Birth.' (Entry of birth? What am I, a ship in the harbour?) This listed the initials of my birth mother's Christian and middle names, as well as her surname. *Her initials only? Why?*

And then suddenly I saw it: my Christian name, my birth name. Bridgette.

Wait a minute. My name is Bridgette? My eyes felt they were opening wider and wider, and I couldn't move them around the document fast enough. In a state of shock, I scanned it for information about my mother and father. But, as per the usual standard in such documents under the Forced and Closed Adoption Act of 1955, there was no name at all listed for my father, and only the initials of my mother's first and middle name – but at least it listed her surname.

Included in the file was a handwritten piece of paper outlining a very brief description of each of my parents – a few words about their interests, their features, religious preferences, whether they had siblings, if their parents were still alive, and a little family health history. Most of the information recorded about my birth father was completely inaccurate, as I was to later discover.

It was a lot to take in, especially since I felt I couldn't talk about it at all with my adoptive parents – my adoptive father especially. He didn't want me to even have this information – he wanted me to be his, he would say. He was in complete denial that he didn't produce me as his offspring.

To top it all off, a couple of weeks later, I also got kicked out of home after a huge, explosive blow up with my adoptive mother. She attacked me physically, pinning me down with her weight, and I had no other choice but to flee to a friend's house for the weekend. When I returned, the entire contents of my room were all packed into boxes – she had wasted no time in getting rid of me after she gave me my adoption file. What *really* hurt was that my adoptive father was the one who told me to get out. (He tried to make up for it later.)

I had nowhere to go. No money. I have no options but to live in my car with my life in boxes and my name in a manilla folder. *Bridgette*: it was now to be written upon my heart.

Oh, and I had broken up with my boyfriend Ben, too. I was madly in love with him, but thought I wasn't good enough, so I called it off before he dumped me. I ensured I was always the one to leave in relationships, but getting kicked out of home was not on my radar that year.

Homeless and couch surfing, looking for a place to live, supporting myself financially as a cook at the local café whilst returning to school to get into university – what better time, then, to search for my birth mother? There was no off switch

CHAPTER 9

with me. Maybe *she* would love me, and maybe I would be able to finally understand and accept who I was, with all my faults and unlovable bits that my adoptive family obviously abhorred.

Somewhere in the recesses of my mind, however, was the reminder of what I had been told: 'Your birth mother gave you away because she loved you so much.' *Would she do it again once I found her?*

I finally found a shared house, and in my tiny room on a cold wintery afternoon, I looked up the Department of Children and Welfare in the phone book and dialled the number. This is in the late 1980...trust me, it was a huge book with thin pages with tiny rows of names and phone numbers to flick through – and I don't mean 'swipe right.'

The department refused to give me the full name of my birth mother. When I asked why, they stated that due to her *unusual* Christian and middle names, it would then be 'too easy' for me to find her. To easy? They explained that under the Forced & Closed Adoption Act they had the power to rule out any information being issued to me of my mother's identity if it was too 'distinctive.' I will never forget how they stated that 'it was their job to protect her from me.' *What was I, a serial killer? I guess I could have been, considering...*

Well, that only inspired me more. I spent hours at the public library, scouring through the white pages and microfiche files. Where were Google and the social media platforms when I needed them? Not that it would have helped really; I only had her initials and her last name, which happened to be a very common surname, like Smith. Seriously.

I searched the electoral roll in the year and the place of my birth, thinking she might have submitted her details at her place of residence at the time. So many initials with a surname like 'Smith' – I was getting nowhere until I heard that voice in my head: 'Look, dumb-arse, you are completely missing the clue given to you from the department over the phone the other day.'

Ohhhhhhhh – I've got it. The Department failed to recognize that on that phone call, they had inadvertently given me information of her Christian and middle names: *both names were 'unusual.'*

Idiots. I would show them. I went back to the public library and rifled through the electoral roll under the year and city I was born - (where she was farmed out to hide and to birth me in secret). I was also looking for a woman with a weird first and middle name. So, in no time, I had stumbled across my biggest lead yet.

I called the department back. They were the bastards, not us adopted people, but that is what we were called. Bastards. These bastards at the department were responsible for taking away my name, my family, and my history, and I was going to get it all back. I had a plan.

They finally answered the phone. 'Oh hello,' I said. 'I am just calling you back as you requested, to verify a name.'

There was silence. Then they muttered a flippant, 'Oh?'

I continued: 'During my previous call, you guaranteed me a yes or no answer if I found a name that I thought matched my mother's full birth name. Could you please get my files first so we can just clear this matter up on the spot?'

I told them my adoptive name and held my breath while I waited for them to return. I just couldn't believe I had come this

CHAPTER 9

far now – this could be it for me! Suddenly they spoke: 'Are you there? Yes, well, I have your file here, just a moment. Can you please state the name to me?'

'Janevieve Laureline.' I ensured my voice didn't give away the fireworks going off in my heart.

'Ummmm...OK...uh-huh...right...yes, it looks like that name you stated is indeed correct. Is there anything else I can do for you today?'

I don't remember how I finished that call. My head was spinning; I couldn't believe it! In just two months since I was handed my adoption record, I had found my mother! I think I went for a run – I had so much energy to release. Within that same month, I also obtained her birth certificate. I saw her name on a real document, as well as those of my grandparents! And on her birth certificate, it also listed her home address! *Maybe her parents still live there?*

I looked the address up in the White Pages, and would you believe it, they were still living there! I was on a winning streak – *I am INCREDIBLE! I have DONE it – the IMPOSSIBLE!*

It was about that time that I started freaking out – this was too real now, and I felt out of my depth. What was I going to do? I had to either write a letter to my grandparents or simply make a phone call. Either way, I knew I had one chance with this, and I needed to get it right the first time.

I called a friend who was around the same age as my birth mother, and I asked her if she would help. We decided she should call my grandparents. Together, we planned a story to pitch to them: that my friend had met my birth mother in the birthing unit at the hospital and had become firm friends, but that over the years they had lost contact, and she wanted to see how she was. (In hindsight, we could have just said they were old friends...)

It worked! My grandmother gave her my mother's contact details and told her that she had two sons! I didn't call my grandparents directly after that – I was afraid they wouldn't like my voice or what I said, and that they wouldn't want me in their lives. I was afraid they would then warn my birth mother of my impending contact with her and tell her I was a despicable person and that she should have nothing to do with me. I had to play my cards carefully – writing a letter to my birth mother was my next step.

I also obtained my first birth certificate, which was stamped with a reissue that my birth name of *Bridgette xxxxxx* (*surname redacted*), under the order of adoption, was to be changed to the one I have now. 'Null and void' was stamped over my original name, Bridgette xxxxxx. *Well, we will see about that!* This was issued to my adoptive parents nine months after I was born, like I was another birth. Literally.

My *new* birth certificate – the *fake* one – was legal. It stated my adoptive name and my adoptive parents' names as being officially *legal*, and my other name of Bridgette and my birth mother were now 'null and void.' Wiped. Erased. Fake. Confusing. Crazy-making stuff. My head was screaming 'BUT MY REAL NAME IS BRIDGETTE!!!'

I am not who I thought I was...I am not who anyone thought I was...not even me! Oh, and I have also just found my birth mother.

Maybe she would love me. Surely, she would! I needed to contact her immediately.

CHAPTER 9

***

I filled several rubbish bins with unsent letters – for *two whole years*.

I just didn't feel good enough about myself and felt that I would be rejected by her again. It was too hard to trust that anything good would happen to me in my life. I wish I had known the phrase 'better to be hated for who you are, than loved for who you are not'; maybe I would have sent the letter to my birth mother sooner.

I was 20 years old when we met. Two years later, after bins full of letters, because I was too insecure to just send it, I did the impossible and made a phone call to her.

I was surrounded by my flat mates and my boyfriend at the time, and they were more of an emotional wreck than me. I was calm and collected, something I had learned to jump into when highly stressed. 'Dissociation – normal reaction' into pathological personality parts, is how I was later able to describe what I would do when I became stressed. This part of me, which was so centred and calm and strong, I think this was Bridgette, and she was finally birthing to life within the core of me.

A woman answered the phone, and after I confirmed if it was her, she jumped in ahead of me by asking if I was her niece calling from Sydney. I suggested that she may need to sit down, and then I told her who I was. I introduced myself using my first given name – my birth name, for the very first time to any human, let alone to a woman whom I presumed gave birth to me. The rest of the conversation is summed up in one punch line:

'It's Bridgette, and I believe that you are my mother.' I mean, am I not stating the obvious here or what?

In a heartbeat, she said that she had been contacted by the government a month ago with my details, and that she was planning to contact me. Well, to say that wasn't a relief…

From there we wrote letters and exchanged photographs, and a few months later I found myself on a plane flying to another country to meet her.

Coach Charlie:

The following powerful statement surfaces regularly on the internet and elsewhere, and it's often attributed to Nelson Mandela. In fact, it was written by Marianne Williamson, specifically from her book *A Return to Love*. It's incredibly powerful, and I do encourage you to read it regularly during your healing process time spent with me!

'Our deepest fear is not that we are inadequate. Our deepest fear is that we are powerful beyond measure. It is our light, not our darkness that most frightens us. We ask ourselves, 'Who am I to be brilliant, gorgeous, talented, and fabulous?' Actually, who are you not to be? You are a child of the Universe. Your playing small does not serve the world. There is nothing so enlightening about shrinking so that other people won't feel insecure around you. We are born to make manifest the glory of God which is within us. It is not in just some of us, it is in all of us. And as we let our own light shine, we unconsciously give other people permission to do the same. As we are liberated from our own fears, our presence automatically liberates others.'

It is difficult to connect with our superpower and our superconscious mind when we keep tripping over our past belief systems that are lying all over the place and magnetizing us back to the past every time we attempt to improve our life in some way. This is where 'Anchoring & Kinesiology' can help you.

What is your deepest fear? Is it being lied to or being betrayed again? Is it the fear of abandonment and rejection happening to you again? Is it a fear of not being good enough or worthy enough to be loved for who you are? Negative beliefs and patterns and programs like this, are the unconscious wounds, created from the womb to the age of around 8. These are also called your 'Inner Child Fears.'

Spend a few minutes connecting into your deepest fear. Remember, you are safe – and I am about to give you a wonderful little technique to assist you in moving out of this fear. It is called *Anchoring*.

Anchoring is a Neuro Linguistic Programming technique, which refers to how a memory stored in one of the senses (smelling, seeing, feeling, hearing etc.,) stimulates a response. We have many anchors that help us to get along in our environments. For example: red and green traffic lights stimulate drivers to stop and start at the right times; the sound of the school bell reminds students that it is time to go to class; the smell of jasmine can remind you of your grandparents' garden.

Anchors provide a way for the unconscious mind to sort and retrieve information through a system known as Kinesiology. This system is used in the complementary health or natural medicine field, defined primarily as the use of muscle testing to identify imbalances in the body's structural, chemical, emotional, or other energy, to establish the body's priority healing needs, and to evaluate energy changes brought about by a broad spectrum of both manual and non-manual therapeutic procedures.

Let's try out a great technique based on the wonderful art of Kinesiology to create an anchor to reframe your inner belief systems. Ready?

To start, get comfortable and take a relaxing deep breath to the count of four, in through your nose, if possible, hold for four counts and release slowly for four counts – repeat four times.

Now, with your non-dominant hand, simply close your forefinger and thumb together & hold. Your non-dominant hand connects with your inner child fears, negative thinking, and outdated beliefs. So, if you are a right-hander, you use your left hand to connect with your inner child by closing your left forefinger and thumb. Whenever we are feeling fear, pain, low self-worth, not good enough, feeling unloved, hurt, or scared – whatever the negative energy – it is actually coming from our 'inner child self.'

To 'anchor', place the thumb and the forefinger of your non-dominant hand together and hold, ask your inner child what 'they' are wanting right now, and what they are feeling is blocking them from having that. Acknowledge their feelings without judgement and lovingly ask them to share with you the memory of where this feeling originated from (as far back as you can).

To 'anchor' a NEW belief, use your dominant hand to re-enact the scene in a new positive outcome focused way.

Be the parent, or carer or adult you needed to have back then and say the words you needed to hear – to heal the fear of the past and erase the 'old file.'

CHAPTER 9

Now, take this even further and connect with one emotion from one situation right now, that keeps blocking you – use the instructions above and give yourself some healing!

Once we 'reframe our brain' we are no longer being 'run by the files.' We can simply recode the past to let it go, and step into the desired reality we want to create. Right now!

Practice this as much as possible – to address old, outdated belief systems. Welcome to your healing time!

Big love to you from me,
Coach Charlie X

CHAPTER 10

The Day I Met My Mother

(Kaiyah)

As the plane touched down on the tarmac, I flew out the window, so to speak. Just a little panic attack – nothing to do with the landing, but *everything* to do with the fact that I was about to meet my birth mother for the first time. I didn't know why this event is called a 'reunion', because the last time we were ever together was in her womb. Unless she had stuck her head up there introducing herself, she had never met me before. A reunion it was not.

I was minutes away from a monumentally life changing moment, and there was no backing out now. No pressure! *What am I doing here? Why didn't I just get her to come visit me instead?*

She did offer to do that – if only I had upgraded the factory settings in my brain before I made the stupid decision to come here. Maybe I could just say a quick hello and book the next flight home? My breathing was now fast and shallow. The guy sitting next to me was tuning in, and I could hear that he was wondering where that spiritual, confident, calm, sparkly 'cute girl' he had been chatting to for the last half day had gone.

Whilst my ability to hear people's thoughts had helped me to survive, I could have done without the added anxiety right then.

Get a grip, Bridgette! But seriously, what the hell was I thinking? Flying to her country to meet her in person? Phone calls were safer. Letters were safer. The distance between us was safer. I was not safe here.

I suddenly became aware that I couldn't exhale the air properly out of my lungs. I fidgeted around in my jeans pocket for my asthma inhaler. Then I checked my jacket pockets – *where the fuck was it?* Then I remembered that it was stowed in my bag in the overhead compartment. I had to get it – I had to get it right then!

Ding Dong: *'Ladies and gentlemen, we welcome you to Sydney. The local time is 10:30 a.m. For your safety and the safety of those around you, please remain seated with your seat belt fastened and keep the aisle clear until we stop completely at the gate.'* 'Oh shit,' I wheezed.

I willed myself to calm down, pressing into the pressure points of the indentation on my collarbone. I closed my eyes and focused on slowly breathing in and out through my nose – I had read somewhere that this can help. Nope, it wasn't. And neither were my unrelenting thoughts of doom: *what if she doesn't show up to meet me? Or worse, what if she turns and walks away once she does see me? What if I don't like her? What if she is bat shit crazy? What if she looks exactly how I don't want to look like when I am her age? Her photo she sent could have been taken years ago…What if she leaves me again?*

CHAPTER 10

One of the perks of adoption (and there *are* some, once you *really* get creative about it) is that you have no idea who you could turn out to look like as you age; there is nobody to compare yourself with genetically. Oh, and another perk is getting some bereavement leave at work when your 'parent' dies. You can always make it up – you can't disprove it, and neither can your employer. Try it out for yourself, I highly recommend it – personally, I lost count of how many times my 'parent' died.

My thoughts were interrupted with my breathing, which now sounded like mice frantically mating. 'Hey, are you okay?' asked Mr. Nice Guy next to me. 'Do you want me to get the flight attendant?'

Great – just what I needed. Attention drawn to me. Though I did need my inhaler, I wasn't going to ask for any help. Seatbelt sign off, I finally retrieved it from my handbag, sucked the life out of it, and assured the nice man that I was 'fine', just fine.

Making my way through customs, I felt…what was it? I felt I actually *was* fine, and that I was unusually…calm. Maybe it was because I was way high on Ventolin, experiencing the rush of oxygen filling my lungs with relief. Or perhaps I had dissociated a little? (My ex-shrink would be delighted!)

I waited for my luggage, hypnotized by the conveyor belt but coherent enough to grab my bag. When my feet shuffled me through the sliding doors and into the international arrivals lounge, I quickly tuned into my emotions: was I really feeling OK now? Why was I so chill when my mind was previously screaming, '*What is about to happen to me is going to change my entire life. Turn back now!*'

Yup. I was just 'FINE.' I held my head high and moulded my

face into what I hoped would best express the outward look of inner calm confidence as I looked around for the lady whose vagina I fell out of 20 years ago.

And. There. She. Was. Wow! She was *real! She showed up for me!*

People in the busy airport disappeared, and it was just the two of us walking towards each other; I felt I was floating to her. She had on a lovely coral-coloured jumper and faded blue jeans with white sneakers, and she was holding a long-stemmed apricot-coloured rose in her hand. She was tall and skinny (*yay, I will be a skinny old lady!*) and had the biggest smile showcasing the cutest dimples. *I love dimples! Why didn't I get those?* I have no recollection of what I was wearing, but I am sure I looked as good as I could. Truth be told, I felt as if I was buck-naked walking towards her – that's how vulnerable I felt.

We hugged immediately – not too tightly, not too warmly, and for not too long and not too quickly. It was just right, like a Kellogg's cereal ad. We stood back, and I noticed she was taller than me. She was giggling and smiling, and it seemed we were both at a loss for words. A little awkward, as to be expected – we both reached for my suitcase at the same time, nearly bumping heads. Laughingly, she suggested we grab a coffee and a seat there at one of the airport cafés.

Whilst there, we just sat and stared at each other, just soaking each other in. We couldn't keep our eyes off each other, and unbeknownst to me, we were holding hands. I didn't feel uncomfortable about this at all. I was aware of how her skin on my skin felt – almost sensual, but so comfortable, like my favourite old slippers. So warm. Her touch...it felt like nothing

CHAPTER 10

I'd ever experienced – it felt like home to me.

I glanced down at her hands and noticed they were the same shape as mine. I remember I had the overwhelming desire to leap over the table and bury my head into her chest and inhale her deeply, just to smell her. As if sensing my rawness and longing to connect, she suddenly started to cry. She couldn't look at me then; it seemed like she was ashamed to cry in front of me. I knew what that felt like, and I reassured her that it was all going to be OK.

I didn't feel any sadness, but that was the way I had to be from that day when I was eight. So, of course, I was composed whilst she was a total mess. It would take the birth of my son, five years or so on from this day at the airport, to open my heart up and fill it with gooey love and squishy, melting moments.

But right now, sitting here at this airport café, she was poking at my heart a little...and it hurt.

We started up some more small talk, to create some space in the intensity. I noticed she had a very high, quietly strained voice. Was that her normal voice, or was it just nerves? Then I noticed she had the same hair texture as mine. Soft and wavy with a bit of the curse of the frizz. She wore it long like I did, in a high ponytail. Her smile was exquisite – oh, those dimples! Her sad eyes were a pale blue, and her skin was sun kissed but soft looking. She seemed very thin. She had boobs! I hardly had any – there was hope for me yet! I tried hard not to stare at them.

I was slim but bigger than her. Her face was long and taut, and quite drawn, whereas mine was rounded and full. Gosh, she was pretty. Was I that pretty? I don't think so. And she looked great for her age (all of 44 years) – she didn't look that old at all! Remember I was only 20 years old back then and anyone over 40 was ancient…

I wondered what she was thinking of me right then. Observations and comparisons abounded for us both, I suspect.

Suddenly, she started to weep again. She scrambled around for a tissue in her bag, and I handed her a serviette. I hoped it wasn't too difficult for her, meeting me. As if reading my mind, she spoke to me: 'I am just so overwhelmed right now. As you must be too; it's a lot to take in. But I just want to say, from the get-go, I am so happy we found each other.'

Relief flooded through my veins like cool water. 'And please feel free to still call me Jan,' she continued. 'But if you ever want to – and when you are ready – you can call me mum…if you like.'

She leaned over to gently rub my forearm and I felt a piercing sting of hot tears behind my eyes, and quite the ache in my throat. Well, *that* was a button that hadn't been pushed before. Depth. Meaning. Love. What she said moved me, and I wasn't at all prepared for it.

'Thank you,' I said, 'that is very special. I would like to think I could call you mum, one day.' I held my breath a bit after saying that, mainly to compose myself. *Did I really mean that?*

She seemed touched that I would consider it. Her eyes said it all – they welled up with tears again, looking bluer than ever. She said, 'I still can't believe the coincidence of your timing – I was just about to contact you too when you called.'

I remembered that she had also been searching for me and had only recently found me a month before I contacted her. I took a sip of coffee and said, 'Yes, knowing you were looking for me felt very reassuring. It totally alleviated any fears I had.'

CHAPTER 10

She tilted her head with a look of surprise. 'Fears?'

I took a gulp of what was left of my coffee, delaying my answer. 'Yup. Fears. That you wouldn't want any contact from me.' *That you still didn't want me.*

She sat back and shook her head from side to side. 'How could I not want to meet you! Look at you – you are beautiful, intelligent, talented! And I was so relieved to hear that you didn't have that awful American accent. I was afraid you would sound...so...American.'

I remember thinking, *well what if she didn't see me like that – would she dump me again? And what if I did have 'that' accent? Would she cringe every time I spoke? And what IS IT with this recurring theme about my accent – is it to haunt me my entire life?*

Then it hit me. 'Jan, I am just curious. Why did you think I would sound like an American?'

She sat back again and looked at me strangely. *Oh god, what is she going to tell me?* She took a moment to compose herself a little. 'Well...when I was handed the final adoption papers, I had to sign some sort of legal declaration allowing you to be taken to the USA once the adoption was finalized. I had to state that I was never going to try to prevent you from leaving New Zealand! So, naturally assumed you grew up there – in America!'

This was quite the surprise for me; I had no idea that this was the original plan for my life. The lies kept stacking on up for me, with every piece of the puzzle I built. I didn't know what I felt, finding out about this.

Jan broke the silence. 'Uh...so....so...wait a minute, are you going to tell me that you *didn't* grow up in America?'

I sensed some sort of panic rising and her voice had an accusing twinge to it – or was that my imagination? *Should I just go ahead and tell her a bit of the truth of what happened after she wiped her hands clean of me?* I wondered. In our previous conversations I had told her I had a happy childhood – I had just wanted to reassure her and make her feel better about the whole thing and deflect from the painful truth. (Bloody Amy and Georgiana are to blame for that.) I should have just told her the truth of it all back then and taken the hit earlier.

I focused in on the colourful chalk written menu on the wall to avoid making eye contact with her, whilst I gathered myself. 'I grew up in New Zealand mostly,' I said. 'My adoptive father was American; my adoptive mother was Kiwi. He stuck around until their daughter was born 13 months later, and then left, only coming back to visit us once or twice a year until we moved to the States when I was 10.'

I turned my gaze to look at her now and couldn't help but notice her stoic expression. There was also a little hardness in her eyes. *Shit. What have I done? Is this it?*

'What do you mean, they had a child?' she asked. 'And what do you mean, you moved there when you were 10?' Her voice was now a little breathless and her neck was craned, leaning in towards me.

Here goes nothing. 'Yup – my adoptive mother became pregnant four months after you signed me over to them. Then, they split up before I was two – their daughter, Erica, would have been under a year old. I was raised by an angry, depressed, psychotic narcissist who favoured Erica over me. It was hell – still is. They got back together when I was 10 and that's when we moved to Hawaii, but only for a few years. Hence the Kiwi accent that you like.'

Jan's face had frozen fixatedly on her coffee cup. I felt like clicking my fingers to bring her back so we could just talk this out right now. She finally looked up. 'But the social welfare department told me the reason why they wanted to adopt was because they couldn't have a child of their own! And *you* also told me you had a happy childhood and to top off all of that, I was also led to believe that you grew up in America!'

Her eyes were wide like saucers, locked onto mine. Now I was sure I heard the accusatory tone in her voice. 'Well, Jan, yes, I lied to you when I said I had a happy childhood; I am sorry. I was going to tell you the truth when we were face to face and… well…here it is! The truth. My homelife was a fucking nightmare. You should never have signed me over to those people. They lied that they were infertile, and they lied that I was going to live in America. You were tricked, and I bet it was my adoptive mother who orchestrated it – I just know it!'

I felt a sudden chill down my spine – even my teeth felt cold. And yet, I was burning up – my heart was beating so fast with the release of sharing this – with anyone, let alone with her – and from the fear that she was really angry at me for doing so. She had the right to know the truth, just like I deserved to know the truth from her about so many things, when the time was right.

We already had so many lies that had separated and buried us from each other. For this new beginning to ever work out, we would have to dig each one up together and work through them. The trouble was, we both had no idea how big a shovel we would need – let alone a location map.

She made the ice crack by suddenly reaching through for my hand and holding it warmly, her gaze softening. I waited for her to say something, anything, but I guess we both didn't really have a road map for this journey. Intuitively, she simply suggested we get out of here. I needed some fresh air, and her car was parked close by – just enough to take in a much-needed walk and a stretch and to breathe in the humid Sydney air and shake the icy moment off.

It was warm for July – back home, it was snowing. Talking about the weather was always a safe play, so that's what we did. The conversation continued to lighten up along the hour drive to her house. Her driving was good too, thank God, as all these cars, highways and freeways seemed intimidating. Eventually, we pulled up at her little villa in the east of Sydney. Cute, yet cozy.

Along the course of the rest of the day, I met my two half-brothers. What a crack up they were – such a relief to have a laugh. They were both so tall, young, and handsome. Ryan was 13, Max was 17, and they both wore braces. My blood brothers. I had the distinct feeling that Max was more than a little infatuated with me; he was like Velcro.

I really couldn't get enough of all of them – they were a breath of fresh air in my life. Even my asthma had completely settled down – it was nearing the early evening, and I was still breathing so easily. I thought that was a good omen. My heart chakra was happy for now – I genuinely felt love here, a kind of feeling that I had never experienced in my entire life. Family Love. Home. Belonging. I already knew it would be hard to leave. I was feeling so lightheaded and giggly and...happy. What an unusual time for me. *Maybe I could just stay on here longer than*

CHAPTER 10

the 10 days? Wouldn't that be magic?

Gifts were shared and jokes were aired, many jokes, but as the night wore on, my happy mood was wearing thin. This meeting was becoming less magical for me, as the reality of how much I had lost was starting to sink in. Yes, I did feel happy that I had found them, and they all were absolutely lovely, but it was also brutally bittersweet, and I could suddenly see why many adoptees do not venture into where I was – because once you do, you can never 'unknow' things. And then all the questions start creeping in: *what if she had kept me? Why didn't she keep me? What if I had grown up with my mother and brothers? Would my childhood have been better? Would I have felt loved and nurtured with these people – my blood family?*

But that is where my spiritual understanding would step in and show me that you cannot change your destiny – it was written before you were born. If my birth mother did keep me, that might have meant these two boys would not exist. She might have stayed in New Zealand and might have eventually married somebody else – or maybe she might have gotten back with my father.

Speaking of which, I wondered when I would get the chance to ask her about him. Right now, was definitely not the right time.

Over the dinner table, my birth mother said that it was indeed quite a shock to my brothers when she told them they had a big sister. They didn't know about me until a month ago. *Why didn't she tell them about me before? If I hadn't found her, would she have told them at all?* I wondered.

My thoughts were interrupted by my brothers, 'But we are sooooooo excited to have you as our sister! Hell yeah! It's so cool!' They were talking over one another, both assuring me they loved the idea of having a big sister and that they had always wanted one.

They already had one, one made 20 years ago. *'I would have been there for you,'* I wanted to say. *'I would have protected you at school. Taught you how to read, taught you how to ride a bike and then chased you on mine, taught you how to swim, introduced you to my hot girlfriends that you would have fallen for.'* I wanted to say all those things to them, but I chose not to. I wasn't used to being in the deep end.

My overwhelming feeling of being loved and wanted by them all distracted me from some of the unease that was creeping up on me like the increased volume of white noise. Yes, they all seemed ecstatic to have me in their lives, even so out of the blue, and I was thrilled to be so accepted by them all. But I was also facing a massive reality shock of what I had lost – I had come out of the same womb as them, and she kept them. They had everything that I wanted: my mother. I couldn't help but notice the sting of other, similarly painful realizations that were beginning to surface, like bubbles of water slowly starting to boil.

Over the course of the night, sitting there making them all very happy with my presence, my water was now boiling dry. Nobody was asking me questions about my story – my version of my beginning, my adoption, my upbringing, my life. We just focused on the surface. In turn, I didn't ask any deep questions either.

I noticed that my parts were fighting as to who was to take centre stage right now. Amy – the forever positive upbeat cheerleader just wanted to jump in and lighten up the mood when it needed a boost. She wanted to keep things nice and happy. Sam, on the other hand, was beginning to want some booze, and there wasn't any, which agitated her – on top of her already feeling cranky that she didn't get to grow up in this much nicer family unit *and* she didn't get to complain about it.

But I wasn't here to disrupt or to destroy – I was here in peace and in gratitude. That's the big part of being Kaiyah, Georgiana, Amy – to stay safe, perfect, and silent, and to be peaceful and positive. Grateful.

Turns out that creating the impression of being the nice girl was to one day lead to the beginning of the end for us sitting here at the dinner table. It would take another 20 years before I was able to confront her about my true feelings towards her actions and decisions that she made on my life – in utero, upon my birth arrival, and then several times after I found her.

Me playing the nice girl was a role that this audience would now only ever want to expect. I had set myself up to fail, pretending to be somebody I wasn't – big life lesson.

Coach Charlie:

Reunion – is it though? Is it really a 'reunion'? In my opinion, this word is incorrect, and we are again misrepresented, much like the cultural lie and agenda of the entire Forced and Closed Adoption era. Relinquishment at birth means 'no contact' with our birth parents or family, and therefore, no actual meeting between mother and baby, and no identifiable information issued to either party. That was the case for my birth mother and me – these were the lawful conditions of the Forced and Closed

Adoption Act. (Again, I am not speaking about open adoptions.)

According to the Cambridge Dictionary, 'reunion' means: 'a situation where people meet again after they have not seen each other for a very long time.' I had never met my birth parents, grandparents, siblings, extended family – how, therefore, is it a reunion?

For me, I would prefer to call it a 'first meeting.'

What do you think about this word 'reunion' as used to describe your own first meetings? What would you call it instead? Would it be called something different, for each family member? For example, I would call my 'reunion' with my birth father a 'complete trainwreck,' but more on that later.

Then there is the fantasy stage. The planting of the seeds in anticipation of the first meeting created all kinds of fantasies, and I fantasized that my birth mother was the beautiful singer and actor: Olivia Newton-John from the movie *Grease*. I was around eight years of age or so when I first saw her on the big screen. I fell in love with the fantasy that she really was my mother. She had similar features to me, I could sing as well, and she was just so lovely and seemed really very kind. She was everything I didn't have in my adoptive mother let alone within myself.

Who is/was your 'mother fantasy'? Did you ever fantasize who your father is/was? I never really did – only much later in life when I started to search for him. What about your siblings? I fantasized that my two older sisters (whom I would find out about years later), would be so happy to have me in their lives, and that they would be protective of me and be people I could look up to – that was far from the truth, as you will discover further along in my book.

Do you remember the first time you spoke with your birth mother? Did you have the feeling of 'falling in love'? How did you orchestrate it? Experts say that working with an intermediary is advisable to ensure a level of comfort for both parties at the first meeting, but I never did that because I thought I couldn't rely upon anyone. I just jumped right on in there – I wasn't really prepared with questions to ask her or responses to her own questions. In hindsight, I wish I had prepared in advance of our first meeting.

If you had the chance to meet her in person, what was that like for you? Have you journalled about it? What would you have done differently? For example, I don't think meeting in a busy airport was the best place for our first meeting. I was too distracted and was also uncomfortable with people glancing at my mother crying. I held back emotionally when I was in the ecstasy of touching her hands. It is a very heightened, emotionally charged first-time event, so maybe meet somewhere more private. That's what I would do for a 'do-over', but you only get one chance at this 'first.'

Even though there was a little tension at our first meeting, we did enter what I would call the 'Honeymoon Phase.' We were infatuated by one another; I burned to dust any further thoughts I had that were negative. I was content to bask in the glow of the aftermath of our first 'date', and my heart was beating with a peculiar feeling of deep, deep love. She could do no wrong; I put her on a pedestal – so high – that it made me work even harder to keep impressing her.

We lived in different countries, so our 'romance' blossomed

via phone calls – but especially letters. In those days, emailing wasn't 'a thing', and this is the time when we really were in information overload with each other. We shared so much, and I still feel charged up when I revisit that lovely slice of life in my mind. What an incredible experience. Until it ended – more on that later, too.

How did your honeymoon phase play out? What were some of the feelings you experienced? Can you still feel the memory of it all now? Or perhaps you haven't found her yet.

Unfortunately, some of the information divulged during that phase was now being processed without the rose-tinted glasses on. For example, after a few months I started to think more about *why* she couldn't keep me – she told me her brother and his wife had even offered to help raise me. I wanted her to tell me more about my birth father, now that I knew she was engaged to be married to him. What happened with their relationship? She was also asking deeper questions about my adoptive mother's behaviour and seemed to want a lot of reassurance that I wasn't blaming her for my traumatic childhood. I wasn't prepared at all as to how to handle this 'phase' of our relationship – in hindsight, we both should have been seeing a specialist, but who was qualified to help back then? Even now it is hard to find a professional equipped enough for the job.

What were some of the challenges you were facing at this point of time in your relationship with your birth mother?

Later, our relationship went from bad to worse. We couldn't compromise on what we needed from each other, and after a few years, she called a time out on me. She needed some space, and she admitted she wasn't ready to take me on board completely as her daughter. She asked that I respect her wishes. You can imagine how painful that was for me – I was devastated.

When she was ready, she contacted me again, but by that stage, I had grown weary of her. I did seek some counselling with an adoption specialist, who referred me to my first books about the journey of the adoptee, books like *Primal Wound* by Nancy Verrier and those by Betty Jean Lifton, especially *The Journey of the Adopted Self*. I also delved into the book *Being Adopted: The Lifelong Search for Self* by David M Brodzinsky. I can't recommend these books highly enough for self-care, insight, and education into the psychological implications of being abandoned and then adopted.

Was there any kind of a 'time out' in your relationship with your birth mother, or any other members of your birth family? What self-care actions did you implement? What books have you read to help you understand your journey prior to this one you are reading? Were you able to move on and make adjustments for your relationship to continue?

Let's talk about the 'instant' thing – what I mean by that is this: we suddenly become an instant relative to our relatives. How did you come to terms with adjusting to when you became an instant sibling? An instant first cousin? Grandchild? Aunt? Uncle? An instant daughter for the friend of your birth mum to befriend?

It's a lot to process, isn't it? I remember when my birth mother remarried for the second time, and how her new husband insisted that he was now my official 'stepfather' and that I was now his 'stepdaughter.' I didn't want that – not at all. He creeped me out, and it was a big lesson for me to create appropriate boundaries to honour my feelings. I didn't like him, but yet I appeased him by allowing him to claim me as his 'stepdaughter.' I compromised myself to 'fit in' with him – to be accepted – and to not rock the boat with my birth mother.

I compromised myself to fit in with *all* members of my adoptive and birth family, and I compromised myself to fit in at work, with friends, partners, dates with strangers, the guy that made my coffee – you name it – until I was in my early 50s.

Did you compromise yourself in any way(s) with your new family culture, and expectations of the role they wanted you to play? Do you still? How?

Look around your family circle. How are your relationships with your birth and/or adoptive family members right now? Are you standing in your power and feeling respected, nurtured, and loved unconditionally, or are you compromising a part of yourself for someone? For everyone? Don't do it. Give that up. *Now.*

Remember, you are a beautiful, sovereign human being, and you have every right to be loved and to feel validated for being who you are. It is your divine birthright to be loved for who you are, rather than loved for who you are not. Remember that.

Big hugs to you. Love you,
Coach Charlie X

CHAPTER 11

Oh, I Remember Those Eyes!

(Kaiyah)

I had been warned about how I was to behave in front of my grandparents, my biological mother's parents who were based in New Zealand.

I was a 20-year-old grown-ass woman, about to walk up my grandparent's driveway for the very first time – and I was being told how to *behave*. A walk that would have been pleasant enough – even if a little confronting – if it weren't for my cousins chiming in on top of one another, giving me instructions on all the dos and don'ts.

I just didn't care, though; these were *their* rules made for *them*, never for me.

There were only three grandchildren that had ever visited who were based in New Zealand, and today I was the fourth, as well as the second eldest granddaughter. My three cousins, in their late teens and early twenties, seemed extremely un-worldly – living at home with their parents, who paid for what they wanted, using their parents' credit cards, getting loads of cuddles in between their parents running around after them, swimming in their parents' pool, and swanning around the kitchen looking for the next homemade piece of fudge. I thought it was pathetic – or was I just jealous? I don't know. OK, I was a little jealous.

It was such a different world from my own, and whilst I was there, staying with my aunt and uncle, I could see how lovely that was for them all – however, I knew I would much rather have the freedom that I had: renting my own place and partying with friends, paying my own way through university, living on my own accord, and owning my life. I will admit a slight itchy twinge of envy, once I knew the life they had growing up – a life I could have also had. My aunt had told me that she and my uncle offered to adopt me, but my maternal grandparents forbade them to do so. To them, I was just not worth keeping.

I couldn't change the past, but I was all about changing up my future – that was why I was there.

I had met everyone else on my birth mother's side, aside from my maternal grandparents. They had my birth mother when they were older, so by the time I had my first contact with my birth mother, they were both well into their mid-eighties. My birth mother was excited for me to meet with them, and she had decided to fly over for the week as well. In hindsight, I think it was a deliberate act of control, to ensure her presence censored my true purpose. But what was my purpose in meeting my grandparents, other than wanting to meet them before they met their maker?

I was still playing nice with my birth mother – not asking

any unsettling questions – and I wasn't about to ruin this next new 'meet and greet' trip, either – it wasn't the right time for such questions.

I was used to my voice being silenced on the outside, and now it was set on silent mode on the inside. I had already been well-groomed by my adoptive parents that my questions about my adoption were unwarranted, insignificant and unruly, which left my questions burning away in an endless, confusing pit of fire. Meeting new family members only added more fuel to that fire.

I didn't know it back then, but I was so fucking angry. I also felt so detached from reality, simply because I had to be so I could cope. I was starting to suffer with physical symptoms, like ongoing chest infections, sinusitis, increased allergies, and I had recently developed adult-onset asthma.

I had been forced out of my family of origin and my 'new' reality was a forced and fake one – but I was beginning to realize that finding my birth family wasn't helping me feel more 'real.' I realized finding parts of the truth of my past, and asking for the 'real' truth, are two very separate things. Just. Like. Me. And Them.

I was two separate 'entities', my birth identity and my adoptive identity. I didn't belong to either family of trees, so I had to exist somewhere else in time and space, somewhere in the middle without any personal rights or knowledge of the true facts of my life. I was uprooted all of the time, floating in the clouds... (as depicted in my book cover).

As we reached the end of the driveway and the last of the steps, one of my cousins rang the doorbell. The sound instigated an alarm that went off inside of me, and I knew I needed to get my thoughts together. I had set a 'note to self' that although these people were my grandparents, they also were my mortal enemies. They didn't want me to begin with. Plus, I had long walked away from any bowing down to the rules of the family hierarchy.

Let's face it with a recap: my grandparents were the ones who pressured my mother to give me away for adoption. *They* wanted nothing to do with me. They didn't offer my mother any financial support after I was born, and they refused the offer from their son and his wife to adopt me. They did the most unloving, irrefutably selfish act - abandoning *and* banishing their own flesh and blood from the family.

And I now found myself walking through their front door and into their living room.

They probably were expecting that had I been raised in this family I would have turned out to be more like my cousins. Educated. Well-mannered. Safe and Secure. Well-groomed. Educated. Reserved. Toilet trained. I was all of that and more, but I wasn't 'reserved' – just unreservedly wary and untrusting. And I certainly didn't feel safe and secure with anyone – that was a luxury not gifted to me.

I was a high achiever, competitive, and one of those highly resilient adoptees – a 'Type A' personality. The one portrayed by the government success factors with their brainwashing narrative. I was the popular, confident, pretty girl at high school; I ran my own business as a singer from the age of 16; I looked after my appearance with strict dieting, perfect hair and makeup, and too much exercise; had a killer wardrobe; and my current

CHAPTER 11

boyfriend was an international sports star. Seriously! To me, at that time of my life – at the age of 20 – nothing was ever going to be a problem. Including myself.

One would think I should feel pretty spectacular, but I can admit to you now that all of that was simply a vortex of protection, a shell of armour to preserve the lost little girl who felt so terribly alone and unseen and unloved. I just didn't know it at the time or didn't want to see.

I kept distracting myself and others by impressing people, so my shell wouldn't crack and reveal the true imposter that I was. Today was no exception, except I was feeling particularly heated about meeting the two people who should have protected me from the life they threw me into.

My cousins were obviously accustomed to letting themselves in through the house. 'Hello! Gala! Gampa! We are here!'

Wow – the house was very impressive. Located just down the road from the beach and cafes, it was a stunning five-bedroom weatherboard and brick home, all Art Deco inside with parquet floorboards, ornate fireplaces, and an elevated living room with big bay windows overlooking the ocean. Big, lush, green oak and willow trees surrounded the house. It would have been a lovely place to spend my childhood. But were the people just as lovely? Based on the decisions they had made in the past; I didn't think so. But then I reminded myself that it *was* my grandmother who gave my friend the contact details for my birth mother, and who told her that I had two younger brothers.

'Hello! Hello! Come on in, we are in the sitting room!' said a lively, melodic female voice. Now I can feel my stomach lining in my throat. This is it – another big *first* in my life. I was about to become an instant granddaughter.

The 'sitting room' could have sat at least 30 people.

My cousin Greta introduced us. 'Gala, Gampa – I'd like you to meet your granddaughter, Bridgette.' Tentatively, I looked across the room and instantly locked eyes with my grandmother, Gala.

'Oh, I remember those eyes!' she exclaimed, as she walked over to me and gave me a stiff hug. She felt so frail under my arms, and skinny as a dried-up fig tree. She had luminescent white perfectly set hair. She went white at 30 years old; she later told me, '*Must have been the marriage,*' I remember thinking. I found out later that she had an affair and wanted to leave, but couldn't bring herself to do it, so instead she had a nervous breakdown and was diagnosed with manic depression. She ended up undergoing electric shock therapy.

Still hugging me, her eyes were like large blue marbles, locking into mine behind her magnified glasses' lenses.

Awkwardly, I pulled back from her embrace; I wasn't used to hugging. 'I do! I remember those eyes!' she gasped.

I walked over to hug my grandfather, who didn't get up. He had a walking stick and a patch over one eye, dark olive skin, and thick white hair. He was sipping what looked like brandy and puffing on a cigar, like a menacing mafia pirate.

'Uh…hello. Well, it's just so great to finally meet you both!' I spoke, but I was a little lost for the right words.

Silence. Then Gala said, 'We met you when you were a newborn, you know? We were allowed to see you, but your mother wasn't. And I will never forget the way you looked right through me, with those big blue eyes. Just like you are doing right now.'

CHAPTER 11

No, I didn't know – and that quite shocked me.

I hoped my eyes didn't betray my thoughts that were on the tip of my tongue. Had I given my thoughts free rein to speak, I knew this little meeting would have ended abruptly. You can probably guess what I was fighting back to say: *I mean, how could you walk away from your own granddaughter, especially after looking at me? Did you hold me? Or did you just see me through the nursery window? But how could you just leave me there like that? To be passed around, taken care of by strangers for weeks on end then to be signed away to more strangers. How could you not help your own daughter to raise her child? You obviously have money, just too much pride and prejudice.*

I was censoring myself from using my words, and letting my actions speak instead. I guess I really was angry. My cousins had warned me to never sit on the floor, and whatever you do, never spread the newspaper out in front of you – and never sip your tea.

But there I was, newspaper sprawled across the carpet, slurping my cup of tea, crumbs flicking here and there, speaking with my mouth full. I could hear what they were thinking. 'Oh dear,' they all said behind their disapproving faces. '*Whatever shall we do with her? Has she complete disregard for basic manners? Or maybe that is just her nature, due to her environment. Or from her father? Thank God we got rid of her. She should know better than to carry on like this in our family.*'

It was just a game to me now, and I was enjoying myself. *Don't say what you think, just act it.*

Out came the photo albums. I don't know which was more painful – looking at photos of my mother as a child and not seeing any resemblance to myself or looking at the photos of her as a new mum to my brother, Max, whom she gave birth to only a few years after she got rid of me. Seeing my great-grandparents' faces staring up at me from underneath the plastic film was fascinating. Because, as I looked deeper at the pictures, I was shocked to see I looked just like my maternal great-grandmother, Josephine. Wow! It was the first time I had ever looked like anybody. I couldn't help but share my surprised reaction with an out-loud 'Wow!'

It was then that I noticed the room had been eerily quiet for there being so many inside of it. It was as if they had all stopped breathing, watching me rifle through the family album. My grandmother broke the silence: 'Please, Bridgette, feel free to take home any photographs you want.' Well, that was most generous of her, considering.

All eyes were on me as I started to take out the photos of my family, feeling I was taking something that wasn't meant to ever be mine to take. Funny that.

The spotlight was beginning to burn my skin, and I needed to deflect the attention onto somebody else. 'Eva, tell us again what happened down at the beach this morning,' I said. 'It was so funny!' She was a great storyteller, and we were in dire need of a laugh.

I wondered what it was like for my grandparents, to suddenly have the ghost of the baby they'd cast out of the family walk into their lives as a twenty-year-old? I guess it's not something they had planned for. Later that same day, Gala shared with me, in front of everyone, that every Christmas, she would raise a glass to me, saying aloud 'I wonder what happened to that little baby girl and I pray she is doing well.'

I don't know what hurt me more – knowing that I was remembered or knowing that I was forgotten. When people I needed love from go and die, I find I no longer suffer from the hope of being remembered. They are dead and my need to be remembered by them is buried with them. It is a sweet relief when it happens, trust me. Birthdays are the hardest, when they are still alive – to be forgotten about is depressing enough, but especially on your birthday, right?

I kept in touch with my birth mother's family over the years to come. We were never very close; it was mainly letters and a few quick visits here and there. My son William was able to meet them both just before Gampa died. I was told by my birth mother Jan not to bring my son to the funeral – actually, I don't even recall her inviting me (we weren't on the best of terms by that stage.) My cousin Greta insisted I come, as did my aunt and uncle. At the same time, however, I was specifically told by the entire family not to get up and speak at the podium.

Gala died a few years later, after my birth mother and I had stopped talking. This time, my son and I were both invited by my aunt and uncle and my uncle even invited me to make a speech! I couldn't believe it. He said to go ahead and tell everyone who I was, and that I was adopted out but had found my birth family and had a few good years of getting to know my grandparents. It was as if he wanted me to 'out' the family for him.

Why would he put me in that position? What was his agenda? If I did what he requested, my birth mother would be 'outed' by me to all of the extended family, as well as her parents' friends and church community. In a way I would be undoing everything they had done. I felt very shocked about my uncle's true motive; I had always felt I could trust him, but now, I felt he was using me as a weapon against his sister. So, I enlisted a friend to advise me of how to best address this delicate matter. I ended up not saying anything about being adopted out, just that I was the second-eldest grandchild and how wonderful Gala was. I caught the eye of my uncle, who was smiling weirdly and nodding, willing me to unlock the secret vault of who I was to the entire congregation. Then I looked at my birth mother, who was sitting there, all tensed up and glaring at me, wishing me not to utter a word. I will never forget that look she gave me; it felt like a death wish.

It was quite the moment. The story of my life. In the end, these people knew nothing of me. I didn't tell anyone at the funeral who I was and managed to avoid any dodgy questions during the reception afterwards – well, except for one person. I was standing next to my aunt when a man marched up to me and literally demanded I tell him who I was – he had never known of this 'second-eldest grandchild.'

I was still keeping a lid on it all, but my aunt wasn't having a bar of it. She put him right in his place. 'This is my niece. She is the second-eldest granddaughter. The reason you didn't know about her is because she was adopted out of the family as a baby and kept as a secret from you all. Please be respectful, as she didn't want today to be about her – we are here to celebrate the life of her grandmother.'

Wow! I wasn't used to somebody standing up for me, let alone speaking up about what had happened to me. Although my aunt and I didn't share a close connection with each other, we had an understanding and a certain level of respect for one another.

The only person who kept in touch with me every year was my uncle, and I would get a message from him each Christmas, wishing me well.

In my early 50s and not speaking with Jan for the last twelve or so years, I thought it was time to try and reconcile with her. Surely my birth mother would want me in her life one day? Maybe now was the right time? Previously she had decided she didn't want me in her life and had told me so via a text, but after completing an interesting family constellation therapy session, I felt...inspired. I reached out to my uncle to ask him if he could please let her know that I was ready to talk if she was, and I was more than willing to try to work things out.

You know what he said? 'Your aunt and I do not wish to get involved.' Just a generation of ostriches, putting their heads in that sand.

And there were no further Christmas wishes from that year on. Maybe I was just being looked after by my 'guardian alien' again.

Coach Charlie:

'Show me a child of seven to eight years of age, and I will show you the adult.'

I don't know where this came from originally, but I like it! I want to share with you some of my teachings about my spiritual beliefs around where our feelings and behaviours stem from – if you already understand about energy centres, then this will be a great refresher. If chakras are a new concept for you, then I hope you will get a lot out of this information here.

By the age of eight, each of the seven main energy centres in our human body pop open, literally energetically. They contain, and then filter out, all the unconditional belief systems and emotional events from our biographies of our first eight years and the epigenetics of seven generations of our family systems. These energy centres can also contain memories of our past lives too! If you don't believe me, feel free to research all that you can about chakras, but, because I am taking my role as your coach very seriously, I will help you out with some information right now.

What are chakras?

Chakras are spinning energy centres located throughout the body. There are seven main chakras that begin with the 'root', or base, chakra, which starts at the base of the spine and ascends in a spiral column up through the crown chakra at the top of the head. They contain all our 'STUFF.'

Each chakra is associated with a particular colour, along with certain functions, and to achieve balance, it is essential that all chakras be open and clear. Energy will flow cleanly and easily once the chakras are cleared, and this clearing can be achieved through a combination of healing modalities. Reiki treatments, sound baths, energetic clearing, and utilizing crystals for healing are especially effective in chakra clearing and balancing. The key seven chakras run vertically through the middle of your body, along the entire spine, from the tailbone to the top of the head. It is important to understand how your chakras can show up in your feelings, and therefore how you communicate to yourself, others, and the world around you. Remember, behaviour is the highest form of communication from ourselves, to ourselves, to others and to the world around us.

So how about we have a quick lesson about each of the chakras and what we can do to balance them out.

The first, as I said, is the **base/root chakra,** located at the base of the spine. Red in colour, it is associated with needs in life. It's the root connection to our source, and it serves to usher life force into the body. The level that is closest to your skin governs the awareness of survival, and it helps us meet our basic needs. The first chakra relates to a person's overall physical health, their sense of stability and security, and their sense of groundedness. An overactive base chakra will show up in your feelings and behaviour as paranoia, aggression, anger, mania, nervousness, and fear. An *underactive* base chakra will show up in your feelings and behaviour as apathy, weakness, depression, passivity, and lethargy.

Here are some wonderful affirmations you can say to clear and balance your base chakra:

I have a beautiful physical body. I assume responsibility for my body. I recognize it is a gift from God and I can trust it. I am safe inside my body, and I take good care of myself. My base chakra is open and balanced, and I am fully grounded and comfortable being me.

The second chakra is the **sacral chakra.** Located just above the pubic bone, it is orange in colour and is associated with *wants* in life – your life force, or your essence. This level consists of two parts. The first records your earthly lessons from this life, and the second contains the lessons from past lives. It indicates how much you let go of control and go with the flow of life. An overactive sacral chakra will show up in your feelings and behaviour as greediness, addiction, tension, compulsivity, and frustration. An underactive sacral chakra will show up in your feelings and behaviour as disinterest, repressed feelings, self-deprivation, depression, and sexual repression.

Some wonderful affirmations you can say to clear and balance your sacral chakra are:

My feelings are healthy. Part of the miracle of being alive is having the capacity to feel, to learn, and to experience the world through my senses. I do not confuse this wonder with the greater wonder of love. I can allow myself to feel without fear. I am guided by the voice of my Higher Self, not controlled by my body. My body seeks only genuine and healing pleasures that are healthy and balanced.

The third chakra is known as the **solar plexus chakra**. Located just behind the belly button, it is yellow in colour and linked with your life force. This is the tier where you subconsciously communicate with others around you – it sends out signals to and receives signals from others. This is where you keep your fear and insecurities or your confidence and courage, and this is where your soul's energy and psychic intuition live. An overactive solar plexus chakra will show up in your feelings and behaviour as subjectivity, bossiness, narrow-mindedness, abrasiveness, or a dictatorial nature. An underactive solar plexus chakra will show up in your feelings and behaviour as wishy-washiness, an inability to concentrate, naivete, passivity, and obliviousness.

Some wonderful affirmations you can say to clear and balance your solar plexus chakra are:

I am receptive to Divine energy moving into every cell of my body. I am committed to expressing my creativity, to accepting my responsibilities, and to making decisions that are balanced and supportive to my spiritual growth. I am guided and receptive to Divine will at all times.

The fourth chakra is the **heart chakra**, which is located in the middle of your chest, at the same height as your physical heart. Green or pink in colour, it is associated with love and is the link between the higher tiers of the aura and the lower tiers. This tier is also known as the social aura because it blends energy with other people you are close to – family or a team, for example. This is your centre of love, self-love, forgiveness, and healing. An open-heart chakra will show up in your feelings and behaviour as patience, kindness, generosity, peace, humour, forgiveness, and love. A closed heart chakra will show up in your feelings and behaviour as loneliness, suspicion, neediness, possessiveness, bossiness, greediness, and jealousy.

Some wonderful affirmations to clear and balance your heart chakra are:

I am loved and loving and trusting in God/The Universe/Superconscious provides all I need. Everything I do, I do with love. I am receptive and open to receiving love. My heart is healing, my needs fulfilled. I let go of all resentments. I forgive others, ask forgiveness, and lovingly let go of the past. I allow the abundance of the Universe to pour into my heart. I feel others' energy but do not attach to them as a rescuer or people-pleaser.

The fifth chakra is the **throat chakra**. This chakra sits in your throat, at about the level of your swallow reflex. Blue in colour, it is associated with how you relate to others. Your thoughts create activity at this level, and the proximity of this layer to the emotional layer depends on whether you make up your mind emotionally or analytically. This is where you express your truth or suppress it in your verbal communication. An overactive throat chakra will show up in your feelings and behaviour as distraction, negativity, saying hurtful comments, resentment, preoccupation with others, and gullibility. An underactive throat chakra will show up in your feelings and behaviour as dishonesty, wilfulness, hostility, confusion, and repressed expression.

Some wonderful affirmations to clear and balance your throat chakra are:

The only voice influencing my life is the voice of my Higher Self and God's/the Creator's superconscious Divine wisdom – all other voices I lovingly ask to leave. I am a clear receiver and producer of the truth. I speak my truth and my inner wisdom with confidence and love.

The sixth chakra is the **third eye chakra**, and it sits in the middle of your forehead. It is indigo in colour and is related to your intuition as well as your solar plexus chakra. The job of this tier is to convey heavenly/divine/superconscious guidance into thoughts and feelings. This is your third eye, your psychic vision, your inner tuition, and how you receive and project from your ESP centres and protect yourself from lower life forces. An overactive third eye chakra will show up in your feelings and behaviour as hallucination, paranoia, and a tendency to daydream or space out. An underactive third eye chakra will show up in your feelings and behaviour as lack of imagination, insensitivity, self-absorption, and narrow-mindedness.

Some wonderful affirmations to use to clear and balance your third eye chakra are:

I can see and think clearly. I see that all is well in my world. I see the solutions to situations in my life and I make positive changes now! I am the creator of my reality, and my dreams are coming true. I am one with the vibration of the infinite potential of my Divine creative force energy!

And finally, the seventh chakra is the **crown chakra**. This sits at the top of your skull. It is violet in colour, and this is the chakra that receives Divine inspiration. This level is pure heavenly energy, and it operates at the deepest superconscious level. This is your immortal soul connection back to the Divine Source of all creation. An overactive crown chakra will show up in your feelings and behaviours as having a 'God' complex, being stuck up or ungrounded, indulging in 'cosmic' encounters, and acting out how 'special' you are. An underactive crown chakra will show up in your feelings and behaviours as a lack of purpose and meaning, feeling unloved or like a victim, anger at God/the Universe/the Superconscious Creator; a negative outlook on life, a fear of dying, and no spiritual connection or interest in working on oneself.

Some wonderful affirmations to use to clear and balance your crown chakra are:

I trust my inner knowing to guide me through life. All people in my life are here to teach me something new about myself so that I can grow and evolve. I trust that everything happens for a reason and that what I do makes a difference. I am balanced between Heaven and Earth, and I am protected at all times from the highest of realms for my highest of good. I am superconscious and I can create the end results of anything I choose for the highest good of myself, others, and the world.

I hope this has inspired, uplifted, or reminded you of how magnificent you truly are, and that it has given you something extra to reflect upon from this chapter.

With love,
Coach Charlie X

CHAPTER 12

In the Name of the Father

(Amy)

'Mummy, can Connor come over to play today? Pleeeeeease?'

My son's big blue eyes were shining up at me with a knowingness that I could never resist his requests. Not that he got everything he wanted, but I ensured he felt his feelings were important and I went out of my way to make sure he didn't go without. I couldn't help but laugh. 'Only if you come over here and give me one of your big cuddles and kisses!'

Immediately, he leaped over the bean bag, nearly landing on the cat, jumped up on my lap, and wrapped his arms around my neck, 'I love you, Mummy.'

My heart melted, every time. 'I love you too, so very much. Now finish your pancakes whilst I call Connor's mum.'

I was living in Auckland raising my then 5-year-old son, William – I had been a single mother since he was six months old. I am just so proud and relieved that I was able to find my maternal family before he was born, and that I had built up an ongoing and reasonably healthy relationship with each of them. Having a child wasn't even on the radar when I was searching, but I knew I had to find out the truth of who I was – not just for myself, but also for my future generations to come. My future family had every right to know the truth of my beginning, because I knew firsthand that the loss of an entire family is one of the most traumatic human experiences, and I did not want my future family lineage to go through that.

William had now met his (birth) maternal uncles, grandmother, great-grandmother (his great-grandfather had passed away a few years back,) his birth great uncle and aunt and his three second cousins – he knew his entire immediate family on my maternal side. I had broken a generational family constellation – what happened to me was NOT going to happen to him and there would be *no more* lost family members or hidden family history.

I know that not many adoptees have such an opportunity to find and share their birth family with their own children, and that I am one of the exceptions. Whilst I am very grateful for that, I do know that without being 100% responsible for actioning the steps spaced out in front of me, none of this would ever have come into fruition. I was the one to create it – I took the action steps. It wasn't luck, it wasn't God, I wasn't sitting there creating and wishing on a vision board or praying to my guides or angels. I took action, and it took guts, determination, and many tears and years of frustration. I therefore commend anyone who takes the same leap into action to find their birth family. Hats off to you – don't ever feel you need to be grateful to a power greater than you for finding your family or for attempting to do so. You did it yourself; you took the necessary steps. Also, Lady Luck shouldn't get the credit here either – your perseverance and resilience got you through the unsurmountable roadblocks that would have potentially stopped you from ever finding your family. And don't I know it!

I don't recall the day when I knew I was ready for my next big challenge – I was around 30 years old and guess I just felt the time was right. I wanted to find my birth father, William's grandfather. I also wanted to find my entire paternal family. I knew how time-consuming and harrowing searching could be, so I gave myself plenty of time to get ready to launch again. I also ensured I was in the right mental state to endure such an undertaking. It wasn't just about the trials and tribulations of finding my father – it was the stress of approaching my birth mother and her family for their help. After our honeymoon phase, my birth mother had indicated he was 'off limits.'

I wanted to know everything about my birth family, especially for William's sake. Whilst we were both healthy, I didn't have any medical history for either of my birth parents, or any of my generational family's medical history in my adoption file. I had to start by questioning my maternal family about their medical history to create my own medical case file, as well as one for my son. I wanted to be aware of any potentially inherited medical conditions, and my maternal family confirmed that there were none.

What if I hadn't found them? I would never know.

I just don't understand why this important legal medical information was not included in the birth files of adoptees born under the Forced and Closed Adoption Act. Why were we treated like third-class citizens, unworthy of the same rights as the unadopted citizens? I was 100% reliant on my maternal family to tell me about any medical conditions, and unfortunately, I would find out years later from my birth mother about a condition she 'forgot' to tell me about. I researched it and discovered this condition has a hereditary component and studies indicate that about 20% of patients have affected relatives. Had I known of this medical condition my birth mother had, I could have given my son the medical treatment required as a child to prevent him from a future of suffering as an adult. But by the time she flippantly mentioned this to me, William was now too old to have received the treatment he needed to prevent the symptoms he had struggled with.

I am getting a little hot under the collar so, let's get back to my father – not that this topic is any easier to deal with, really.

Basically, after our honeymoon phase, asking my birth mother about him was like dragging a vampire from their coffin and putting them into the sunlight. It was such a scary and painful ordeal, when her teeth would snarl at me, and her hair stood on end with her fiery eyes piercing my soul. Plus, the last time I attempted to do so, she insisted I wasn't to hound her any further about it. I had learned very early on in our relationship to give her space from asking about him – years of it – and then push myself to ask her again. It was always the same result: glare, sneer, and block. She was like a father-blocking-ninja.

More secrets and lies, more silencing and control, threats, and coercion – first from my adoptive parents and now from my birth mother. Obeying and placating was really stretching my people-pleasing quota – I had a right to know about him, who he was. I had a right to know what happened between them as well. What had led me to be cast out of my family?

If people didn't want to be questioned about the consequences of their actions in the future, then they should have behaved better in the past, right? Now I have changed this sentence to: *'If people didn't want to be written about in regard to their adverse actions, they should have behaved better.'*

I had been waiting so long for the right time to revisit this with her, but I also wanted to keep my thread of a relationship I had left of us intact. Questioning my birth mother about my father's identity was like placing my head inside a door frame and asking her to repeatedly slam the door onto it. Why was I always in this same position, searching and asking for answers, literally begging for the story of my life, to be able to put myself together? She had all the power, just as she always had, right from the start. She never asked for my permission; she just made decisions for me by putting her own needs first. I am even pretty sure she wished I didn't exist, especially when I was the little dog with the bone, asking questions about my Daddy.

My existence was a ghostly reminder of a past she wanted to forget. Maybe that is why some birth parents choose to leave the past in the past and do not want any contact with us.

Her 'motherly' duty of care for me was more like an arrow aiming towards her own needs. Why did I feel compelled to take care of her needs too, before my own? This self-neglect transferred into other significant relationships in my life, leaving me powerless, taken advantage of, and psychologically and sexually abused. I was a narcissist's dream dinner.

I don't know what it was that finally motivated me to pull

up my big girl pants and bravely embark through these treacherously forbidden woods and demand the answers from her, but the forest was covered in thick weeds from a family generation or two of lies and deceit – there was no clearing in sight. Questions were swatted off like mosquitoes, left to buzz around in my head. My birth mother had drawn more than just a line between the truth of my past and what she would reveal – there was a great chasm in the earth around her, and between us.

I found myself in the most precarious of situations with her. She had offered for me to move in with her temporarily when William was around six, as I had fallen onto hard times financially (again) and had walked away from a short-lived, extremely toxic relationship (again,) and I needed a place to stay whilst I found my feet (again). Finances, housing, friends, relationships, jobs, family – these areas in my life seemed to suffer the curse of the constant leakage from my adoption wounds. I just couldn't make anything stick; I just never felt worthy of having a happy life and I kept proving this to myself.

✱ ✱ ✱

'Cup of tea?' I asked.

It was a warm but windy Saturday morning in summer. We were out on the balcony, sheltered from the wind, overlooking the western vista of the Auckland suburbs. There were plenty of houses on hills covered with trees, and I loved to imagine the trees were dancing on their own, not because of the wind.

'Yes, sounds lovely, thank you darling.' Wow – she seemed in good enough spirits today.

CHAPTER 12

Living with her, I had noticed she was even more melancholy than I had thought, at times quite depressive – was it me? Her eyes were always so red-rimmed, as if from crying, her face sullen, and sunken, especially in the mornings. She would become fatigued easily in the mid-afternoons and disappear for a sleep.

Was it my fault she was so miserable? I think she was deeply depressed, and I really did try hard to cheer her up…when I wasn't asking questions. She certainly never sought any counselling for herself, and I didn't see any self-help books lying around the house. (Except for mine, of course).

Kettle boiled, teapot warmed, I made a delicious English breakfast tea and then loaded up the tray with some of her favourite cheese and crackers. Tea for two outside on a warm summer's mid-morning.

We sat for a while in silence. We did that a lot those days – I didn't know who was veering more out of the way so as to not run into the other. The embers were always crackling underneath, threatening to flare up between us. Especially when I asked about 'him.' But I will never learn, so I topped up her teacup and dove in with my forbidden questions. Well, it *was* a nice morning for a while there.

'Oh my *God*, Bridgette, I told you I don't remember much about him!' She said it as if spitting out a fly. 'Although, I will say that you do look and act more like "him" every day.' She shot me a look of disgust.

I reached for a cracker and felt nearly as cracked as it was in my teeth. I really didn't think she could stand me anymore now that I knew I reminded her too much of 'him.' To whom she was engaged to, whom she had been deeply in love with. Him, whom her parents didn't want her to marry. He, who arrived at their engagement party late and drunk. Him. *That can't be the only reason why they broke off the engagement?*

The next time she spoke, more than a fly flew out of her mouth. 'He is a horrible, terrible, disgusting person,' she spat out, 'and that's all I've left to say on the matter, so please stop bringing it up. It's very hurtful of you!' Ticked off and line crossed. *Is that why I remind her of him? Because I am a horrible, terrible, disgusting person?*

'Yeah, but surely you can remember his *name?*' I retorted. Yikes – you know that feeling when you've gone too far?

I don't know if it was my pressing for his name, or the stress of having my son and I living with her for a month, which made the wind take a turn for the worse that morning. But my perseverance was about to pay off, even if it would cost me dearly.

Without looking at me she said, 'His name was Ron. I don't remember his last name, but he broke my heart by sleeping with my best friend, my bridesmaid-to-be, so I called the whole thing off. I had no idea I was pregnant until a month or so afterward. When I told him, he wanted me to get rid of you. He wasn't offering any support. And that is all I can tell you.'

She looked up at me and her glare sent an arrow that pierced a burning hole through my heart. It was such a look of hatred. I'd grown all too familiar with glares, constantly copping them from my adoptive mother, but this one was intense. *Great, now they both hate my guts – how did I manage that in one lifetime?*

'You have pushed and pushed me way too far, Bridgette. I am not telling you anything more. I can't believe how insensitive and how utterly selfish you have been towards me. I let you and your son live here, and all you do is hound me again for information about him. You have his first name, a few other details – that should be enough for you to find him! But you won't like what you find, and that will be your problem and not mine!'

She stood up to go inside. I instinctively grabbed her arm to get her to stay and talk things out, but she shook me off her, yelling 'No! I have *nothing* left for you. This conversation is *over! And so are we!*'

She slammed the sliding doors shut and went up to her room – this really was quite the sliding door moment. *Do I chase her, fill her with my apologies, and beg her to forgive me? Or do I let her be?* I chose the door with the sign that read, 'I think I am done with her, too.'

I was playing with William outside, quite stunned by her coldness. *God, I hoped he hadn't heard us.* I started to internalize her projections and fell into blaming and shaming myself. I didn't know which part I was more concerned with right then – was it the shame I felt? Was it because I was that awful, that I reminded her of him? Or was I more concerned with the fact of finally knowing why they broke up? Maybe it was the fact that she had now just asked me to pack up our things and leave?

As if divine intervention was reading my mind, she yelled out the window at me, 'Please, do as I ask and get the hell out of my house now! Just leave me alone!' And then the window slammed shut, just like her heart.

Well, at least this time she *asked* first before she abandoned me again – *always looking at the bright side, huh, Bridgette?*

So, of course, we left. I had another place to stay with a friend until I got myself a job; my son and I would be okay.

Over the next few months, I just pushed it all aside, including her, and got on with my life. I found a job, a rental, and a great school for William. I was good at this, this 'survival' thing, this life without being loved by a mother. It wasn't a problem at all because I was so used to it; I didn't think that feeling unloved and unwanted by my two mothers was a problem, but it all sure did seem to wreak havoc in other areas of my life. It was built into my subconscious to be unloved and unwanted everywhere I went. I just lived with it.

A year later, after a promotion at work, things started to brighten up a bit. William was thriving at school, I was focused on my career, and I felt the sudden itch to search for my birth father. I had journalled every clue and I just felt ready. So, I hired a private detective. I had a few clues, but his last name was still very conveniently forgotten, not just by my birth mother, but by *everyone* in that family. The man my grandparents threw an engagement party for at their house – nope; can't remember his full name. I was determined to find him, but it turns out you can't find a long-lost father with just the name of 'Ron.'

I paid the detective handsomely. Back then we didn't have ancestry.com or DNA spit kits to find your daddy, and the chances of finding any of your birth family were slim to zero, especially without a full name.

I needed to compile all the clues I had collected over the years for my first meeting with the detective. I looked at my scribbled notes. Luckily, during the honeymoon phase with my birth mother, when she and I shared and bared our souls to each other, I had asked her quite a few questions about how they met and I had recorded it all in my journal. She seemed

CHAPTER 12

more than happy to share.

Over that same year, after she kicked me out of her life (again) that day, I had also asked different family members about him. I continued to keep notes in my journal on everything I found out. I was happy to see that my due diligence was starting to create a little picture for my detective.

For example, Jan had told me he sailed his own catamaran, which he had built, from Sydney to the Northshore of Auckland in the late 1960s. They met on the beach, him in his sailing whites and all-American kilowatt smile, and she a tanned and long-legged young thing, pouncing around in a hot pink bikini. The two of them sparked instantly, dazzling like diamonds in the sun.

My uncle had told me that he liked to party, gamble, womanize, and generally run amuck. He had a bachelor pad and lived the high life. He told me he was also about 15 years older than her – God, she was barely a woman. Game and set for a total mismatch.

Jan had also divulged, in our honeymoon period together, that he and his sailing friends had earned the name 'The Rat Pack' from the locals. She said his smile would light her up as he flaunted his extravagances – he had money, lots of it. He booked out the honeymoon suite at a swanky hotel, proposed to her, popped a massive rock on her finger, and ravaged her. Gross.

It was quite the night, she said. He choked on an oyster too, she remembers, rather too fondly. He recovered enough to help conceive me later that night – or wait, it could have been one of the many drunken party nights on the boat. It all happened quickly; it was a six-week heated whirlwind summer romance of dining, wining, and sex. And oysters.

Other than my birth father, my grandparents, and my uncle and aunt, nobody knew the truth of why she went away for the next six months. Arrangements had been made to ferret her to the south of the country to hide us. The delivery was to be kept secret, in a secret place for unwed mothers.

It was my birth grandmother who told me that a week before Jan gave birth to me, Jan told her she saw him, and that he saw her, too, across the street one Sunday afternoon when she was allowed out from wherever her secret prison was. He would have seen that she was about to have their baby, and that she didn't abort me after all.

I wonder what it felt like for Ron when he saw that I hadn't gone away as planned. I am sure he would have been unpleasantly surprised, but he had already wiped his hands clean of us and had gotten on with his life. I was just looking forward to the day when I'd knock on his door. Surprise!

Back to the detective. My savings in my account dwindled, with absolutely nothing to show in return. He was meant to be the best in the field, but he couldn't find him at all – I think he was one of the best at ripping people off more like it.

Coach Charlie:

I cannot stress this enough: use your 'honeymoon period' as much as you possibly can to drill down information on *everything*. And I mean *everything*. This is the time when you and, most probably, your birth mother/biological mother/first mother are 'in luuurrrve.' Compatible. If she has agreed to meet with you or has initiated first contact, you are in the prime position to get as much information as you can. Remember, it can be a short window of time when you are in the 'honeymoon phase' – so you need to make haste.

You *must* be prepared with your questions. Not only that, but you must also get those questions answered NOW, during this cozy honeymoon period. Trust me please – these answers to your questions are one day going to be the most important and valuable questions you could ever hope to get answered.

Trust me, and your future self will thank you.

Have a journal and pen on hand, record on your phone, type away on your laptop, write on the back of your hand – anything! Your chances to gather as much information as you can about your life are statistically much higher at this point of your relationship, so you MUST DO IT or you will miss out, like Bridgette potentially did.

BE LIKE THE GODDESS NIKE; JUST DO IT.

(Please do keep in mind that I am speaking to those of us who were victims of the Forced and Closed Adoption era, pre-1986, and whose maternal family were aware of who their father was. The chances were higher that we were not permitted to have access to our files.)

Some of your questions to ask could be:
1. Who is my father?
2. What happened in your relationship with him? How did it end?
3. Why was I adopted out?
4. What is his name? (Straight to the point!)
5. Where did you meet?

6. Where was he raised?
7. What can you tell me about him? (His childhood, his family, his profession, his interests, his personality)
8. What did you love about him? What did you hate about him?
9. What do you know about his parents?
10. What was your first reaction when you found out you were pregnant?
11. What did you do to cope? Not cope?
12. When did you decide to adopt me out?
13. What help was offered to you? What were your options?
14. What family support did you get? What happened?
15. Do you remember much about the delivery of me? What do you remember?
16. Was I a Caesarean baby?
17. Was I premature or overdue?
18. What drugs did you take during the labour?
19. What happened to me after delivery?
20. Did you see me/touch me/hold me? Who else did?
21. Who met with the welfare system? Who wrote out the details about you and my father?
22. What did your parents do to help?
23. Where did you spend your time during your pregnancy?
24. Where were you working during your pregnancy?
25. Where did you stay during that time?
26. What support did you have financially?
27. Did you know anything about my adoption?
28. What did you know about my adoption?
29. How did you cope after my adoption?

30. What happened in your life after I was born – chronologically?
31. Do I have any siblings prior to my birth and/or after my birth? Who are they? Have you told them about me?
32. Can you please outline your family medical history – ailments/allergies/mental health?

What other questions do you think could be/may have been useful at this first meeting, during this honeymoon phase?

With love,
Coach Charlie X

CHAPTER 13

So Which Mother Did You Come From, Dear?

(Amy)

It had now been several years since I had given up on finding my birth father, Ron, but then, a miracle happened: I received a letter from my 97-year-old maternal birth grandmother giving me the biggest lead yet. She told me that she had suddenly remembered his last name and wanted me to have it. This was incredible! I wondered why she was telling me now, after all these years. Was she wanting to come clean as she was nearing the end of her time? Did she suddenly regret casting me out of the family, forcing my mother's hand before she met her maker?

I wondered if my birth mother knew what she had just told me. Things were so strained between Jan and me – we barely spoke, and this would be the last thing we needed to come between whatever shred we had left of 'us.' I decided that it was *my* journey now, for *my* self-discovery – it was not about her anymore.

My maternal grandmother (Gala), just couldn't remember the correct spelling – it was a tricky last name, as there were many ways to spell it – and was it a 'Mc' or a 'Mac'? Bloody Celtics! It was then that I realized where my paternal bloodline had originated from!

I grabbed my 'Find My Father' journal and wrote out all the variations that one could possibly spell his surname. As I revisited my notes, I realized that now I had the most important missing piece of the puzzle, and it was time to recommence my search. The first obvious step of action was to place an advertisement in the 'missing persons' section of major newspapers in the two countries where my research had led me to believe he had spent much of his life.

I received a phone call the following week.

It was a woman, who stated that she believed her father and Ron were old friends from the early 1970s. We spoke for about 10 minutes or so, and I captured it all in my journal.

As a child, she remembered him visiting her father often. They had met at the local pub, and he carried suitcases of cash to the house and would have long business meetings with her dad in his 'beer cave.' She said that in 1978 he moved back to Christchurch, the same city I was relocated to for my birth! She went on to tell me that he was a boat builder and sailor, and that the last time she heard anything, it was that he had moved back to the North Island and was selling BMW cars at a dealership his best friend owned – she didn't know the name of the friend.

She added that she doubted he was still alive, as he was a big drinker, smoker and gambler who was also doing many dodgy deals on the side. She gave me a couple of leads to contact but had no other information. Wow! Much of what she said confirmed what I had known and more. This was a strong lead.

I went back to my notes and wrote everything out and reviewed my journalling. In doing so, I noticed a name I had recorded years ago. Jan had mentioned the name of his best friend and that he had lived on the North Island – could it be a match? Strange how she could remember his name and not my father's...

I did a Google search and found a few names on the North Island that were the same as his best friend's. I dialled up the first name on my list, and a jovial voice answered the phone in a country area outside of Auckland. I asked him if he could help me, and after I asked my questions, he said he used to spend time with him – and yes, they had been best friends, but not anymore.

When I asked if he knew how to spell his last name – he said he had no idea. When I pressed him about Ron's life, his marriages, his children – he firmly stated that he had no idea. His voice was now agitated, but he gave me the name of another person who might be able to help me. That person then referred me on to someone else, who referred me on to yet another person, and so on. It felt like everyone had one thing in common: they didn't want to talk to me about him, and they couldn't get off the phone quickly enough.

But even still, I did get tiny bits of information here and there. Each phone call I made, I simply said I was researching my family tree and that I believed I was related to this person. Through the course of my investigations, I found out that he had owned several catamarans and houseboats, and that he had made quite a good living out of an invention for the telecommunications industry that he created. I found out from one of these leads, that my father had called him three years ago to invite him to stay on his houseboat for a vacation – was he still living on that houseboat? I obtained the location from him and commenced another search.

There was only one person of that name listed in that area, and that afternoon, I found myself possibly speaking to a man whom I thought was my father! I was beyond excited and filled with trepidation.

As it transpired, he wasn't my father, though he had the same last name – *but he actually knew my father!* He told me that he lived on a houseboat in that same location as him, with an unlisted phone number. Then he actually gave me the name of the boat: *Orion*. Another great few leads there! I asked him when he last saw Ron, and he said he had drinks with him about six months ago.

I called the local pub – since I knew he was a drinker – and asked the publican if he knew my father. He told me he most certainly did know him and that he had last been seen at the local boat repair yard – he even gave me the name of the company. I immediately contacted them, but there was no answer. I searched every boat registration company to see if I could trace the ownership details of the boat, now that I knew it was called *Orion*. I phoned the pub back and asked if he could give me some names of Ron's friends, this time stating that I needed to contact Ron as he was a member of my family, and that it was urgent.

I was getting bolder, but my nerves were wearing a little thin from getting so close, then falling so far away again all in one afternoon. I needed a drink. Several, in fact.

Later that afternoon, I pushed myself on. The publican had

kindly given me the details of a couple of his drinking buddies to try my luck with. I dialled the next person on my list.

'Oh, hello, Bob? My name is Bridgette. I am wondering if you may be able to help me – do you have a second? Sorry to call you like this – you don't know me – but I believe that you may know a family member of mine, Ron, from the pub? It's just that there's been a bit of a family emergency, and I need to speak with him, but I've misplaced his number.' I held my breath for the umpteenth time.

'Ron? Oh, yes, I sure do know him – in fact his boat is five minutes' walk from here. I don't have his number but how 'bout I head down and get it for you? I'll call you right back.'

Sure enough, after 10 minutes, my phone rang. He said he was so sorry, but Ron was no longer living on that boat – there were new owners residing there. The good news was, they offered to help me as much as they could and gave him their number for me to call. I did so immediately, explaining that I was searching for a missing family member, and that it was urgent.

They were able to give me the greatest lead yet: the details of the broker who sold my father's boat to them – they said that he would have his details. So, I called the broker, who then asked me to email them with what I wanted. What did I want? I wanted his full name spelled correctly, and I wanted his new address and phone number.

They replied to me the next day. I finally had the correct spelling of his full name, and his full contact details. I then contacted a friend who owned a private credit search firm and hired her to run a search based on that information. She was able to give me his date of birth and confirm that these details were indeed correct.

I had finally found him! I tried to obtain his birth certificate, but I was prevented by Births, Deaths, and Marriages to obtain it as I didn't have his authorization.

I guess I would just have to call him then.

✶ ✶ ✶

'Hi, is that Ron?'

There was a brief silence before I heard, 'Yes, who is speaking?' from a rich, deep baritone voice.

'Oh, hi, my name is Bridgette. I am calling you because, well, I believe you are actually my father.'

Now, ordinarily, a man might deny such an 'accusation.' They might fend the accuser off angrily, shouting expletives or at least demanding to hear some cold hard evidence. But for my father (and this is why our first phone call was so memorable other than the obvious), his response was classic:

In a very relaxed, melodic tone, he casually asked, 'Oh? Which mother did you come from, dear?'

I thought it was the funniest thing I had ever heard – great stand-up comedy material. I held myself together to stop cracking up with laughter (or tears), and prompted his memory of meeting a tall, blonde tanned woman on a beach in Takapuna, Auckland in the early 1970s. 'You know, the one you proposed to and got pregnant and cheated on and left?'

That seemed to jog his memory.

✶ ✶ ✶

CHAPTER 13

A few months later, I flew to Wellington to meet him. My first impression was...to run.

Upon looking at me for the very first time in his life as his daughter, he said with a big grin, 'Oh wow! I thought you were really a Russian bride looking to marry me for citizenship; but you are not fat and ugly – wow, look at you!'

Did I have to remind him of who I was? I really didn't know how to process so quickly on the spot. I knew that I wanted to turn and run away from him, but I'd journeyed this far. Give him a chance. *Bridgette, Bridgette, Bridgette...don't you remember the two-second rule? Your first impression is always correct. You should have run darling.*

After a couple of hours, I was done. I didn't like him, not one bit. No longer the millionaire he had claimed to be, he was weird and dressed weird and acted weird. He was swarthy, rotund, and looked a lot like Pavarotti. It was obvious he was a hoarder – his small council housing unit was so filled to the brim with junk that I could barely fit in the living room. As the afternoon progressed, it was obvious that he was more interested in striking up an opportunity to start a business with me. Not interested in his daughter that he'd never known, he just focused on my career and my talents. Aside from that, he didn't ask me *anything* about my life, and he avoided any questions to do with his family or his other children, or his family origin in general.

Overall, it really was a huge disappointment. I had even created a beautiful, leather-bound photo album of my life for him. Hesitantly, as I handed it to him, I hoped he wouldn't perve at my photos later.

I finally got back to the airport and just bawled my eyes out, sobbing uncontrollably. I was doing it so loudly, and I couldn't stop. I didn't know what was wrong with me – I never cried! I had even totally disconnected from caring what people would think, which was not at all like me. But I felt so very alone in that moment, and so far away from where I was. I shook and gulped and cried a river of tears, loudly, unable to stop.

That scared me – why couldn't I stop? I was out of control, and I remember thinking I really needed help. My very first panic attack as an adult. People were coming over to me, seeing if they could help – what should I tell them? 'Oh, thanks, I am okay. I just met my father for the first time, and he preferred that I was his Russian mail order bride.'

Thank God for the airport bar – I had a few hours to drink my feelings away before I could get on that plane!

I returned to Australia and thought about it…and thought about it and thought about it – too much. I didn't speak about it to anyone. Once again, I convinced myself that I was 'just fine.' I should have booked some kind of therapy session immediately but I didn't. Maybe hiring a therapist for this episode would have helped me to stop attracting and placating to that same type of man.

***

A week later my tough and protective personality part, Sam, decided to play a game with him. I began calling him every two weeks, after I drank a good amount of wine to numb myself out. He was very inappropriate in the way he would speak to me at times, making sleazy comments about my body shape and how pretty he thought I was. But the more alcohol I downed, the easier it was to overlook.

One day, I called him when I was only two glasses in, because I wanted some specific information and that required a clear head. It was 5:00 P.M. on a particularly dreary and rainy day, just the kind of day I felt most comfortable in. I had all my notes in front of me, my scribbled writing splattered with drops of red wine. I had written down some very important pieces of information gathered from my arduous talks with him, and in the pile of papers was my one-page document from my most precious adoption file – a handwritten description of him. It stated: 'Only child, parents deceased.' I compared this with my notes in my journal: 'he has a sister called Adele. Father died in 1973; mother died in 2003.' His parents were alive when I was born AND he had a sister – more lies.

'Hello? Hi! It's me! How was your day?' I said in an upbeat, warm, and friendly manner that I knew I needed to conjure up to be able to speak with him again.

After some chit-chat I launched right in: 'So, where did you say you grew up again?'

I took a deep breath in again, prepared for deflection from him, but my timing was good – he was in a most jovial mood. 'Oh, I grew up on a sugar plantation.' Wow! That was another huge clue he had just given me.

I continued: 'You mentioned you had a sister? Adele?'

'Adele, yes. I don't want to talk about her.' I paused just enough for him to want to fill in the space. 'My parents and her – they were all weird. Christians – you know the type. They didn't love me and pretty much wiped me out of their lives. I haven't heard from her – she could be dead for all I know.'

I pushed on. 'Oh, I am sorry to hear that. Uh, didn't you say you also had a daughter named Roxy?' I spoke with extra warmth in my voice – I wasn't going to let him change the subject. This was my chance to go into his secret stash to fill in missing information.

'Oh, yeah, she was born in NZ. Can't remember when or anything else to tell you – I don't speak with her anymore either.'

'Do you have her current surname, or details of her mother, your wife at the time?'

I sensed that I had gone too far off the track and had now run sheer out of luck. He validated that with a firm and grumpy, 'No.'

Then I filled my glass to the brim. I was getting so tired of placating him, and the energy had begun to spiral. I decided to change the subject and ask him about his boat building and sailing days. It was then that it began to get very, very…weird.

'Enough about my boat,' he said. 'Hey, what are you wearing? I love it when I know you are due to call; I always like to get undressed and lie down in my bed when I talk with you. What are you wearing right now? Tell me.'

Oh fuuuuuuuuck. I was suddenly on a call with a guy that wanted to have sex talk. My own father. Had he been thinking about me like this all along? Had I denied that he was? I felt sick – but if I didn't play, would he never take my calls?

Me being me (as Amy), I just played further along down this rabbit hole. Sam would have told him where to go. 'Oh, I am wearing cargoes and a cute pink T-shirt; it's one of my favourite outfits. Barefoot.' Awkward fake giggle from me.

Well, he seemed to really like that. I don't know how I got

through that conversation, but I deflected it before it got anywhere more degrading for me. I shut it down by making up the excuse that I needed to make dinner for the family and that I would call him in a couple of weeks and couldn't wait to talk with him again.

I had already made my mind up before I said that: I was never going to speak with him again. Why would I? Why would any daughter want to continue down that line with their father? I was a grown woman being subjected to sexualization by my father. If I were a child, raised by him, and he thought I was attractive, how far would this have gone with me as his daughter?

I didn't call or speak with him again until 2016, when we spoke very briefly. I had just found his sister, Adele. We had an instant and beautiful connection. She and I spoke over the phone together and she informed me that Ron had told her I had made contact with him years ago, but that he refused to give her my contact details. She was so happy I had reached out and told me she wanted to meet me immediately – and that now I also had five first cousins who wanted to meet me too!

I travelled interstate to spend a few days with her and to meet my cousins. I felt so embraced by them all – especially by my Aunt. I adored her so much. She was truly the kind of mother I dreamed of. One night, she told me that she called Ron every month for a catch up, and that this month's call had already been scheduled for the week I was there. She suggested that we announce that I had found her together, and as I was sitting right next to her, she could perhaps say that I wanted to speak with him. She thought that maybe I could finally get some information on my sisters. Yes, she had just told me I had *another* sister, Liz. He had kept most of us a secret from her (except for Liz, but more on that in a later chapter).

Her plan did not end up working out – he didn't fess up, so I finally exploded at him and said he was a rotten human being and a disgrace as a father. He died a year later. Good riddance.

After that last phone call with him, later that same week I had a conversation with my best friend at the time, discussing my plan to continue the search for my sisters and my extended family. She was 100% totally against it. I was surprised, and eventually she admitted that she couldn't understand why I needed to keep searching for people that never knew about me, or why I would want to search for parents and grandparents that had left me for dead. She said she also couldn't understand why I couldn't just be grateful for being adopted – I had a roof over my head, food, clothing. She said I should be grateful that I had the names of my original parents who had abandoned me and just leave it at that. I was extremely shocked and upset to realize that was how she felt about the whole thing – all along, I had been under the impression that she was supportive and respectful of my decision to search. I told her I couldn't believe what I was hearing and that I needed to take some time out to process this. In the end, we could never repair the relationship, as it was impossible for me to be friends with somebody that could not respect my feelings about my abandonment, my adoption, and my search to find who I was.

I should be grateful. If I had a dime…

In that same week, the truth of two people had been revealed to me. Two people who should have treated me with the exact level of respect I gave them. I never spoke with her again, either. But that was my style then – I cut people out for good and never looked back. I was taught by the best.

Coach Charlie:

For far too long, too many adoptees have been the target of what I call 'adoptee shaming.' Much like body shaming, when people hear negative comments about their appearance, it leaves them feeling self-conscious, ashamed, depressed, and anxious. *Adoptee* shaming is when people make inappropriate, uninformed, judgmental, and negative comments about our lived adoption experiences, often leaving us feeling self-conscious, ashamed, depressed, guilty and anxious. But nobody is recognizing this 'adoptee shaming' because nobody has ever spotlighted it like I currently am. Or are they? Are you?

I have been branded an 'angry adoptee,' an 'ungrateful adoptee,' a 'self-centred adoptee.' I was threatened to be punished as being a 'naughty adoptee' if I ever told anyone I was adopted by my adoptive mother. I have actually been on a personal development retreat where I was told to 'get over it' and that I am 'better than that' and to stop my lamenting because my adoptive parents are my '*real* parents,' who gave me 'food, clothing, and shelter.' These criticizing, gaslighting, shaming, condemning comments have come from my friends, teachers, family, people on my social media, and other individuals I am not even close to or don't even know. I have even been shamed by the adoptee community itself – apparently, it is offensive of me to call myself an 'adoptee.' In addition, it is offensive to apparently call my mother who left me my 'biological mother or my first mother' and it is offensive to call my mother who purchased me, my 'adoptive mother.'

A long-term goal of mine was to collate my entire lived experience and put it all into words one day – and now you are reading it. I have been wanting to get this book written since my early 20s, and now, in my early 50s, here it finally is. Why did it take me so long to write it? Well, to be honest, if I wrote it in my 20s you would only have a tenth of the book! But I wanted to get this published 7 years ago. I just couldn't write it all out cohesively. I didn't believe that my story was worth writing about.

From my research and training as a magnetic mind superconscious coach (sounds impressive but what a mouthful), I realize now that it was because of the dysfunctional belief systems living in my subconscious mind. The unconscious agenda of my ego state has held me back, telling me to never, ever, ever write this book in an effort to protect me from further shaming. Protecting me from failure, from further rejection and judgement. Most of all, my subconscious mind had been 'trained' to never speak about my adoption – or I would be punished. That particular belief was rammed hard into me from my adoptive mother during my formative years when dysfunctional beliefs such as these are created. Like the time she drove me to the orphanage and threatened to leave me there when I was around five years old.

We all need to create the space and time across our lives to include setting personal goals and taking the obvious actions to fulfil them. Once fulfilled, we can naturally go on to create the next goal and the next. But the number one roadblock in setting up a goal is getting caught up in what the goal will *give* you versus what it is that you really want to *create*. For example, you want the shiny new car, but you really just want to *appear* as if you are successful and therefore *feel* like you are good enough/successful enough/worthy enough. You want to impress others to then feel accepted/admired, and getting the shiny car will then give you the desired feeling of being accepted/admired/good enough.

So, what is the ultimate goal here? It obviously isn't the car. It is to feel accepted, to feel good enough. For me, my goal in writing and publishing my book was initially to feel understood by the people who I wanted and needed to understand and accept me. So really, my goal was not to write my book – my goal was to feel understood and accepted by others. I was needing to *fix* something about myself. I was problem solving and not creating. We can all unconsciously sabotage ourselves from ever reaching our goal by going for something to 'fix' what we consciously feel is wrong with us.

This is because we are getting caught up in what is called our 'dysfunctional patterns.' These are structures that we have subconsciously set up as steps that we can take to sabotage ourselves from going for what it is that we want. This is a program that is running out of our range of conscious awareness, as it sits in our subconscious mind, creating us to fail instead of creating our success. Knowing our dysfunctional patterns will assist us to create the desired end result.

These patterns filter their sabotaging ways into all corners of our life: relationships, career, health, business, money, love. No matter what it is, I can guarantee that it is the same dysfunction that is sabotaging these areas in exactly the same way. It is imperative, therefore, that we unpack what these dysfunctional patterns are and become aware of them when they rear their ugly heads!

Being stuck in our patterning is a hidden egoic agenda, set up initially to protect us from the very thing it is now keeping us stuck in. For example, if a pattern is set up to protect us from failing, it will ensure that we never go for what we really want – because of that fear of failure. Or, if a pattern is set up to protect us from abandonment, it will ensure that we never allow ourselves to be vulnerable or close with anyone, therefore creating that very same dysfunction by abandoning our desire for closeness at the get-go.

All we need to do is understand what our dysfunctional patterns are, becoming aware and recognizing how and when we unconsciously set up the scene for the same patterning to sabotage. This is the gateway to our personal empowerment, and to break the cycle of these sabotaging patterns.

In a nutshell, as mentioned earlier in the book, we each carry one or more or all of the following six sabotaging dysfunctional belief systems:

- I am not perfect.
- I don't belong.
- I am not good enough.
- I am not capable enough.
- I am insignificant.
- I am not worthy.

These beliefs unfortunately can be developed in our first seven or eight years of life. Look at the previous chapter, where I talked about our chakra systems – you can see when these belief systems stepped in, where they sit in our body, and how they 'act out' in our lives. They come from our family systems, both epigenetically and collectively, by conditioning from our caregivers, teachers, friends, siblings, extended family, and even strangers.

The good news is this: you can reprogram these beliefs by stating the following affirmations aloud every day, and imagining and feeling what it is like to exist 'as if':

1. I could not be any more 'perfect' than I am; therefore, I am perfect just the way I am.
2. I could not 'belong' more than I already do; therefore, I belong wherever I am, just the way I am.
3. I cannot be any more 'good enough' than I am; therefore, I am more than good enough just the way I am.
4. I am already more 'capable' than I am; therefore, I am more than capable of doing anything I want to do just the way I am.
5. I could not be any more 'significant' than I am; therefore, I am more than significant just the way I am.
6. I could not be any more 'worthy' than I am; therefore, I am more than worthy just the way I am.

To reprogram your old belief systems and patterns, you can also do some wonderful, guided meditations, recodes and hypnosis, NLP, and anchoring techniques I previously talked about.

Just choose to reclaim your power back. Focus on creating a life you love instead of problem-solving your way through life, and step into the superconscious being that you truly are.

Wishing you love and magical creations,
Coach Charlie X

CHAPTER 14

The Undoing

(Sam)

When I was in my late twenties, I decided to commence yet another new career and I signed up to train to be a counsellor. After a short stint at being a professional singer, I'd tried my hand at being a primary school teacher, but it was too dogmatic and regimented – the day they refused to let me teach math through playing my guitar and singing – was the day I quit. Professional counselling just seemed like a natural fit for me. Throughout my life, many of my friends and ex-band members would come to me for advice; they thought I was a 'wise old soul' and could problem-solve their issues away within minutes. I figured counselling as a profession mustn't be that hard as I was already doing this for free, and I thought I might as well make a living out of it. I could also do it part-time in between daycare for my son.

So, I researched the next available course nearby. As you may have gathered, the events in my life had equipped me with the skills required for troubleshooting, problem solving, reading people's motives, and developing strategies to become highly functional and resilient. Plus, I had already devoured many books in child development, inner child healing, mindset, and meditation – anything to do with spirituality and personal development. And of course, I didn't think that there was anything that I needed to explore within myself; I felt invincible. From my perspective back then, it was everybody else and society in general, who were broken.

Much to my dismay, the counselling course that was available within the next few months required that I undergo 12 weekly therapy sessions in order to complete the diploma. This may come as a surprise, but at that point I had never been to see a counsellor or psychologist in my life. I honestly didn't think I needed to; I thought I was managing just fine, working it all out on my own. Plus, I knew that the suffering I had endured was not even considered an area of importance within the curriculum of psychology and counselling.

And this is exactly one of the reasons why I wanted to finally train up – to become an expert in the field of adoptee trauma. I certainly had the lived experience to give me the credibility as a trailblazer in the industry back then, and I thought that I truly was a shining light, unaffected by my past and ready to lead the way for others going through such adversity.

In all honesty, at the time, I felt that I was left completely unscathed by my past.

I started class in early July. Day one of the semester started off as one of those frosty, overcast, dark, dreary wintry mornings. Walking the several blocks to my college, the frozen solid

CHAPTER 14

grass cracked under my feet, and my lungs felt as if they were burning with each inhalation of the negative-three-degree air.

Twenty minutes before class, the students were already gathering in the foyer. There was a mix of nervous glances amidst the small talk, all of us cozying up near the oil heaters lining the walls. I had just spent the night reciting how my story would go, how I would present my family background, where I grew up, how *great* my life had been. I was more than prepared to divulge a complete life of fantastic lies that were nothing like the ordeals of my past. The less people knew about me, the better – that way, nobody could use my adoption against me as a weakness in my character, a flaw to pick at, a vulnerability to give them the upper hand.

I didn't want people to feel sorry for me or look at me through a 'pity lens' – even some of my closest friends didn't know.

Just as I suspected, once we settled in our seats, we each had to each stand up in front of the room and introduce ourselves to the group, stating our name, where we grew up, and why we were here, as well as our biggest adversities and our proudest accomplishments.

I was intrigued to discover that none of the 25 students in my cohort had been adopted or orphaned – or maybe they were just clever enough not to admit it. Some had experienced abusive childhoods, early parental deaths, family suicides, or drug abuse, and some had recently left toxic relationships. Some were already working in the mental health industry but wanted to step up further in their career, and a few were reiki master healers, energy healers, or kinesiologists, all looking to improve their rapport and skills to create a more professional credibility and connection with their clients.

After the break, our lecturer issued us a profile list of psychologists. She informed us that we were to each select a psychologist whom we would like to work with for the next 12 weeks, reiterating that it was compulsory for each of us to attend all 12 counselling sessions in order to pass the diploma – no exceptions. She said this would be completely confidential – the teachers would not be privy to any counselling session notes – but that the payment rates, while heavily discounted, would be added to our final tuition fee. Judging by some of the students' reactions, they had obviously not read the fine print.

I made my choice quite easily. Anna Hershey specialized in trauma and hypnosis, and I just got a good vibe from her profile. I also assured myself that while whatever I divulged *was* confidential, I wasn't going to *really* fall for that – I was sticking to my plan, and my full adoption story and any feelings associated with it to date, were to remain locked in a vault.

* * *

'Welcome Bridgette. Please, take a seat. My name is Anna Hershey.'

I surveyed the room. It had a fish tank, which I didn't find relaxing. My stomach churned with the caging of any animal, as it reminded me of my adoption – taken out of my natural habitat, rebranded, and re-owned to survive in a completely unnatural environment.

The room was lit up with harsh fluorescent light, and there was a tall green palm in the corner and a desk with lots of papers scattered across it. *Careful, I thought, that could be my file lying*

CHAPTER 14

there in the future for all to see. How unprofessional! The couch was very brick-like to sit on, so I searched for a cushion and grabbed one that was all crocheted with peacocks. The carpet, however, was plush, and the tall, unlit lamps were all Art Deco in style. There was a little heater glowing a soft pink in the corner which didn't do much to warm up the room, aesthetically or not.

With her red framed glasses and her cropped white hair with pink frosted tips, Anna looked like a woman who appeared to be going through a mid-life crisis. She wore a crisp white shirt with her collar standing up, corners facing downwards, a long blue and green paisley skirt with wedge-heeled burgundy boots. She looked very purposefully 'put together.'

The grandfather clock in the other corner of the office monopolized my attention because it was ticking so abnormally loudly – it was as if it was trying to distract me. *Why would you have such a thing in a counselling room?*

Anna interrupted my agitation: 'Well, it's great to meet you, Bridgette. Uh, look, let me just start with asking you this; I am curious, what has led you to want to study to be a counsellor?'

That answer was too easy. Still not divulging the obvious, I rattled off how I thought I could make some coin professionally doing what I naturally seemed to be good at – getting into other people's heads and finding the solutions. 'Oh, and I have also trained as a life coach and hypnotherapist,' I said, 'and thought this was the next obvious step for me.'

Go on – ask me something deep. Let's see what you can dig up, 'Hershey Bar.'

Anna peered over her thick red rimmed glasses. 'Oh, that's great. Well, it seems to me that you have already discovered a natural propensity to help others. What do you think gave you that inner drive, and that innate ability?' She did look intrigued.

Well, I wasn't giving away my game hand, no way. This counsellor was going to be *my* plaything. If she was to have 12 weeks with me then, I was going to enjoy myself. Total non-disclosure of my feelings. Which was easy to do of course.

Let's see, where shall I start with such an answer to her question?

'I was raised in a *very* toxic family environment. My adoptive mother is probably an undiagnosed Schizophrenic and displays deeply set narcissistic traits that she inherited from her unresolved bullying issues from her own narcissistic mother. She always believed she was the black sheep of the family and consequently, she felt ostracized. She deluded herself into a hasty marriage, as her parents were certain she would forever be a spinster, considering she was 28 years of age when she did so. Whilst she was propositioned by many a fair-weather friend, she settled on my introverted, empathetic, and mostly pathetically obliging father. He was an alcoholic, and a military machine workaholic robot of a man. His mother died when he was two, leaving his father with seven children to raise on an egg farm in the Midwest of America, before his father remarried to a woman who had six kids of her own. My father was raised without enough love, food, clothing, or money, and joined the Navy at 17 to escape. He never really grew up; Peter Pan Syndrome would be how I would define him.'

Always running away looking for his Tinkerbell; his 'mama.'

'OK, alright, thanks for that. And do you have any siblings, Bridgette?' Anna didn't even look up, as she was too busy scribbling a ton of notes.

CHAPTER 14

I took a sip of water. 'One younger sister. She was a complete anomaly for my parents. Her name is Erica. She displayed high-level masculine qualities by the age of five and was ruling the household by seven. She was a child genius and – not quite the pretty little thing. She loved ballet and piano but was terrible at both, still she was the star in my adoptive mother's eyes. When she came out of the closet at 18, a piece of my adoptive father's heart died along with his dreams of his daughter being the woman he wanted her to be. My adoptive mother put it on herself to protect her daughter Erica from any judgement or condemnation from him, and this created a huge impasse between them. My adoptive parents had ended up cheating on each other for years when we were kids, and this went on long after we grew up and left home. I cut ties with them years ago.'

The room was feeling very warm, and I took off my coat to settle into the session now.

'My adoptive sister Erica always knew what she wanted. She wanted me to be a surrogate mother for her, but ethically, of course I couldn't do that! Unfortunately, explaining my stance on the matter and refusing her generous offer created a nasty reaction from Erica. She and her partner went out of their way to ensure I would know how any enemy of theirs was to suffer their wrath.'

Anna's glasses were nearly sliding off the tip of her nose and her pen was now probably nearly out of ink. She looked at me, but, also through me, as if she was somewhere in her mind's filing cabinet, searching for relevant theories and secret potions... The clock was ticking loudly, signalling that the hour was nearly up. *Was she ever going to ask me any questions? Like, oh I dunno but how about, 'do I know why I was adopted? Or how did it feel to be adopted? How old was I when I was adopted? How did I discover that I was adopted? How was my adoptive homelife? How do I think it has impacted my life?'*

This is a typical avoidance reaction I've experienced from one other so called 'therapist' I had spoken with in the past.

Gathering herself she said, 'OK, well... I think we have covered a lot of ground here for our first session. I just get the feeling that you have many layers – there is something huge going on behind those eyes and I hope to earn your trust so I can reach you and help heal your wounds, Bridgette.'

It never ceases to amaze me that people in this profession seem to never want to explore my lived experience as an adoptee. They never seem to take that into account for what may have brought me here in the first place. I believe it is because it intimidates them – they are not equipped to deal with it. Once again, it is going to be me who opens up this discussion at the next session. I just couldn't help myself.

Walking out however, I felt a strange spring in my step, a sudden feeling of lightness, like a part of me had been lifted out of the underworld and was floating upwards. Because only Anna knew more about my past than anyone and it felt good, not disempowering at all. In fact, I had never experienced such a feeling of euphoria.

Even if she didn't ask anything about my adoption. I had an hour in my life where I gave myself permission to talk a little bit about it!

I was really looking forward to our next session now. It actually felt good to share but I felt a little unhinged.

CHAPTER 14

And as I drove myself to day care, to pick up William, and then later, prepared our dinner...it was as if I wasn't there at all. I was floating again, and the view seemed so much better from up here.

***

I did eventually initiate our sessions to go deeper into the discussion of my feelings around my adoption experience, and whilst she did pry a little into it, she never really made me think that my lack of trust in others, my inability to bond intimately, or my disconnect from my own feelings into the world around me had *anything* to do with my adoption. In fact, she was more focused on other trauma experiences such as my friend James being murdered, or me being abducted by aliens, or of me being abused by my adoptive mother and my ill treatment from previous boyfriends and friends. She never once discussed how my abandonment as a newborn child – or how being an orphan – could have impacted my life. It was just as I suspected: my adoption experience would be unvalidated and deemed insignificant and unimpactful to my long-term well-being.

This was extremely unsettling as you can imagine. *Why isn't somebody able to help me understand what I can't put into words or feelings? Was I ready to access my feelings? What would I feel?*

This insight from my counselling experience propelled me forward even further on my quest to be a leading counsellor for adult adoptees. The trouble was, we didn't cover this topic in class, and I couldn't locate any material that I could personally relate to on the matter. That is, until one day, deep into our second semester…

We had all now completed our 12 weeks of psychological sessions, and as my teacher paced up and down the room delivering his new lecture on 'Complex PTSD and Learned Helplessness,' the summer sun was warming up the classroom through the big bay windows. Suddenly, the room started to spin. The more I listened, the faster the room seemed to spin, and the harder my heart seemed to pound. I didn't know what was happening – what was going on with me? Was I coming down with something?

'Are you okay, Bridgette?' my classmate Rachel asked. She was leaning in, looking at me with concern. 'You look…flushed. Are you feeling hot?'

Her voice seemed so far away, yet she was right up in my face. Too close – I wanted to push her away. I wanted to run out of the classroom. I still never cried, but I was sensing the block I was feeling in my throat was like a massive water balloon of tears that would soon pop and drown everyone in the room. *How embarrassing; this isn't like me. I wish that bloody teacher would change the subject.*

My lecturer continued regardless: '…And studies have shown that 'Survival Personality Disorder' stems from what is known as a 'Primal Wound,' when the process of 'hominization' is impacted. We mustn't underestimate that a baby is born with a base need to feel the touch of that skin, from the bond with the birth mother developed in the womb. If this is compromised within the first three years of development, then they will be injured and fractured into their future selves. But it is an invisible wound.'

CHAPTER 14

Oh shit. I couldn't feel my arms. I was aware of my heart pounding, but I wasn't in my body. Where had I gone?

Tom, the lanky dark-haired 21-year-old student sitting across from me in the semi-circle asked, 'So, how does this play out in their lives? I mean, surely this 'fracture' would create massive anxiety and attachment issues as an adult?' For a young guy, he certainly seemed mature – and I wanted to punch him in the face.

'Yes Tom. Without this intimate bonding still intact with 'mother,' the impacts are huge: low self-esteem, lack of regard, emotional mismanagement, increased risk of psychological disorders, anxiety, dissociation, and of course the inability to form lasting relationships, because they tend to not trust anyone. The fear of rejection is also insurmountable.'

Wait – did my teacher literally just rip my clothes off and pull my heart out in front of everyone and throw my body naked and bleeding into the centre of the room? I was feeling validated yet at the same time I was in total shock. I had resonated to the truth of hearing this for the first time. It took every ounce of whatever measure of resilience I had left to stay in my seat; I thought that my cover would be blown if I reacted. But I couldn't move anyway, and I went into freeze mode, because the worst thing imaginable that could possibly ever happen to me was to feel vulnerable or exposed.

I had prided myself on my steadfast abilities to lock my feelings in a vault and catapult them light years away from this lifetime. But the words he spoke were like 1,000 paper cuts in my ears, slowly bleeding me out with the things he was saying. Not knowing the repercussions of what happened to my emotional development as a baby kept me intact, but now I had heard it – game over. I had not only heard it, but I also *felt* it, and I felt it deeply. It took me over – I burst into loud, uncontrollable, sobbing tears, sobbing like a fucking baby with those deep, gulping, and staggered in-breaths, *Stop it, Bridgette. STOP! STOP! STOP!!!*

The group was in total shock: *Bridgette? Upset? But…why? But…what about her eyeliner? I thought she had nothing inside, that nothing fazed her. She was always so put together.*

I could hear them, even amongst the 1000 paper cuts. Plenty in the group had their fair share of crying from subject matter and case studies, but for me to lose my shit? This was epic. I didn't know what to do or where to go. Maybe I could just…well, I could just run, right? Or walk. Calmly. Out of the classroom.

I excused myself, saying I wasn't feeling well, and I went home early. Straight to bed at the same time as William. I was drained, extremely embarrassed, and, well, yeah…I didn't really know where I was or what I was feeling.

* * *

I took the rest of the week off, claiming I had the flu. By the following Monday morning, like Humpty Dumpty, I had 'put myself back together again.' I went back to class, saying my head cold had messed with my emotions, and I thanked those who had approached me for their concern, assuring them I was 'fine' now. I was JUST F.I.N.E. – Fucked up. Insecure. Neurotic. Emotional. *Now, please. Stay. Away.*

But, as fate would have it, and to make matters even worse,

the following week, we were introduced to a guest lecturer – and in walked my very own private psychologist, Anna.

This was to confirm the anecdote of the theme to my life: shit sandwiches for every lunch. To say I felt stripped naked when she walked into the room is an understatement; I freaked out and nearly pee'd myself. My immediate thought was that she was going to reveal my secrets to the class, telling them my story and all about my adoption. I was sure she would betray me and make a mockery of me to the group, who would then turn on me and peck at my flesh until I was begging to just simply disappear for good.

This is how my mind would attack me, like a bee stinging and swelling up every fibre of my being. Why did I feel so ashamed of what happened to me? As if it were my fault?

OMG, has she already told my teacher? It was all too much for me; my heart was in over my head, and I couldn't pull it back down. I had lost complete control over the entire situation.

I walked out and never returned. I pulled out of the course; I was done. My dreams of becoming a counsellor sunk to the bottom of the ocean, into the vault that was buried with the rest of my secrets, my goals, and of course, my feelings.

I just wasn't ready to learn about the undoing my adoption did.

Coach Charlie:

'*She never once discussed how my abandonment as a newborn child – or how being an orphan – could have impacted my life. It was just as I suspected: my adoption experience would be unvalidated and deemed insignificant and unimpactful to my long-term well-being.'*

– Sam, Chapter 14

I have heard this so many times from adult adoptees. They go to a counsellor or a psychologist for a particular concern, and as they recount their life story, their being adopted isn't even clocked by the therapist. It is as if being adopted is as insignificant for the therapist as what they may have had for lunch the day before. I often wondered if it was me who was at fault for minimizing my adoption experience – if I gave the impression that it was no big deal – or, if my lived experience as an adoptee was just whimsically dismissed in the therapist's brain as nothing of importance. That recount of my experience happened in the late 1990s, but even in the 2020s it still seemed like it should have been the elephant in the room standing in between my therapist and me, but it never earned the naked spotlight, only a little torchlight now and then.

I recently contacted the Department of Social Services in New Zealand to obtain more information from my files, but what was sent to me I already had, and what I wanted was completely redacted. I asked them if they could provide any specific counselling services with professionally trained experts in the field of adoption trauma. Can you guess what the answer was? Correct: 'We don't have anyone on our books we can refer you too. It is on the 'to-do' list.' Obviously not on their 'ta-daaa' list.

Have you ever been to counselling before, or had any type of therapy? Did you want to discuss your experience with a professional in the field of adoption trauma? Have you brought up your adoption experience?

What has been your experience with therapy in general?

CHAPTER 14

Have you given your adoption the credit it deserves for how it has impacted your mental health and well-being? Or have you not taken what happened to you seriously enough? Where are the therapists in your community who are trained to assist you professionally, if and when you want to explore your adoption experience?

In the next chapter, we will explore resource therapy – also known as parts therapy – and I hope that it will encourage you to seek out a therapist in this field, if you feel inclined to explore your amazing personality parts that helped you to survive and thrive in your lived adoption experience. Personally, I am so happy I stumbled across it in my magnetic mind coaching course a few years ago.

Read on my friend!

With love,
Coach Charlie X

CHAPTER 15

47 and Rather Discombobulated

(Sam)

Thirteen years later, when I did eventually finish my diploma of counselling, I was only beginning to scratch the surface of the causes and effects that my adoption was taking on my life, but I was at least opening to it a little more and seeing a therapist or energetic healer here and there. This was mainly to investigate why I felt so displaced in life, like something was missing inside of me, or why my self-esteem and self-confidence had never ever developed. Why did I keep moving to different homes and cities, creating one bad relationship just to leave for another one and restarting a new job after two to three years? Why was I constantly reinventing myself – hair short, hair long, weight on, slim, hippie or chic – or looking so totally unrecognizable at times? And why, oh the fuck why, did I keep attracting narcissists wherever I went?

Some psychologists didn't even focus on my abandonment and my abusive adopted home life at all to account for the reasons behind these concerns. It wasn't until I hit the age of 47, that I realized I needed to talk to someone in more depth about the pains of my past. Because this 'past' had suddenly caught up with me, and I had no idea how to navigate it. I had now discovered my paternal family, and I wasn't really coping with it at all – it was as if my north star had walked out of the southern door of the theatre stage, screaming, 'I quit.'

I was 47 and discombobulated.

I decided I needed to find a new psychologist after years of giving up on them. The criterion was that they lived far enough away from my neighbourhood to dissuade the chances of them ever crossing over into my private life. In walked a guy by the name of Harrison. He was referred to me by my doctor, who issued me with a mental health care plan, saving me a percentage of the session fee each time. She thought he might be able to help as he specialized in identity therapies, and that could be a great fit for my adoption trauma needs. I had also heard that Harrison was a very handsome, single, sought after author and psychologist. *I don't know why, but Georgiana was making a big deal out of it.*

***

I wasn't myself today at all and I really needed to get going. Myself? Well, *who the hell is she/me anyway?*

This dress with wedges and bangles? Or jeans and a T-Shirt and Converse – no bangles? I don't know if it was the weather pretending to be a warm, cloudy threatening-with-rain kind of day, or if it was the toxicity of my anxiety invading me like floaties in my bloodstream – I think it was the fact that I would

CHAPTER 15

soon be meeting with this 'Harrison.'

At any rate, I did not want to look like I had made any effort to dress for the occasion, but at the same time, I wanted to make a good impression. *Why? To appear that I really have my shit together, regardless of what has happened to me? Or, because he is, apparently, 'hot?'*

I downed a couple of reds to help me relax – Shiraz was my miracle worker – a quick fix until it wasn't. *I'll only have two glasses. Good.* I decided on the faded ripped jeans, high top Converse, and blue and white striped quarter sleeve tee – and oh, for extra confidence, my old faithful biker jacket. *Cool.*

This wasn't a fashion show. It wasn't a date. *For God's sake Georgiana, fuck off, would you? It's just a session with some shrink.*

The elevator to get me to Harrison was the type you would find in a 1950s horror movie. It had a folding caged door that you had to pop a bicep to pull across, and then you instinctively felt the urge to move to the far corner, praying the door didn't open mid-floor. The bumpy ride up seemed to take as long as the bread to toast when you were in a hurry. Eventually, I pushed aside the heavy caged door and stepped out, only before making sure it had safely reached a solid floor surface first.

Immediately, I was overwhelmed by the smell of Pino-Clean mixed with Pledge. Somebody had gone to no expense spared with shining up that 1950s brown and white checked linoleum – were there blood stains to hide? The hallway was long and skinny, and the linoleum checks seemed smaller in the distance. There were tall wooden doors staggered on either side of the corridor. All we needed was the grandfather clock at the end covered in spider webs.

I walked further along the checked floor towards door number 13 – my lucky number. There was a wooden chair waiting for me, but no waiting room. *This* was the waiting room – the chair that was positioned to the right of the door. It was an antique and made of oak, with carvings of flowers around the burgundy leather seat and back. I sat down and immediately it introduced itself to me with a sound that threatened that I was too heavy for its structure. Gingerly, I sat very still and prayed for it not to break.

I could hear a male voice and the distinct stifling of sniffles. There was a crack under the door that was in dire need of one of those weighted snake things; the kind that stops the airflow *and* the 'ear-flow.' I could hear more than anyone on the other side of the door should – it wasn't right. This man, whomever he was, was very upset that he couldn't get access to his kids that weekend. It was his birthday, all he wanted was to spend it with them. I couldn't hear the response back from Harrison, as he was not near the door. *Smart*. But it was so remiss of him – this could be me in there with some random like me, listening in!

I really did feel for the upset guy. Lucky kids he had; he obviously wanted to be with them so much. *If only my two fathers had felt the same way about me...*

I don't know where I went just then, but the door was suddenly opening, and the client was walking out. One puffy red eye caught my eye, and I gave a shy closed-lipped smile and darted my eyes downward to hopefully convey that I didn't hear everything...only a little bit. But I probably knew more about him as a stranger now than his work colleagues did; his private life had been totally ambushed by a frikken missing door snake.

CHAPTER 15

And now it was my turn to be overheard by the next stranger sitting on the rickety chair. The only semblance of comfort I had was that hopefully the room didn't have the same aroma as the hall. My stomach was churning enough already, and those cleaning smells had always disturbed me on a deep cellular level. *Maybe I should kick the session off with that?*

'Bridgette! Hello! Welcome! So great to meet you and thank you for booking in with me!' Harrison said warmly, opening the door and shaking my hand.

'Ah, well you can thank Doctor Layla for that,' I said, 'or else I doubt I would be here!' I think I was blushing; I felt hot. I was trying not to notice how handsome he really was. 'I mean, well, without the healthcare plan...you charge a pretty penny!' *OMG! I sound like I am from the 1950s – must be the ghosts here hacking my thoughts.*

'Come in, come in. Take a seat wherever you like.'

I chose the red leather couch with a soft silver mink thing on it because it was the furthest away from the door. I blurted out, 'You do know that if your client sits close to the door, they can be heard from the waiting area, right?' I sounded like I was snitching on him – this was not how to make a great first impression.

'Ah, yes, I am aware of that and have been waiting for the superintendent to fix that gap in the door. But thanks for the reminder – I see why you have chosen the red couch. But just so you know, you are the last appointment for the day. No spies on the other side.' He said in a deep voice in some weird Russian accent trying to be funny. I didn't think this was funny; I was always of the mindset that I had spies everywhere.

He made me a coffee and I took a quick gulp – it was so bitter.

He sat back into the opposite chair, watching me intently. 'I do love my coffee – I hope yours is okay. Now, let me begin with my unofficial spiel about me and what I can hopefully do for you. Then perhaps you will tell me what brought you here today other than fulfilling the expectations for your doctor?'

Turns out Harrison was not only a psychologist – he also had a background in hypnosis and NLP with a focus on trauma healing, and he was trained in something called 'conscious creation coaching.' He was a huge believer in the metaphysical world and past lives, and he had studied a lot about neuroscience. He had the kind of aura about him that matched his voice: relaxing, nurturing, deep, and colourful. I really liked his shirt, too. And his shoes. His socks were interesting…

'Bridgette? Ah sorry, but do you need more time to respond?'

I had completely zoned out. 'Sorry, Harrison, could you please repeat the question?'

He asked me again about what I was hoping to get out of our sessions.

'So yeah…well, I have been really worn out lately. Very tired. Work is stressful as I have been feeling a little bullied and harassed from upper management for a few years now. I thought I could handle it but maybe I'm not? I know I am not making great lifestyle choices, which are all probably affecting my sleep. I just feel a little overwhelmed with stress lately.' It felt good to finally say this to somebody. I usually never admitted any failure on my behalf of any kind in the past to anyone.

'This bullying at work is a concern. Have you reported it?' Harrison seemed like a no-nonsense kind of guy.

I simply said that I didn't think I needed to, plus, there was no Human Resources department to take it to. It wasn't affecting me that badly, was it? I mean, sure, well, I guess I did have some grounds for bullying, but really, was it anything I couldn't handle on my own? *I am not here to talk about that. Focus on why I am really here and stop detouring around it. Stop looking for excuses. You are here to uncover what is lurking beneath these situations, remember?* As if he could sense I was stuck in overthinking, he asked, 'uh…have you experienced any bullying before in your career, or in your childhood?'

In my career? Never. In my childhood? My first response was to say no, but something made me stop and get real with myself. 'Yes, my mother was a bully all my life until I completely cut all contact with her several years back – just before she died.'

Jotting down notes he said, 'OK. So, tell me about your childhood. Take your time. Tell me as much as you feel you want to and start anywhere – we don't have to cover everything today of course!'

'It wasn't great,' I said. 'I mean, it was a little more than the usual ups and downs, but nothing I thought I couldn't handle as a kid. My mother raised us on her own until I was ten years old – and she took out her suffering on me. I wasn't her favourite, so I got the brunt of it. I was constantly on edge with her, but I had comfort in knowing she wasn't my 'birth' mother and that helped a lot.'

Boom: bomb dropped.

'So, you were adopted?'

I told Harrison everything I could in the next 25 minutes we had left.

I concluded my recount with this: 'After my adoptive mother died, my adoptive father continued his affair with a woman who went to school with me, 32 years his junior. He and I are not speaking, nor am I speaking to Erica. Oh, but I do still speak with my adoptive mother sometimes. So, I guess this all gave me my special ability to want to help others.'

I drew in a deep breath and wished I had a ciggy – had I said too much? I observed him shifting in his seat. 'Well, thank you for sharing all that Bridgette. Uh, you mentioned…um…well you said that you *speak with your mother sometimes*? Didn't you say she had passed? When was that?' He had one eyebrow cocked, and I noticed one front tooth suddenly protruding forward. Still handsome though…

'When was what? When she passed away – or when I last spoke with her?' Harrison looked at me with a face that was implying sincerity or neutrality, but I knew what he was really thinking: This girl is batshit crazy! 'Oh, ah…can you tell me about the time after she passed – can you tell me more about those conversations that you had with her then?'

I paused for a bit. I was impressed. 'Well, she first visited me about a month after she died. We had a good, long chat, and she asked for my forgiveness. After that, she came to me again and we talked about the afterlife and the karmic lessons she chose to work out with our family whilst she was in the role of my adoptive mother. But to be honest, it has been a while since she last visited me.'

Maybe it was because I did say to her that in her next lifetime, she would need to balance the karmic scales and come back as a child with a mother as narcissistic and unloving and unkind as she was towards me. I said that I was able to survive (as always) but I doubted she would be able to get through it. I had my tongue in my cheek, as I wished her luck, and told her she would need it. I gave her my blessing of forgiveness, but I stated that I will always remember her as the horrible, back-stabbing, gaslighting, bully of a woman that she was. Forgiveness? Yeah, right.

This didn't seem to faze Harrison one bit. 'I may not have mentioned this, but I specialize in Adoptee Trauma. Or to be more politically correct, 'Adopted Persons Trauma.'

He went on to share that he too was adopted, and under the Forced and Closed adoption laws like me. He said he really couldn't get over how that hideous law forced us from our family of origin and gave us no access to our original identity, or any rights to citizenship or rightful inheritance.

'Wow, Harrison! That's fantastic! I mean…well, you know what I mean…' I was so wrapped to have found a specialist in this field – I felt I was in very safe hands now indeed!

'A typical question I know, but have you found your biological mother or father?'

It was me who asked Harrison. He said by the time he found his birth mother, she had passed away. As for his father, any chances of finding him had sadly died with her. Like a true professional, he was quick to turn the conversation back to me. 'OK, Bridgette, your turn. What about you?'

I assumed he wanted to start with my birth mother. 'Yup, I found my biological mother when I was 18 years old, before the internet search bar – you know, back in the days of microfiche, electoral rolls in the city library and the white pages in a telephone book. It was amazing that I found her, considering the lack of clues I had. So proud of that accomplishment.' I really was. Not many of us from that era have had similar outcomes. Too little, too late, like in Harrison's case.

'Oh, and I just recently found my biological father and some of my external paternal family,' I said. 'Actually, I only just found out about another half-sister – another daughter he had.'

'Great! Wow! I can't wait to delve further into that with you. And how are you and your birth mother going now?'

'Well, let's just say, I went on to let her abandon me two more times after I found her. I ended it with her last rejection of me, which was years ago now. Regardless, I am just glad to have found her and my entire maternal family of origin in general… well, that and also, I am aware of most of my paternal family of origin. I just followed the breadcrumbs after asking the right questions and taking the next obvious steps to action.'

Harrison seemed impressed. That's what I was aiming for, but this felt genuine from him. 'How long have you been searching for your family, Bridgette? 'Oh, only for the last 30 years of my life.'

He asked if he could focus a little more on how I felt about my birth mother's actions. 'The highest form of communication is observed through behaviour,' he said.

I'd been so caught up in the search, the discoveries, the first meetings and the aftermaths, that I realized I had no idea how I felt about her behaviour as a birth mother. Actually, I still had no idea how I felt about anything that had happened to me. Full stop!

✳ ✳ ✳

CHAPTER 15

Walking out of the session that day, I didn't feel that well at all. I knew I was now committed to unpacking my feelings around my adoption experience and I felt full of trepidation and doom, like I'd just said yes to training for a marathon. I felt nauseous.

For the next two weeks, everywhere I went I kept bumping into parts of my story, my 'self' – all I had to do was write it all down, as instructed by Harrison. As I wrote it all down, I had to ask myself how I felt. That was the hardest part. It would be the first time I had taken myself below the surface and through that door. My writing made the truth of the lies, and the pain of my past come to life, and I couldn't deal with that at all. Drinking helped. If I wasn't meditating. Such a contradiction I know. Ah, my conflicted parts!

At the next session, Harrison didn't move his body the whole way through my recount. I had never felt so held. 'Bridgette,' he said, 'thank you so much for sharing that with me. I am wondering what is going on inside you right now. Where are you? Are you feeling the chair and the floor underneath you?'

I thought about it for a moment. 'I feel strangely far away, as what I've shared with you is beyond painful but at the same time, I am called inwards to myself – to feel more real than ever before.'

'I asked you to write this down and to read it aloud to me,' he said, 'not just for me. For you. And I hope you don't mind me saying, and it's just an observation, but you look very different today, Bridgette, in a very cosmic, bohemian kind of way. Did you intentionally dress like this, or is this what you normally wear?'

Actually, I hadn't really made a connection to my appearance until right then. I looked down at my flowing dress and silk scarf, and the many crystal bracelets on my wrists and rings adorning most fingers.

'Here, stand in front of the mirror,' he said. 'It's OK. I want you to look into your eyes, look over your body in the mirror, and think about what you just shared with me about how you met your birth mother, and how it ended up. Really connect into what you are feeling; connect with your feelings now. Being abandoned by her, searching for her, finding her…what you discovered, how it ended.'

He positioned me directly in front of the long mirror. 'Who do you see in the mirror when you think about these things?' he asked.

I honestly couldn't recognize myself at all – my hair was in some kind of loose braid, and I had no makeup on. The rest of my outfit was definitely… gypsy-like. Had I ever recognized myself in the mirror? I felt I was too busy covering myself up. Hiding. Not existing. Being rebranded into something else. 'I look very feminine and bohemian-like today, yes.'

'Good. Now come and sit back down on the couch and I want you to gently close your eyes.'

I floated back and settled into the couch with my eyes closed. I heard Harrison say that he was going to take me on a little journey, a guided meditation, to meet a part of myself that I saw in the mirror today.

He put on some beautiful, relaxing meditation-type music in the background. I heard him telling me to breathe in through my nose and relax each part of my body as he counted down from 10, 9, 8, 7…

And then I saw her – I hadn't seen her since I was five years

CHAPTER 15

old. My alien, my guardian angel. Or was that me? She told me my name was Kaiyah, and that I knew about the power of acceptance, that it was the backbone beyond forgiveness – to accept my past would be more powerful than forgiving those who hurt me, and that in time, I would come to understand this, she said, and it didn't mean that it was necessary to forget, because that meant I had learnt my lessons; it was important to be able to accept.

This was really peaceful and calming to me, but I felt her being pulled away, getting smaller in the distance as I heard Harrison's voice counting me back into the room.

'…And three, two, and one. Good, Bridgette. You're feeling lighter, brighter, happier, and grounded. You feel complete and whole – authentically you. Take a few long deep breaths, have a stretch out, and slowly open your eyes. Welcome back! How was that experience for you? Please share!'

It took me a while to come back. 'I don't know if I've been hypnotized or just had a guided meditation, but I have a very vivid recall of what just happened. A part of me, like another personality part, spoke to me, saying, 'I am the eldest of us and my name is Kaiyah.'

I looked at Harrison and waited for his response. He asked if I would mind if he could record the rest of the session for his own research. I agreed. 'Can I now ask you to please describe Kaiyah to me in detail – does she have a back story? Where did she grow up? What are her interests? What does she look like? Just take your time – you OK for me to record this?'

I nodded slowly whilst I went back to Kaiyah in my mind. He asked me to just relax, and he counted me back down with my eyes shut.

This is what he recorded:

'Kaiyah – is the eldest of us, and she displays resilience by firmly holding onto her spiritual beliefs and purpose – focusing on being positive, glass half-full, lives in the fifth dimension, not the third dimension, detached from emotions but uses her spiritual understanding of life to excuse the 3-D and to stay resilient here.'

I went on: 'Kaiyah is a spiritual seeker; soul centred. She is a loving, caring, and empathetic yogi and hippie who works as a psychotherapist/hypnotherapist. Single, never married – loads of friends but no kids. Always looking at the higher reasoning behind pain, the karmic explanations, and the spiritual lessons behind the adoption. She is a quiet, kind, and loving soul and doesn't like to dwell on the negative impacts of adoption – instead, she looks at how she chose this experience as a soul, as part of her ascension process. Spiritual Escapism is a part of her belief system, as she feels she doesn't belong in this 3-D world and so stays 'up there.' As a justification, she states she is the one who found her birth mother – and has coped with the fall out, because she doesn't dwell on being a victim of adoption. Transcendental Meditation has helped her over the past 30 years to also assist.'

Then I described her features: long, straight, thick blonde hair; light olive skin; green eyes; tall; slender; no make-up; wears hemp clothing; and is mainly vegan or vegetarian and loves smoothies and organic produce…I think that's all I have.' I didn't wait for Harrison to count me back; she was in my consciousness now.

CHAPTER 15

What was going on here? I mean, I knew I had a great imagination, but this seemed a little more real than some imaginary friend. The detail I was able to relay about Kaiyah to Harrison was pretty full on! Who was she to me? Why was she so familiar?

'Bridgette, this is truly amazing information here. What you have been able to access and bring through into real time about Kaiyah – it's incredible. Even down to the spelling of her name. Did you read it, or did she tell you?'

Harrison was busy scribbling down notes, probably along the lines of, *'Bridgette is certifiably insane. We must lock her away for the safety of others. NOW!'*

'It was as if I just knew her name,' I replied, 'and everything about her was just sort of sitting there for me to see, like she had been waiting for me in some time and space.'

I wasn't feeling very grounded – more discombobulated, which had become my favourite word of the year.

After Harrison unlocked Kaiyah, I wondered what the hell he had done. Who else was inside of me, waiting to come out?

Coach Charlie:

'Knowing others is intelligence; knowing yourself is true wisdom.'
– Lao Tzu

What experiences have you had in your life where you have felt compromised, intimidated, angry, or freaked out? What did you do? Why did you feel this way? What was happening at the time? How did you recover from it?

Do you know you have a 'part' in your personality that helped you get out of that sticky situation with grace – or with maybe not so much grace?

Let me begin by asking you: what work have you gifted yourself with, to garner an understanding the undoing your adoption has done to you? Do you intuit that you may also have a part that could be similar to Bridgette's part named Sam? The part who would step in and protect and fend off any potential person or event that could threaten you, even before it happens? Sam's early role was pretty exhausting, considering that Bridgette was training to be a counsellor and therefore had to explore her fears, disappointments, trauma, and confusion, inevitably going into a deep process with it.

Sam wasn't having a bar of it, not at all. Her worst fear, losing control of her emotions – let alone in a public forum like this chapter – was too much to bear. Sam should be a marathon runner, because she certainly has run the distance keeping Bridgette's emotions far away from any potential triggers. Backwards and forwards, up and down – the constant battle and upkeep, the on-point hypervigilance required at a moment's notice is keeping your cortisol levels maxed out and your serotonin at an all-time low.

So, I ask you again: do you also have a 'Sam?' What would their name be if you did? When was the last time that you removed yourself from a tricky situation, or a time where you felt unsafe or compromised?

Maybe you have an 'Amy,' who just made you put up with it, and look at the positives of it all – and cheered you on for staying in a compromising situation way beyond its use? If so, how do you feel about compromising yourself like that?

Perhaps you have a 'Georgiana,' who is too busy trying to

see the perfection in the situation and is focused on saying and doing the 'right' thing to appear like she can handle it. She has superpowers of the highest levels of resilience, whilst inside she may be feeling painfully uncomfortable because she knows being so resilient is actually a toxic, self-gaslighting response?

Maybe you have a 'Kaiyah,' who chooses to approach any stress or discomfort by detaching herself from the world and escaping into the higher realms, whilst life is blowing up all around her?

Or perhaps you may have experienced the sinister 'Voice' that made you do terrible and highly unpredictable things, good or bad, seemingly out of the blue?

However you handle your stress, and whoever takes over, I urge you to decide right now to consciously tap into your resourceful personality parts and start by giving them some thanks. Maybe you might allow them to introduce themselves to you, so you can get to know your whole self now and diffuse the conflict going on within you – or at the very least, give them some recognition.

Remember, we all have personality parts – and no, it doesn't mean you are crazy or have identity disorders. *You have survived the unthinkable trauma of being abandoned by your birth mother, so it's an easy road from here, right?* (Sam, shut it. Sorry about that.) Look, I bet you are extremely good at 'reading' others, but maybe not so sharp at understanding yourself? It's time to connect your dots, my friend!

I have been studying resource therapy, which was created by Professor Dr. Gordon Emmerson. He confirms what I didn't even realize I was doing when I was misdiagnosed as having dissociative identity disorder – this misdiagnosis led me to want to understand why I had compartmentalized these parts of myself and given them names and identities. I finally understood their purpose, and it also helped to give me a sense of peace and perspective – which is how I was finally able to articulate and deliver my memoir to you.

Essentially, our personality parts are resources that can allow us to 'do' something when another part of us thinks it is impossible. They can be in conflict with one another, overpower each other, and sometimes they make an allowance, but what I have learned is that I need to talk to the one part or parts that are upset, are in conflict, or feel abandoned and rejected.

For me, that was the tipping point to my healing – I finally had the tools to be able to identify and speak with that big broken part and let her exist. That big part is me – Bridgette. Only through working with all of my parts could we all get along and thus enable me to finally write this book, let alone make many significant and positive changes with my mindset for a better life. Now more days than not, I live the life I have always wanted to create – and I will never stop creating! But some days are not so great at all, and you know what? That's ok too!

Professor Emmerson's resource therapy work gave me a theory, which is a theory of personality that accurately recognizes the causes of psychological stress, and a clear intervention strategy to enable me to locate and resolve these causes. Here are some questions to use as starting points in getting to know 'who is who' within you, why they are there, and how to resolve your psychological stress:

1. How do you tend to react when you feel disappointed,

confused, intimidated, threatened or sad?
2. If you could give that 'tendency' a name, what would you call her/him/it?
3. Describe their characteristics – look/personality/purpose.
4. What has been/still is their role in your life?
5. What do they need you to know?
6. What do they need to feel right now from you?
7. If you could thank them, what would you say?
8. Are they acting out in a positive or negative way in your life?
9. Are they in any conflict with another part of yourself?

If you would be interested in a resource therapy session with me, please see my contact details at the end of the book.

With love from all personality parts,
Coach Charlie X

CHAPTER 16

Love and Other Strange Occurrences

(Amy)

I was about to embark yet again on the thrill of another 'first meeting.' Several of them, in fact. I had found my birth father's sister, and she had given me the contact details of her five children. Five first cousins! More instant family members! I scheduled a phone call for the initial introduction with each person, as speaking over the phone was less intimidating than a video call at that point. Over a month or so of chatting regularly with one of my cousins, Damian, I was starting to develop a bit of a 'love addiction.' It was more than a crush – I was in way too deep for that. *What was I doing? What was happening to me? This is incest! He is my first cousin! Maybe it is this phenomenon I'd heard about from other adoptees, known as 'Genetic Sexual Attraction'? WTF? What is wrong with me? Is it my fault that my birth father said what he said to me that day?*

I had heard that GSA can happen, both to us and from us, when we meet certain family members we have never met before. But just to check, I decided to research what genetic sexual attraction was all about so I might be able to at least fucking forgive myself.

According to Wikipedia, genetic sexual attraction is 'a theory that attraction may be a product of genetic similarities. There is 'little scientific evidence' for the position, and at least some commentators regard the hypothesis as pseudoscience. The term is also used for a supposed phenomenon in which biologically related persons separated at a young age develop intense feelings – including sexual attraction – upon the restoration of contact.'

How can it be a 'restoration of contact' when we had never met before? 'This' can't be 'that'!

I dug a little deeper and upon further research, I discovered that in the 1980s, the term *genetic sexual attraction* was originally coined by Barbara Gonyo, who ran a support group for adoptees and their newly discovered birth relatives in Chicago, U.S.A. She herself was a birth mother and had developed sexual feelings for her son when they first met. Some psychologists have theorized this genetic sexual attraction (or GSA), is due to the *lack of growing up together*, stating that had they grown up together, it wouldn't happen. This lack of sexual attraction to 'lived with' family is known as the '*Westermarck effect*,' where the attraction to biological relatives with whom they have been raised naturally reverses any sexual imprinting because they are desensitized to each other sexually.

But how does that account for sexual abuse by family members who *are* living together? It doesn't make any sense.

Genetic sexual attraction, according to psychologists, is

why biologically related persons who are separated from each other forfeit the Westermarck effect, leading to possible genetic sexual attraction when they meet later in life.

It could happen when we meet 'in person?' Well, in my case with Damian, we hadn't met each other in person, not even over a video call. I concluded that whatever was happening, it wasn't GSA, and it most certainly wasn't this 'Westermarck Effect' either, obviously.

Research aside, I had to admit that I had fallen deeply into my distorted desire for him. I couldn't help myself; I couldn't stop texting, emailing, or calling him, and when I wasn't, I fantasized about all of the ways he was thinking of me. It completely took me over – sometimes I wouldn't eat or sleep. And we still hadn't even set up a video call or exchanged any photographs.

What was really happening to me, and why was it with him, of all people? Sure, I was miserably married at that time, but I thought I was…well…happy enough, wasn't I? Then again, when it came down to it, I didn't know any other kind of so-called happiness. My homeostasis of any feeling of happiness was permanently set to below freezing so I guess anything was better than that.

I was so mesmerized by Damian's voice – the timbre, the deep tone, the warmth of it. I was in love with the sound of him – his articulation, his intelligent words, his emotional connection with me. He was the only person in my life who seemed to really want to understand the undoing of my adoption, and that was so attractive. We would talk for hours over the phone, and I couldn't wait to wake up the next day and do it all over again. He tapped open a part of me that had remained dormant, untouched. He had complete power over me.

I couldn't get enough of him, and I hadn't even met him; I was in love with the 'concept' of him. I was in love with the fantasy of who he might be – not who he really was. By the time we had shared photos and a video call, he could have had three eyes, two heads, and a tail; it didn't matter what he looked like. To me, he was perfect. Until we did meet in person. I spent two weeks getting to know him thinking this was to be the love of my life, and I ultimately had absolutely zero physical or sexual attraction to him. He felt the same way. Admittedly, it did get a little messy at times. We remained the best of friends for years, but as I write this, we hardly speak these days as we've grown apart. Such is life.

Eventually I woke up.

The whole experience totally spooked me though. I mean, I didn't even know the guy and I was giving myself in to such intense, intrusive thoughts and desires about him.

He was my first cousin AND a *complete stranger*.

Had this searing intensity ever happened to me before? Yes. It. Had. And there was an actual 'word' for it!

I attended a book launch for a memoir of another adoptee recently, who wrote a book called *Crazy Bastard*. Written by Abe Maddison, he talks in the book about this phenomenon, called 'Limerence,' which his psychologist had diagnosed him with. According to the *Oxford English Dictionary*, Limerence is: 'The state of being infatuated or obsessed with another person, typically experienced involuntarily and characterized by a strong desire for reciprocation of one's feelings but not primarily for a sexual relationship.'

This fellow adoptee wrote about his infatuation with a girl at his high school, and how those feelings never seemed to dissipate, even well into his 40s. It struck me that I had experienced the same situation with not one, but four people. Initially, it made me internally very uncomfortable knowing that there was an actual diagnosis for such a thing.

I threw myself into finding out as much as I could about this 'limerence' phenomenon.

In his book, *Foundations of Psychology*, Nicky Hayes writes:

'It is this unfulfilled, intense longing for the other person which defines limerence, where the individual becomes obsessed by that person and spends much of their time fantasizing about them. Limerence may only last if conditions for the attraction leave it unfulfilled; therefore, occasional, intermittent reinforcement is required to support the underlying feelings.'

He also notes that: *'it is the unobtainable nature of the goal which makes the feeling so powerful, and that it is not uncommon for those to remain in a state of limerence over someone unreachable for months and even years.'* I couldn't help but think that maybe this is what happened to me with Damian before I met him?

Where did such a name or concept even come from? Psychologist Dorothy Tennov created the descriptive word in her 1979 book, *Love and Limerence: The Experience of Being in Love*, in which she described a concept that she had observed and developed in the mid-1960s from her clients. She had interviewed over 500 people on the topic of love, and she used the word *limerence* to describe an involuntary and intense infatuation or romantic obsession. According to the Gottman Institute, in their blog, *the 3 Phases of Love*, Dorothy Tennov created the word limerence as observed from her clients, to describe what happens in the first stage of love, characterized by physical symptoms (flushing, trembling, palpitations), excitement, intrusive thinking, obsession, fantasy, sexual excitement, and the fear of rejection.

Limerence, which is not exclusively sexual, has been defined in terms of its potentially inspirational effects and relation to attachment theory. It has been described by psychologists Lynn Wilmott and Evie Bentley as being 'an involuntary, potentially inspiring state of adoration and attachment to a limerent object (person) [and] involving intrusive and obsessive ruminations, feelings and behaviours from euphoria to despair, contingent on perceived emotional reciprocation.' They also remark that limerence has received little attention in scientific literature.

Some theorize that limerence could be considered a psychiatric condition, due to the level at which it interferes with everyday functioning, but it isn't listed in the DSM-V. Perhaps this is because so-called 'healthy' people can develop limerence too, and *they* seem to be able to cope with life and recover from the entire episode unscathed.

I was extremely intrigued to dig into the reasons behind why I thought I may have experienced limerence with Damian – there had been such an intense obsession with him, even before meeting him in person. Had there been others? Was it due to my abandonment and lack of human affectionate bonding with my birth mother, and then experiencing the same thing from my adoptive mother? Did this indeed have something to do with the attachment theory? *Had I obsessed over a fantasy of the ghost of my birth mother?*

CHAPTER 16

Around the same time, I stumbled across 'limerence,' I was exploring a concept called 'mother hunger,' as introduced in a book by Kelly McDaniel, who is a licensed counsellor and author. In the book, she explores insecure attachment and maternal deprivation in adult women. Regardless of how you identify your gender, I hope you can still connect with this interesting 'mother hunger' theory if it resonates.

In her theory of mother hunger, Kelly states:

'The term almost speaks for itself. Like cancer, mother hunger invisibly eats away your insides, slowly digesting any strength, dignity, or agency you've gathered. Hunger pains need relief. Food, sex, romance, work, alcohol...something to numb the inner longing for a love that's missing.'

She explains that 'mothers provide daughters with three important developmental needs: nurturing, protection, and guidance. If any one of these three is missing, a daughter grows up with an achy loneliness that distorts her self-concept and capacity for healthy relationships. Well-meaning mothers regularly miss one of these critical developmental needs when raising their daughters. Since most women are impacted by the toxic stress of patriarchy, a mother can't give her daughter what she doesn't have. A daughter learns to love the way her mother loves her, and mother hunger is passed intergenerationally between women. For example, perhaps your mother was loving, cuddly, and playful. You felt her love and enjoyed her affection. But she had difficulty making decisions, managing her moods, and you often felt confused or worried about her. You learned that you couldn't look to her for solutions or guidance. As an adult, you wrestle with anxiety and confusion, often feeling younger than your age. You find powerful people irresistible.'

Well, no wonder I was literally starving, trying to fill my bottomless cup. And now I was finally beginning to further understand how being a motherless daughter – not just once, but twice – was jeopardizing any chance of having a fulfilling life. At least I had found the words to describe what I wasn't yet equipped to be dealing with. I had never known what to call it in order to seek out the help I needed.

McDaniel goes on to say that mother hunger 'exists on a spectrum and names the invisible wound that emerges from missing comfort, or safety, or guidance from your mother.' If your mother was abusive and you missed all three of the needs, this is called 'third-degree mother hunger.' Third-degree mother hunger 'is essentially disorganized attachment and shares symptoms with bipolar disorder, borderline personality disorder, or major depressive disorder. But mother hunger isn't pathology or a disorder – it's an injury, an invisible wound that hides from awareness until you find a name.'

✷✷✷

So now I had discovered two new breadcrumbs – words to define parts of me – along the journey to my self-discovery. Limerence and mother hunger. Whilst the GSA part was intriguing, it didn't apply to me at all.

When I start to think about my limerence and my hunger for my birth mother, I am taken back into the time when I was first completely obsessed with my first 'victim.' From the moment my adoptive mother told me my birth mother gave me up,

I fantasized about her secretly watching over me, or how she might just walk into my life at any given moment. I was obsessed with her, dreaming up ways she might be thinking of me too. Of course, I was also starving for her at the same time. Then, of course, there was my abusive adoptive mother who deprived me of love, which impacted my self-love and self-worth.

These injuries impacted my human potential in so many devastating ways, and I grew to become a lesser version of my true self because of them. When I was eight years old, I became obsessed with a girl in my class, Tabatha. She and I explored each other sexually, and even though I was only eight, her touch sent me through the roof. I remember how desperate I was to be touched, wanting to even pay my adoptive mother just to get her to hold me, tickle my back, hold my hand – anything. I fell completely for Tabatha; I worshipped her. I would do anything for her, even share her with the other girls at the time. To me, she was my object of adoration, even if it wasn't reciprocated.

I was so confused about love and I still am. I didn't know what it was like to feel loved. My adoptive mother wouldn't touch me, but said she loved me. My friend touched me, but said she didn't love me. Eventually she stopped touching me altogether when we were teenagers, because she was told it was wrong to touch another girl. I was heartbroken – I had been under the influence of limerence and mother hunger, and she was my medicine. Even though I felt she never truly cared about me, I was already identifying myself as somebody who wasn't worthy of being loved, so it didn't really surprise me.

I quickly discovered that boys were more than willing to go further than just a touch – and for free! So, of course, I willingly went there. I was way too young to be going all the way, but I had no boundaries when it came to quenching my insatiable desire for touch and intimacy. The pain and ecstasy – attachment bonding and maternal nurturance is what I craved and was missing, but I would also discover that giving my body over to fill that never-ending empty cup only led to a never-ending cycle of disappointment, betrayal, neglect, and abuse, of myself and from others.

Eventually, I would just get drunk, sleep with men on the first date, and then throw them away.

In her e-book, *Mother Hunger Surrogate Comfort*, Kelly McDaniel writes about touch deprivation for females:

'Lack of maternal nurturance leads to touch deprivation. Touch deprivation has a mind of its own. Before girls who lack maternal nurturance get older and have access to drugs and alcohol to comfort their touch-starved bodies, they touch themselves. Before they starve or binge or purge, they touch each other. Before they cut, burn, or bang, they meet their desperate needs with siblings, pets, or anything warm and soft. Little girls without maternal affection are especially vulnerable to those who might take advantage of them. They don't recognize inappropriate touch, because it's better than no touch... Like food, orgasm medicates emotional starvation.'

My next limerence obsession (LO), was with Ben, the boy down the road. For years, I watched him from the living room window as he would bike past my house in his cricket whites on his green ten-speed, with the wind in his curly hair and his arms crossed, trusting the handlebars to guide him home. God, he was gorgeous – an all-American kind of guy, but you could tell he would fit in just as easily at Eton. I was too scared to venture outside into the front yard to catch his eye, partly out

CHAPTER 16

of shyness but also because of the nosey neighbours across the road who I thought would be watching me. So, I just hid and watched and waited for a time for our paths to cross.

And one day, my dreams came true – and yes, this was the beginning of his time as my long-term object of limerence.

At the time, I was one of the few 16-year-olds that had a driver's license *and* a car, and I was dating a guy who asked if I could pick a few of his friends up on our way out to a nightclub. I would be the responsible, designated driver. I had been nightclubbing since I was 13, as no ID was required in the 80s – just shitloads of makeup and hairspray.

My instructions were to head back to my street, drive further down past my house, and stop at number 20 to pick up his mate. We waited on the street and then out his friend walked – and my heart stopped still. It was him, handsome cricket guy! Suddenly, he was sitting in the backseat of my car. I was mesmerized; driving was difficult to concentrate on, as he was literally eyeballing me in the rear-view mirror. I tried to avoid his eye contact, but I finally steeled myself and met his cheeky gaze.

I picked up three more people before we all decided to grab a few beers from the bottle store and go down to the river before the club would be pumping. My boyfriend pulled out a joint. I'd only had a few puffs on a ski-field once, so I felt a little bit inconspicuous, but Ben came up beside me and said, 'Do you want a shotgun?'

The energy from him being so close to me was exquisitely electric, and yes, I wanted to do a shotgun with him…I'd have done anything with him.

'Oh, you haven't done this before?' he asked.

I admitted I was a rookie. Suddenly, he inhaled and pulled me into his arms, signalling for me to open my mouth and slowly inhale. His lips brushed in between mine, and he blew the smoke softly, gently into my lungs. I inhaled, and it was the most delicious moment of my life. We did it several times and I literally was blown away. I didn't even care about my boyfriend; I think I was in love.

We all sat by the river for hours, drinking beers and smoking cigarettes in between joints. It was a balmy, starry summer night and I had never felt so intoxicated with life – not just from all the chemicals, but from the endorphins that came from the realization that my fantasy guy on the bike, with the all-American smile and the cricket whites from Eton, was soon going to be *all mine*. It was just a matter of time, but I was going to have him, no matter what.

I was on a curfew – the rules were that I could drive my car at night, but I had to be home by midnight. I had grown to respect most of my parents' rules, especially when it came to my driving, but it was slowly creeping past 11:30 p.m. and we hadn't even made it to the club yet. I hadn't had much to drink, and only about three puffs of those delicious shotguns from my 'future boyfriend,' but we had to leave if they wanted to get to the club.

I told the group that sadly I was expected to be home soon. They all tried to talk me out of it, and Ben was the only one to respect my honouring my parents, defending my decision and saying that the others needed to respect me for that. I imagined that he came from a good home where morals were also adhered to – I liked that in a man.

Long story short, I drove them all to the club and they gave me instructions as to how to get home, as it was miles away, on the outskirts of the city. It was the 1980s, so there was no GPS to come to the rescue. Ben was the one to patiently give me a visual of how to get to the motorway – my boyfriend was too busy flirting with another girl in the group.

Still uncertain about Ben's instructions, and sad to be leaving him, I sighed heavily, bid them all adieu, and watched them all head into the club.

He was all I could think about on the drive home. *Did he say go left or straight?* I had been too busy looking flirtatiously into Ben's beautiful eyes to listen properly – I just wanted to drive straight into his arms.

The night had cooled down, and it was eerie out, with a light misty fog suddenly everywhere. I could vaguely see a railway crossing and a bridge coming up ahead. There seemed to hardly be any streetlamps as I approached the bridge, and as I crossed the railway line, the streets were even darker, and the mist was getting thicker. A very strong shudder ran through my body as I cranked up the fan heater. As I approached an intersection, I knew I had to turn right. There was no give way sign, so I had to be very careful about my timing, as cars were speeding down the bridge toward me, and it was so hard to see when the next one was coming.

Then I heard a voice. You know the one – we've met him before. Cain.

'Hey. What are you waiting for? Go on, do it – just plant your foot down and go. Don't look – it'll be fun. The next car is coming, can you hear it? It's speeding. I dare you to floor the gas pedal and feel what it is like to crash!'

No, not again! This was the voice inside my head that I thought had left me years ago. I called him 'Cain.' He had taunted me as a kid, sometimes telling me to do great things, sometimes not so great. *No, not now. Please.*

I felt paranoid. Was it the shotgun? *Do you want me to hurt myself or kill somebody?* I wondered. This voice had a way of making me do bizarre things in the past, but never something as evil as this. I squeezed my eyes tight, turned up the music, and tried to shut it out.

But the voice of Cain drowned out the music. It must have got through the gatekeeper in me, because of the smoke I had inhaled. To calm myself, I tried practicing my breathing exercises and mantras, but tonight I was powerless. Before I knew it, without even thinking, my foot pressed down hard on the accelerator, and I felt a massive adrenaline rush as I drove straight onto the path of an oncoming car. I was doing 60 kilometres an hour, but they were speeding at over 100.

When I came to, the bonnet was crunched up onto the railings on the bridge. There was a distinct smell of burnt rubber, and I heard terrifying screams in the distance. I managed to push open what remained of my door, but I couldn't see properly – it was thick with fog outside and warm blood was oozing down into my eye.

Then I vaguely saw the other car on the road, upside down! The screams were coming from the people inside it.

I don't remember hitting the car, I just remember the voice praising me and instructing me to brace for impact, telling me I was going to be just fine.

I sat on the curb in shock. There were lots of flashing lights,

CHAPTER 16

and I became aware of a silver blanket being wrapped around me by an ambulance person, whilst someone else checked my eyes and bandaged my bleeding head. I looked at my car. OMG! *What did I do?*

'Concussion. Judging by the injury, I would assume she was knocked out. She is going to need stitches. Call ahead to the hospital – let's get her there now.'

They had my driver's license somehow, and I told them to call my parents, but I couldn't hear my own voice. I couldn't hear *that* voice, either. 'Their phone number is...'

I passed out with the last thought in my mind being *I hope they are not going to be too upset with me.* Weirdly, it wasn't until I saw my parents that I even thought about the people whom I crashed into. They were all okay, thankfully – not a scratch on them, I was told.

***

'Well now, what is a gorgeous thing like you doing in a place like this and at this time of night?'

A male nurse propped me up onto the pillows of the hospital bed.

'Oh, slowly,' I moaned, 'my head really hurts.' I was so thirsty, so I asked for some water.

'Well, my pretty, you are lucky that cut you managed to get is not going to ruin that cute little face of yours. Here, I have a mirror for you. See? It's not so bad!'

My head was wrapped in a bandage and there was a huge bundle of it on the right side of my temple. Ouch. 'How many stitches?' I enquired.

'Well, if you keep touching it, we will need to increase it to 20 – you have three, now, so hands off! Now I want you to take two of these painkillers, please.' *What an ordeal.*

'My parents, have they...do they know...'

'Yes, darling, they are waiting in the cafeteria. I will just pop out to alert the staff to let them know you are awake.' He returned quickly. 'But I just wanted to talk with you. You were not over the limit from our tests – do you remember what happened tonight?'

This nurse was very handsy, touching me on the shoulders and placing a hand over mine that was resting on my lap. He didn't creep me out though; I think he was gay.

I was lost for words. What was I going to tell him? That a *voice inside me* told me to do it?

What were my parents thinking right now? *Where are they again?* I was utterly overwhelmed, and I burst into tears. The nurse was now holding my gaze and my hand, and I felt quite comforted by him. 'I...I don't...I don't know...but I think it was... it was...the...it wasn't me; it just wasn't! I would never do that! It wasn't me! It was this...this voice. That I...I get in my head, and it tells me what to do!'

The nurse looked at me thoughtfully and gently patted my hand. 'Listen, I know I am not supposed to say this, but I can see you are such a lovely, sweet soul. You are a child of God, and God is here for you. If you ever want to come with me to my church and let the voice of God into your head instead, please call me.' I watched as he wrote on a business card. 'Look, this is just between us, OK? Here is the name of my church group, and here is my home number. Call me, I can help you. I've been there, kid.'

Before I had the chance to respond, the doors to the ward flung open, and in rushed my panicked parents. As usual, my adoptive mother could be quite nice – when she was in a public place with me.

I don't know whatever happened to the nurse's card, but boy oh boy, when I got home the next day, guess who was waiting at our door with flowers?

Ben. *Sigh*...

We were inseparable from that day on. I was well and truly in love – or in limerence – and this limerence with Ben outlasted the three-year relationship between us, by over 20 years.

I still dream about him, and we even email a bit, even after years of no communication. It is wonderful having him back in my life, even if it is only via a message or two – at times it has felt quite euphoric. I still dream about my childhood girl crush, too...

Writing this memoir about my forced and closed adoption has not only encouraged me to research the ramifications of the forced and closed adoption law, and its consequences on adoptees as much as possible, but to also delve into my world of my own confusion, introspection and insights and put it onto the page. For me, having the awakening through the discovery of words and definitions for feelings, like 'limerence' and 'mother hunger' actually validates my homeostasis of 'crazy,' 'lost,' and 'fucked up,' and it also brings me a sense of 'identity.' I wish I had read a book like mine years ago.

That is really what I hope you can take away, too – if, through sharing my innermost self, I can introduce you to parts of yourself and give you a platform to dive deeply into your own 'crazy,' then my purpose for this book is done!

Coach Charlie:

Adopted or not, I believe that the more our sense of identity is rooted in the superconscious realms within us – if we live consciously as creative beings versus living unconsciously as problem solvers – the more aligned we are with the creative field, and the more power we harness in our life force. When we do this, we will then be not as controlled by the hidden agendas of our conditioned belief systems from our subconscious mind.

To dedicate our creative power entirely to action towards creating our true end results – our desired reality – we need to truly know ourselves in all our aspects. I have already covered information about our energy systems, dysfunctional patterns, and our resourceful personality parts, which all help with such self-integration and awareness. But right now, considering what was covered in this chapter, I want to talk with you about another part of ourselves, which is called our 'Shadow Self' – also known as our 'dark side.' This is the part of us that we don't want to meet, and for some, this can be confronting.

The wording sounds ominous, I know, but the good news is that understanding this shadow/dark side allows us to reclaim our hidden superpowers, which have been lying dormant after being pushed away during our first eight years. Our true identities have been buried in the basements of our psyches, waiting to be released and returned to us. When we uncover our shadow/dark side, it truly is a life-changing opportunity, and it turns us back to a more enlightened sense of self.

With no more energy needed to keep separate what has been ours all along, we can place our focus consistently on the highest potential of possibilities, create with superconscious awareness, and live in coherence with all our personality parts working together. Imagine harnessing such superpower! You can really start to live as a whole person, which is your divine birthright. We all have this challenge, adopted or not, and we all have this incredible potential to integrate all parts of the self. The goal is to become whole, but the first step is to have an awareness regarding what is lurking in the background of our modus operandi – then we can send it to the light with love and gratitude.

The dark/shadow side is a part of our ego that is always trying to create the conditions it believes must exist before it is possible to create a life you want. Your dark side is defined by the conditions you believe you can't have, as it is an unconscious protection from further wounding.

We are all wounded in relation to who we truly are, adopted or not. We all have a concept of how our true nature is not feasible or even applicable, how we can't be who we are. The truth is, all of our suffering comes from our struggle to create a more acceptable substitute or version of ourselves, as opposed to our true nature. For example, I proved to myself time and time again that I could survive being bullied, so I continued to be bullied to reinforce I could survive that. Some may prove their belief that money is the root of all evil, money is bad, or the rich are selfish – and therefore they will continue to prove that they can survive with money struggles.

I didn't know that I could survive AND not be bullied. You can survive AND have money.

Our dark side is what we fear exists in us and what creates the conditions that oppose our hearts' desires. And as we resist and deny and suppress, we only give power to our fear; what we resist, persists. But what we fear is an illusion.

FEAR is an acronym for *False Evidence Appearing Real.* FEAR. This FEAR prevents us all from going for what we want. That dark side that keeps your real self hidden and protected, is not *really* you; it is a shadow part – a personality part - of your true whole nature.

Today, we are going to meet your dark side through a guided meditation, and then you will have time to write about what came through for you. Your dark side will appear to you by many means – some perhaps a little scary or unsettling. It will happen through a symbol, an animal, an entity, or a memory. It can come as a vision or a feeling, or it can speak to you. But do not be afraid; it will never hurt you, and after meeting it you will soon see its positive aspects. This is your moment of destiny to heal your soul karma. Once your dark side reveals itself to you, it is no longer controlling you. You will not only become fully aware of all of the information it contains about your dark side, but you can thank it and release it from your karmic records. Best of all, you can embrace your dark side and leave it healing in the light. Remember: your shadow side/dark side isn't meant to appear as a friendly, loving, peaceful being – it is going to be a little confronting. But you are ready for this. You can do this.

The fact that you are still reading this means they are eager to share with you today, right now – so are you ready to begin? NOTE: I suggest that you read this meditation through to yourself, then maybe record it on your phone in your own voice, or perhaps get a loved one to read it to you or record it for you. Have a pen and paper or laptop or phone memo app ready for notes afterwards. Now get comfortable, and free from distractions, and go for it!

(This Shadow Self meditation is a reconstruction, inspired from my magnetic mind coaching training and resources such as Chris Duncan's https://consciouseducationcompany.com/).

* * *

Close your eyes and imagine that you are walking through a path in a tranquil, peaceful forest. You feel completely safe and relaxed. Let's create a full sensory experience of this forest path – you can hear the birds singing and feel the cool breeze in the warmth of the sun and you can smell the scent of fresh pine and flowers. Breathing in and out slowly, you can create a full experience of what you see – taking it in, one foot in front of the other – taking in the breath through the nose and out to the count of four as you breathe in and out.

You get to a familiar fork in the road and normally you turn right but this time you turn left. You walk further down the path on your left, and as you are walking down this path you are taking it all in. It is so beautiful and safe and feels familiar, but you haven't been here for a while – lifetimes in fact. As you are walking down the path you get the sense that this is a very important moment in your current lifetime, and if you believe in your spirit guides and angels, you can see or sense them beside you now. You thank them for showing up to be with you along this journey.

Breathing to the count of four as you breathe in and slowly out, see yourself walking until you see a clearing. You go out into this clearing, and you are struck by beautiful scenery, filled with grassy hills and the most beautiful pond – it is as if it were painted by the artist Monet, and the light is reflecting in the deep blue green water of the pond. Willow trees are lapping the water, and you see big white lotus flowers floating on top. You look out and you see a waterfall in the distance, and as you sit down in the soft grass next to the pond and feel the breeze that is softly floating around you, you feel just so serene and relaxed.

You are settling in and taking in the moment, and you get this feeling like something powerful is about to happen – you can feel the anticipation – and you fix your gaze out across the pond. You see that something is rising from the water, and you just imagine you can see that what is rising out of the water is some kind of a being or a symbol – it is a representation of your dark side, your shadow side.

You feel safe and protected as it rises up out of the water now. You can now see that it might change a little – it might be an animal or a symbol. Notice what it is, notice what you feel as it moves towards you – you know you are meant to be right here, right now, and you feel this is meant to be. You feel safe and secure, and your guides and angels are right next to you, too.

You can see it now as it moves towards you. You get to greet this being – a living symbol or animal, or something else that you can't explain – but you somehow feel you connect with it, heart to heart. Connect with it now, experience it heart to heart in this crucial moment when you meet. Ask your dark side – your shadow that you have met now – to share with you all that you need to receive now so you can understand and acknowledge it finally, with love, so it can finally be released from you. Ask what its role was in your life, what *was its purpose? How was it protecting you, and from what? Tell it that you are going to take over now and thank it for the amazing job it has done in your life, but now it is time for it to go to the light.*

You see it appear to be looking up at what looks like the golden sun. As it is looking up, you see it lifting up in the air, floating into the golden sun until it vanishes completely. It has been absorbed by the light, and it is now being healed and transformed. You feel so peaceful and relaxed because you too have absorbed the bright healing light. You feel healed and transformed now! A big shift has happened for you, and you are excited to live your life free from your shadow now.

Breathing in and out as you normally would – you are so ready to come back now – slowly open your eyes, stretch out your body, and feel refreshed and revitalized.

When you are ready, I want you to now write down or record everything that occurs to you about your experience. Here are some questions to use as prompts for your recall:

1. What did 'it' look like?
2. What did it say or convey to you?
3. Did it have a name?
4. How did you feel about it? How do you feel about it now? What was it saying about all that you are not allowed to experience in this life? (e.g., what are you never allowed to feel, have, say, or think?) What don't you acknowledge about yourself?
5. What does it show you that you deny from yourself?
6. What was its job in your life?
7. What does it really want for you now?
8. What are you going to do differently for yourself now that you are free of the past shadow?

9. Who is the opposite of your shadow/dark self?

Keep this record for you to refer to when you feel you need a reminder of your shadow/dark self to show you the opposite – to remind you of the truth of who you really are.

Love and light,
Coach Charlie X

PART THREE

ME

CHAPTER 17

The Nazi Regime and the Forced and Closed Adoption Act of 1955

(Bridgette)

I was a healthy, white, blue-eyed, blonde-haired baby – the Nordic stereotype. Due to my physical appearance and healthy disposition, in the 1970s in New Zealand, my chances of being adopted right away were significantly higher than those of others. Had my appearance been compromised due to either my colouring or my physical health, there was a much higher chance that I'd have ended up in an orphanage. In my opinion.

Why were babies who looked like me such a popular 'brand'? And what about any possible hereditary flaws that weren't actually visible lurking in the shadows?

Thank God there was nothing untoward listed on my adoption file about my birth father's true character. (For example, when I was born, my birth father was nearing 40 years old and was an alcoholic, heavy smoker, and gambler. From the observation of others, he was also probably bipolar or manic depressive, and he was a womanizer who had already been married three times.) I doubt that would have helped my chances. Lucky for me, such details were not recorded, as no one wanted to dissuade the sale from the marketing of the features and benefits of my outside packaging. Selling me was the solution to the problem of my birth, and everyone else won.

Now that I had found most of my family members and was working on myself, peeling off the band-aids one by one and getting the help I needed, I felt strong enough to do more research on the history of the New Zealand Forced and Closed Adoption Act of 1955, and to face the real personal and social injustices of it all. I had questions that I wanted answered, such as: where did the concept of the Act originate from? Who was responsible for such an inhumane atrocity? Why were the records of adoptees up to the 1990s closed and sealed in New Zealand? I was also curious to find out why babies who looked like me were most sought after for white, middle-class families? Did this also apply to other countries during the same era? And if so, why was this the case? And what was the deal with taking newborns, fresh from the womb, and forcing them to be immediately relinquished from their birth mother? Why couldn't they be nursed by their birth mothers? Why was the baby *forced* from their birth mother immediately after they were born?

And suddenly, the Nazi Regime marched into my life.

In 1925, Adolf Hitler wrote in *Mein Kampf*:

'Everything we admire on this earth today—science and art, technology, and inventions – is only the creative product of a few peoples and originally perhaps one race [the 'Aryans']. On them depends the existence of this whole culture. If they perish, the beauty *of this earth will sink into the grave with them.'*

Historian Richard Evans indicates in his book, *The Coming of the Third Reich*, that the Nazis then acted on Hitler's belief, to ensure the existence and strength of the 'Aryan' race prevailed. He stated that, 'what mattered to them above all was race, culture, and ideology...the strong and the racially pure had to be encouraged to have more children, the weak and the racially impure had to be neutralized by one means or another.'

According to the *Holocaust Encyclopedia*, the term 'racial hygiene' was first employed by German economist Alfred Ploetz back in 1895. Also, the term 'eugenics' was coined by the English naturalist Sir Francis Galton, from the Greek word meaning 'good birth or stock.' These concepts illustrated and confirmed Hitler's perspectives and led Hitler and his followers to devise an ideology that combined racial antisemitism with eugenics.

Eugenicists of the late 19th and early 20th centuries believed all social ills - alcoholism, mental illness, poverty, criminality, and physical disabilities, and deformations – were all initially thought to have developed from hereditary conditions only. Eugenicists went on to 'shame and blame' that the decline in public health and morality was due to hereditary influences, and that society required a more *biological* solution, deeming the 'problem' as thus.

This belief wasn't just rife in Germany, but also throughout Western Europe and the United States. Edwin Black, an American historian and author of *The Horrifying Medical Roots of Nazi Eugenics*, wrote:

'Eugenics was the racist pseudoscience determined to wipe away all human beings deemed 'unfit,' preserving only those who con-

formed to a Nordic stereotype. Elements of the philosophy were enshrined as national policy by forced sterilization and segregation laws, as well as marriage restrictions, enacted in 27 states. In 1909, California became the third state to adopt such laws. Ultimately, eugenics practitioners coercively sterilized some 60,000 Americans, barred the marriage of thousands, forcibly segregated thousands in 'colonies', and persecuted untold numbers in ways we are just learning. Before World War II, nearly half of coercive sterilizations were done in California, and even after the war, the state accounted for a third of all such surgeries.'

After the eugenics movement was set up in the United States, it was launched in Germany. California eugenicists produced literature promoting eugenics and sterilization and sent it overseas to German scientists and medical professionals. By 1933, California had subjected more people to forceful sterilization than all other U.S. states combined. The forced sterilization program engineered by the Nazis was partly inspired by that of California.

Did you know that the Rockefeller Foundation helped fund the German eugenics program, and even funded the program that Josef Mengele worked in before he went to Auschwitz? Just another interesting and most shocking fact that I read in that same article by Edwin Black.

As stated in the *Holocaust Encyclopedia*, Charles Davenport was an American advocate who promoted eugenics as a science 'devoted to the improvement of the human race through better breeding' and who hoped to 'encourage better families to reproduce.' It is also stated in this book that members of the eugenic community in Germany and the U.S. also viewed the racially

CHAPTER 17

'inferior,' and poor, as dangerous: 'they maintained that such groups were tainted by deficiencies they inherited, [and] they believed that these groups endangered the national community and financially burdened society.'

By late 1935, a program that was governed by such racial ideology and eugenic theories was created by the SS, led by Nazi Heinrich Himmler. This was called the Lebensborn Program, *lebensborn* meaning the 'Fountain of Life.'

It was designed to advance future generations of Germany's healthy 'Aryan' population, a mythical race of racially and culturally superior people whom Nazi authorities deemed 'racially valuable.' SS Leader Himmler was of the notion that all SS men were the elite race due to their bloodline, loyalty, and bravery, and through selective breeding - the population of Germany would advance the Nazi goals of owning Eastern Europe. A generous financial incentive was offered to SS men to encourage them to have large families with such Aryan women. Applicants for financial family assistance were accepted only after the SS established that *both* parents were of good Aryan stock, by examining their medical histories and family records. They had to have a clear record from any familial physical, mental, or psychiatric disabilities, which the SS called 'racial impurities.'

I concluded that the infiltration of brainwashing and propaganda regarding this Aryan race originated from the Nazi regime and was rolled out by Himmler. I still wanted to more accurately pinpoint where the concept of the Forced and Closed Adoption Act had originated from, and as I researched further, I concluded that the Lebensborn program could be responsible for influencing this unlawful Forced and Closed Adoption Act of 1955 as well!

This is my opinion only.

Throughout the 1930s, the program was now capitalizing upon the stigma, scandal, and financial pressures faced by unmarried and pregnant Aryan women. The SS attracted these 'mothers-to-be' to the program, with a tantalizing brochure offering financial support, food and shelter, by accommodating them in private maternity homes (away from the scrutiny of society,) and by providing healthcare for their pregnancy and delivery – and, inevitably, adoption services. The brochure even stated benefits of medical supervision, legal support, and job placement after labour.

This not only strengthened Himmler's goal to prohibit abortions of 'good stock' by offering such financial support, but to also ultimately assume guardianship of the babies and control where they would eventually be raised.

During World War II, according to the Holocaust Encyclopedia, the *Lebensborn* 'homes' were now being established across German-occupied territories. Himmler feared that the huge loss of racially viable soldiers as casualties of war would cost the nation dearly, inhibiting the production of the hereditary health of the future of Germany. He devised a plan for the German SS, military, and civilian personnel to date or rape women in German-occupied territories – especially Norway, for that Norwegian look – with the goal to impregnate them and lure them into the *Lebensborn* homes. If the offspring of those encounters proved to be of good quality 'Aryan' stock, the Germans then stole the child from the birth mother and placed them (for a fee) with German families. If they established the birth mother and child were indeed not 'Aryan,' they were either murdered or

CHAPTER 17

sent to the concentration camps. The Germans also kidnapped thousands of 'Aryan ancestral' or 'Aryan-looking' children from their families – mainly from eastern and southern eastern Europe – and the *Lebensborn* establishment sold them to German families. *Like pieces of real estate. Just like we were. Pieces of real estate.*

These adoptive families were told they were orphaned because of the war.

According to Wikipedia's information on Lebensborn, after the war, children born in Norway to Norwegian mothers by German fathers were allegedly often bullied, abused, raped, and persecuted by society and by the government, and they were allegedly sent to mental institutions where the same abuse continued. In addition to the site information it stated that, 'the Norwegian government attempted to deport Lebensborn children to Germany, Brazil, and Australia but did not succeed. Some of the Lebensborn children sought compensation from the Norwegian government, whom they implied to be responsible for their mistreatment. In 2008, their case before the European Court of Human Rights was dismissed as the events had happened so far ago in the past.' Eventually, an offer of £8,000 in payment was made as a claim to each Lebensborn child – now an adult – from the Norwegian government.

Interesting fact: Did you know that ABBA star Anni-Frid Lyngstad is a child born into the Lebensborn program? According to an article in *The Guardian*, 'Torment of ABBA Star with a Nazi Father,' after the war, her maternal grandmother helped Anni-Frid and Anni-Frid's mother avoid such persecution by relocating them to Sweden. Anni-Frid did eventually go in search of her father, and, after meeting him, their relationship was unsuccessful. As is the case with most of us adoptees, when we search and find our birth families. In my case, to be completely honest with you, my focus was really just to find them – I never had the goal to have any thriving relationship with them. Who am I to have it all!

※ ※ ※

I have concluded that New Zealand's Forced and Closed Adoption Act of 1955 was initially designed around this concept of eugenics and the Lebensborn program. Eugenics was still a big selling point for adoption agencies – housing these unwed mothers-to-be in secret church-run homes or in 'hostess system' homes, to prepare and deliver – then signing up the government to sell their healthy, white, Aryan-looking babies. A money making business and a striking coincidence to the *Lebensborn* program, don't you think?

Just as I thought I had it all figured out, I realized I had to address the next question on my list: why was it the preference to sell fresh newborn babies as opposed to selling older infants?

I stumbled across a concept called the Clean Break Theory, explored initially by Sigmund Freud and his daughter Anna and later endorsed by John Bowlby, the founder of the Attachment Theory. Unlike eugenics, this theory is based on the idea that babies' characteristics are formed by their *environment* rather than their genes. It led to the widespread belief that putting the babies of single mothers up for adoption to white, middle-class married couples as early as possible benefitted the development of their personalities, claiming they were a clean slate to be moulded by their new family. Like a 'paint by numbers kid' for the parents to create as I discussed earlier in this book.

Therefore, the way I see their reasoning is that by relinquishing the baby at birth from their mother and placing the child in an adoptive home within the earliest possible time frame, was the primary way of safeguarding that the child would turn out to be nothing like their obviously tragic and irresponsible birth parents.

The Clean Break theory, according to Psychology.org, in their article 'Past forced adoption policies and practices in Australia: It's time to make amends,' gained widespread acceptance following World War II. Stemming from their research on attachment theory and bonding, Sigmund Freud and his daughter Anna promoted this new rule of adoption – early separation of mother and child. Anna carried on her father's legacy after his death in 1939, and she became well-known in her own right as a developmental researcher, a child analyst, and a theorist of psychological parenthood, promoting an early break for baby and birth mother.

According to this article, this theory was encouraged by the influential British psychologist, psychiatrist, and psychoanalyst John Bowlby. He recommended immediate separation of the birth mother and baby with the view to prevent any early experiences from disrupting personality development. This concept was formulated from his research on attachment and loss, and it greatly influenced the government, the legal system, the adoptive parents, and even the birth mothers, to believe that adopting newborn babies who had an early *clean break* would create stronger bonds between the adopter and the birth child of another.

However, for those of us who were immediately separated from our mothers at birth, this caused a primal wound trauma, which is where our current life's challenges usually stem from. The Australian Institute of Family Studies, in a 2012 publication entitled 'Past Adoption Experiences,' conducted a large-scale research study on the impacts on people like me who were affected by the past Forced and Closed Adoption Act. Some of the injuries reported include depression, anxiety, suicidal ideation, grief, and loss; disenfranchised grief; trauma symptoms; substance abuse; physical or medical illness; relationship and parenting issues; identity issues and impacts on self-worth. Where was the help for us? Why are we not compensated?

* * *

In 1973, three years after my adoption, a benefit payment was offered to single mothers in New Zealand and Australia so they could keep and raise their child if they so choose. According to the legislation of the Social Security Amendment Act 1973, No. 117. Wellington: Government of New Zealand, 1973 - they introduced a domestic purposes benefit (DPB) to New Zealand's social welfare system. The initial basic weekly rate for the DPB was $23.70 (the same as the unemployment benefit and national superannuation for someone living alone,) plus $3 for the first dependent child and $1.25 for each additional dependant. The weekly adult minimum wage in 1973 was $45 for men and $34 for women. The average weekly male wage in 1975 was $95. The median monthly rent was $55, and petrol was around .50 cents a litre; food prices were in line with today's inflation. At the time of publishing my book, taxes were even higher back then, and for solo mothers, living off $26 a week would have been very challenging financially; family might have rejected them, and there was still a societal stigma attached as well.

No wonder forced and closed adoptions flourished in New Zealand, especially in the 1970s where it reached its peak.

Single mothers were paid way below the minimum wage for the most important job any human could ever be responsible for performing – being a mother *and* a father. It was set up to force single pregnant women and single mothers who had zero financial support, to have no other choice but to relinquish their children under the Forced and Closed Adoption Act of 1955.

It was a crime against humanity, and nobody is accountable for it in New Zealand. At the time of me publishing this in 2024, there has been no official apology from the New Zealand government, no adoption specific counselling services set up or paid for by the government, and no compensation offered to acknowledge the trauma of it all and the devastation it has left upon our lives.

Coach Charlie:

Let's face it: we haven't had it easy as adoptees here on planet Earth. Right at the get-go, from our first birthday breath to our current situation, we have suffered the inhumane and the unthinkable. We have been stolen, hidden, discarded, gaslit, and minimized, beaten and murdered. We have been deeply wounded by others, and the world around us ever since that day. We have been victimized by other people's circumstances and condemned to a life sentence under the control of the laws and government. We are victims of the ongoing cultural ghost of the world whose lens does not represent the truth of what we have been condemned to endure. It is hard to shift out of that persona – the identities of who we have been forced to become – let alone to live a life free of the curse of adoptee trauma.

But what if I could give you a little gift to nurture your soul and to help create a new reality – starting today?

It all starts with what you *focus* on. For example, when you focus on lack, you create lack. When you focus on abundance, you attract greater abundance. When you focus on self-worth, you create deeper self-worth. When you focus on pain and anger, you create more pain and anger. When you focus on giving, you create what you want to have in return. Ever get out of bed and stub your toe, then find that the rest of the day continues to 'stub' you?

There is a way of 'being,' a way to be, and a way to be given what you want. All we need to do is focus on the things that we *want* to *create* and *who* we want to become, and then act as if we already have it all! Einstein said, 'Everything is energy and that's all there is to it. Match your energy to the mindset frequency of the reality you want, and you cannot help but get that reality; it can be no other way. This is not philosophy – this is physics.'

It isn't even about you fixing yourself – it is about you letting go of old ways of being and giving yourself the permission to be given to, by giving to yourself first. If you give yourself the right framework of focus to create what you want, the rest will follow.

CHAPTER 17

You want a promotion? Give your boss a reason for it. You want more money? Give more where you can – make a charitable donation, help out a loved one, and so on. You want more love? Be more loving. You want more respect? Be more respectful. When you give first, you will see it come back to you. The way you build up your new way of being is by stepping into the energies of other people who represent the energy of the life that you want.

Here is a powerful exercise to help you connect to the feeling of being supported, loved, motivated, and encouraged to change the things you can right now. Just go through each question – you may like to take some notes – take your time and enjoy! When you take time for yourself like this, you are truly giving yourself a gift – you are making yourself a priority, and for some of us, even that in itself is a huge step.

This following activity is going to help you feel more loved, inspired, supported, and motivated than you have felt in a long time. I believe that when we think about the following questions, we fill up our love tank – we replenish our heart with love and magic, and we become more of who we really want to be. Are you ready to experience what I am talking about? Okay, let's go!

1. Who is someone who has an outlook on life you would like to have? How do they give you a better perspective that you would like to have in your life? Become them: see with their eyes, breathe through their lungs. What does this feel like to be them? How do they think about challenges? What is it like to be this person? What is it that you would love to imbibe energetically from this

person to bring into your own identity? Feel it, bring it into your chakra energy centres, and breathe it through. You feel the clarity of self and your inner power rising within you now.

2. Who is a fictional character who has attributes you would like to have? What are their skills or attributes? Why do you like them? Become them now; notice what it feels like to be them. What are their special powers or characteristics? How would it feel to be them? Decide which of their skills you would like to add to your identity and imbibe that feeling and breathe it through your chakra energy centres. Notice how good you are already feeling. You are feeling inspired and confident now.

3. Who is a family, friend, or ancestor who supports you? Who is somebody who appreciates you? Who in your life wants the very best for you? What is it like to be completely supported by this person? What does it feel like to receive such support like this for yourself? What do they want for you? Become this person who supports you – how does it feel to be them supporting you? Bring this feeling of love and support back, breathe it through your chakras, and add it to your energy. You are feeling loved and supported and nurtured.

4. Who is a wise counsellor or mentor who has the wisdom you seek right now? They can be someone you know, or whom you've never met. Become this wise counsellor who knows what you need and tune into feeling what it is like to become them, doing what you need to do for yourself. Ground yourself in this feeling of knowing

what to do and breathe it through your chakra systems as you feel so amazing now with all this new insight, wisdom, and guidance.

5. Who is a role model who has what you would like to have, in one area of life or more? A business role model. A health and fitness role model. A happy, heart-filled role model. Become this person by connecting into having what they have, and who they are. What do they do each day or week to have this? Become this person who has what it is that you want in your life. Feel the feeling of a dream come true, of having it all now, of actioning your big end result. How does that feel? Breathe it all through your chakra centres now and feel yourself starting to grow into a new way of being right now! How does this feel to be that role model now?

6. Who is someone you love, admire, or adore? This can be an animal, alive or no longer alive. Feel the feeling of loving someone and feel how they love you. Feel your heart expanding now, so full of love for them and receiving so much love back. Breathe it through your heart chakra and feel it flooding through your entire body and add it to the feelings you have just experienced and stay in this beautiful, loving energy.

7. Now, ask yourself, what is it that you need to give yourself to, in order to have what you want? What do you need to give more to, so you may now receive this? What will your action be? You are now giving what you need to give. Feel the feeling of moving forward in momentum, stepping into the future you who is now a little

ahead on your journey. With all the love, wisdom, magic, guidance, and support you will ever need, just fully step into your future self now. Breathe in this magical superconscious state of being – integrating your future self – and ask yourself how you feel.

8. What will it feel like to be at the end of your life, looking back at all you created? What is one thing you will look back on and feel proud of creating? Look back and see and feel the satisfaction of having lived a happy, successful life; you did everything you needed to do to have a life well-lived. What is it like looking back at the end of your life and knowing you had it all? Claim this position of your new identity and focus. You have oriented a life from this perspective so you can create your new identity from your future. Give back to yourself from this new orientation of you – and love the life you live now.

9. What is this going to allow you to do now? What are all of the great things that this is going to give you? How will you now give back to the world from this place of magic? What are you going to do differently?

Take some time now to write about what you experienced and reflect on this daily to propel you to practice the act of giving to yourself – giving yourself a new identity, the best version of you, the person you were born to be.

This is the greatest gift you can give to yourself and to the world around you. You now have the invisible victory that precedes the external victory. *What you become on the inside – you create on the outside.*

I hope I have helped you to receive the greatest gift of yourself because you are truly amazing.

Loving your creation of you,
Coach Charlie X

CHAPTER 18

I've Never Been to Me

(Georgiana)

I have been obsessed with the song 'I've Never Been to Me' for as long as I can remember. It illustrates how I too spent most of my own life running around living outside of myself, too scared to go within. I was distracted by the illusion of seeking out the experiences of *doing*, never fully settling into truly *being*. I wasn't ready to delve into the unknown of my 'beingness,' for how could I ever have 'been to me' when my original identity was stolen from me, and I was raised to behave as somebody else? The 'me who is Bridgette' was never to exist in this cult, so to speak, as that secret adoption indoctrination cult, isolated me from society, treated me like a third-class person with no rights, brainwashed me, threatened me, and forced me to hide away as a fake identity until I gave myself permission to exist and sought out the right help. I knew who Bridgette was and where she came from, but discovering who my first parents were, was *not* what led me to truly knowing *myself*.

That knowledge came through learning how to change my mindset, creating and honouring my own personal 'bill of rights,' and indeed through writing this memoir, a process that has opened up such self-introspection and awareness. In fact, giving myself the time and the space and the *permission* to write and publish my story has been the biggest act of love to myself *and* from myself, and it has been a *right* to birth myself into existence. I finally realized it was my *right* to tell you this story if I chose to. It is my *right* to finally be seen and heard, and it is my *right* to know what my potential is now and to love myself and to feel that I do belong in this world.

My life really started to change when I learned how to stop feeling I was still living in my 'adoption cult' and to instead begin living on my own terms of my new *personal bill of rights*. I learned that it is *my right* to be loved. It is *my right* to belong. It is *my right* to say 'no.' And I learned that I have every *right* to feel, act, and do whatever I choose to, for the highest good of myself and others. And *others* are now in their rightful place – they are now second, and I am first.

I will admit that for years I blamed my inability to just be me, and to not love me, on my adoption. Thoughts would run repeatedly in my head: *If I wasn't adopted out, who would I have become? If I was adopted into a loving, supportive, caring family, who would I have grown to be? If I had my first parents who cared for me, my life would be so much better.* I was convinced that being adopted was the reason why I feel I don't belong, and why I don't know who I really am. I thought my adoption was why I don't/can't love myself enough to be worthy of having the life I desire.

I didn't want to *heal* it – I much preferred to *blame* it, or ignore it completely – but what we resist, persists. Deep down I felt sorry for myself, and I was angry at myself for doing so. I was angry at the world and the people responsible for my rebranded, fake, traumatized, cult-like life. I had no idea that I was using my adoption (my abandonment and abusive adoptive home life) as an excuse not to thrive. My pain and anger all festered away, and consequently I went on to live out my whole life feeling I didn't have the right to belong or to be loved. I believed these rights were taken from me and that I had no right to reclaim control over my life. And what we feel on the inside is always reflected on the outside. Therefore, much of my life has been a complete mess.

You would never have guessed it was that bad because I worked extremely hard on making it look as if it wasn't. Still, I kept on attracting people and situations to prove to myself that I can still survive 'not having the right' to live a happy, healthy, wonderful life. I kept on creating adverse events to prove that I didn't have any right to belong. I couldn't hold on to anything great, and nothing good would ever stick – a boyfriend who was actually kind to me, money in the bank, a job that I enjoyed, the feeling of happiness. I would self-sabotage my way out of having those things because I didn't feel I had the right to be worthy of anything good. It's how I was wired; I was coded up to believe that I didn't deserve a life I loved, and so I created a life I didn't love and a life of never being loved.

My first mother left me, because I was told she loved me so much she gave me up, and that created my first belief system: *if somebody loves me, they will leave me.*

So, I went on to create a life that affirmed that belief. Either I would leave first, or I believed *they* – my first meeting with my birth families, my half-siblings, adoptive parents, adoptive sister, friends and boyfriends, my husband, bosses, colleagues, money, the feeling of happiness, success, health, God – would all leave me. The only person in my immediate family whom I have never left and who hasn't left me at any stage is my son. As if reading my mind, he literally told me the other day to stop thinking that he would. He said he is never going to leave me and that he loves me very much. And even though I believe him, there is still that *voice* in my head...

I do believe that I was brainwashed by my adoptive mother and sister into believing I was completely dysfunctional, disgusting and unlovable. Not only did they make my life hell growing up, but I was also attacked by them as an adult. The ways in which they gaslit and controlled me were cult-like and therefore, I couldn't shake it off – I was powerless to it. I didn't know what was going on, or that this was a thing called narcissistic abuse; I was so used to living in fear of their toxic energy and attacks that I didn't realize I was submitting to their constant psychological abuse in order to survive. I believed the terrible things they said about me, and any chance of me truly 'finding myself' and feeling comfortable in my own skin were zero. I didn't know these narcissists were programming and controlling my belief systems, and I had no idea of the true extent and trauma of suffering that would come from such long-term abuse, or how that was impacting my overall wellbeing. I had never grasped the true concept of narcissism until much later in my life and after many, many relationships with them – these so-called soul 'teachers.'

When my adoptive mother died in my mid-40s, I wasn't invited to the funeral, but I wouldn't have gone anyway. In fact, I didn't even know she had died – it was my son who found out, and who told me. She and I had been estranged for a few years, but that didn't stop her from writing me disgusting, soul-destroying letters, making nasty phone calls to me, or even trying to turn my son against me by telling him that his father was a much better human than I was and that he should live with him instead.

She enlisted Erica and her wife to also do her dirty work as well – they would call me on the phone and abuse me, defame me on my Facebook page and at my place of work, and send me and my son nasty letters with newspaper clippings about his father – saying all the time how heroic he is and how I was wrong to keep William away from him.

William's father certainly demonstrated that his son and I were not a priority in his life by cheating on me when I was pregnant with his child, refusing to pay full or regular child support, or by not showing up when it was arranged for him to see William. But when William was 14, his father happened to be one of the first responders during a huge natural disaster and was suddenly revered as a hero overnight. Erica and her wife, along with my adoptive mother, were manipulating William in letters addressed to him, making him feel guilty for not wanting to have his 'hero' of a father in his life and blaming it all on me.

All the while my adoptive father just put his head in the sand. Or in the wine bottle. Either way, he couldn't be there for us. This greatly impacted my quality of life even further.

When I heard my adoptive mother had passed, I remember feeling so unusually light and happy. She was finally dead! I was free! The rock she had buried me under all my life, had completely lifted. I never once felt guilty for my joy – all of the bullying, nasty letters and phone calls and horrible memories, even the threats from Erica, died along with her. (I did have very vivid dreams leading up to the time of her death, where she was asking me to come and visit her back home, and I am glad I didn't follow through with that.)

Last year, I decided to seek out a psychologist who specialized in narcissistic abuse recovery. On a very chilly morning, I was sitting in the waiting room by a cozy fireplace. Jasmine scented aromatherapy candles were lit, and the sound of soft jazz was playing in the background. Most of the seats were empty, which is the way I liked it – no small talk before a heavy psych session.

'Bridgette? Hello! I am Katya – welcome! Come on through – it's the door on the left.'

The room was spacious, with a white leather couch and coloured cushions, a batik large coffee table with a vase of native flowers, and another couch to the left. She gestured to me to take a seat on the white couch. There was a soft, creamy, thickly woven blanket that she offered to drape over myself if I was cold.

She asked some general questions, getting to know me a little. After doing some mindful meditation, we discussed the topic of forgiveness. We spoke about the damage my adoptive mother had inflicted and when I told her she had passed several years ago, Katya responded with: 'So, why are you keeping her

CHAPTER 18

alive then?'

I didn't realize that I was. 'Seems to me that you are living your life through her 'lens of you,' she said. 'You minimize your obvious talents and skills and dehumanize your feelings. You put yourself down and use humour to deflect from me ever having any chance to go deep here. You well up with tears, then deflect your pain by making jokes. To me, it sounds like she is still controlling you, as if she is still here. Is she still here, Bridgette?'

I was blown away. My subconscious self was still tuned in to my adoptive mother's conditioning, like she held the remote control of my soul. I didn't even think about her, and yet here I was, carrying on as if I was still under her power. I looked at Katya, and this time I didn't run away – I burst into tears, and they didn't stop.

Katya just gave me the space to cry. She encouraged me to release, and just held the energy there for me to feel safe enough to do so. She suggested that I write a letter to my adoptive mother telling her exactly what I thought of her. Saying everything my inner child and personality part wanted her to know. There was to be no holding back – it would be my farewell letter – and I was to share it with Katya by reading it aloud at the next session.

Doing this felt amazing! Incredible! To share these words with somebody as my witness to all of the pain and misery my adoptive mother caused me was cathartic. The next step was to gather up every photograph I had of her and give her my own cremation, burning the photos and the letter. Then I was to discard the cold ashes into the bin the next day. I actually ended up doing this with Erica as well. I highly recommend you try this for yourself! Such an energetic cleansing!

And with that, I was done.

My adoptive father died a few years after my adoptive mother – and to this day, I still don't know how I feel about that, though I do wish that he may rest in peace and have a happier time wherever he is now. Just before his death, he admitted to me that there was to be no inheritance at all for me or my son, that he had 'no money.' He told me that a few years back, Erica had coerced him to hand over all of the money in his savings account. As if that wasn't enough, he then gifted Erica all the money from the sale of the family home after my adoptive mother died, because those were the wishes of my adoptive mother. My adoptive father did apologize, and then he even asked if I could help him and his new wife to somehow get the money back.

I hired a lawyer to fight for it, but I didn't win. Legally, it was Erica's as it was deemed 'a gift.' You can't contest that – adopted or not. The facts are that it was a gift from my father to his youngest daughter. I just had to get over it.

This was all happening around the same time that I was experiencing my divorce and some workplace bullying and slander. My life was certainly pushing me to finally look within myself. I quit that job and relocated elsewhere in the country to be with my son. Best decision I ever made. I thank Sam for that. I then went for a deep, deep dive into learning how to become a conscious creator, and to live in my superconscious power. I was well below rock bottom, and that really was the turning point in my life. I needed to understand what had happened to me, and who I was. Why I was here and where I was going.

A few months into my desire for some kind of awakening, the magic happened when I finally awoke to this realization:

It doesn't matter about my past; it was all perfect for my individual growth and purpose. It all gave me the chance to connect deeper with others and to inspire, educate, and help change the worldview on past adoption practices! The past is over, and it no longer defines me, but I can use it to my advantage now and help others who are where I was. Now, if only I could decide on a title for this book...oh, and write it!

Whilst I realized that being adopted and feeling unloved throughout my life had made me believe that I wasn't worthy enough to be loved or to belong or have any rights, I also understood that many people who are not adopted can feel the same way. To have a sense of self – a sense of our true identity – and to belong in the world as our true self is something many of us are searching for. Just like the song says, 'I've been to paradise, but I've never been to me,' I found comfort in knowing that I wasn't alone in this feeling. We all want to be free of our old agendas and belief systems and the pains of the past.

We are all searching for ourselves on some level, aren't we? Adopted or not, we have all had our true identities stolen from us by our conditioning that our past experiences, family systems, internalized thoughts, and dysfunctional beliefs all created.

We all want to become who we choose to be.

Coach Charlie:

In my opinion, the adoption laws in New Zealand under the 1955 Forced and Closed Adoption Act and subsequent legislation, such as the 1985 New Zealand Adult Adoption Information Act, potentially violated several human rights and the rights of adoptees in various ways:

The Right to identity: These laws often sealed the original birth records of adoptees, preventing them from accessing information about their biological parents, ancestry, and medical history. This denial of access to their own identity information infringed upon their fundamental right to know and understand their origins. Particularly for Māori adoptees, being denied knowledge of their whakapapa (genealogy) and iwi (tribal) affiliations infringes on their cultural rights and connection to their heritage. This is especially critical given the significance of lineage and heritage in Māori culture.

The Right to family: Closed adoption laws sometimes permanently severed legal ties between adoptees and their biological families, denying them the right to maintain relationships with their birth parents and extended biological relatives. This separation could deprive adoptees of their cultural and familial heritage.

The Right to information: Adoptees and their families were often not provided with sufficient information about the adoption process, the legal implications, or the reasons for the adoption. Lack of transparency in these matters undermined their ability to make informed decisions and understand their personal histories.

The Right to privacy: While closed adoption laws were intended to protect the privacy of birth parents, they also extended to deny adoptees access to their own personal information. This restriction on access to their own records limited their ability to assert their privacy rights and manage their personal information as adults.

The Right to non-discrimination: Adoptees faced potential discrimination based on their status as adopted individuals, particularly in contexts where access to information or rights differed based on adoption status compared to non-adopted individuals. Like our right to citizenship!

The Right to legal recourse: Adoptees often encountered legal obstacles when attempting to access information about their adoptions or challenge the legality of adoption processes. This lack of legal recourse hindered their ability to assert their rights and seek redress for any injustices or violations they experienced.

What right did anyone have, doing that to another person? What right did I feel I had to exist as my true self, when I didn't know who I really was?

It takes time to shift into our true identity – to integrate our personality parts and let go of our outdated beliefs and conditioning – whether we are adopted or not. We ALL believe in false orientations that our personality parts and damaged aspects keep pulling us back into. But when we step into the sheer wonder of possibilities, we realize that our past is just a cellular memory, causing us to fall back into these old beliefs, emotions, parts, and aspects. We are here to step fully into our original selves, our amazing creator selves. Our superconscious selves. *This* is where our true selves exist. They already live inside of us, but we need to first be aware that we can create new results in our lives and become who we want to be – and exist in our full potential – by releasing the conditioning that comes with reliving our old stories. We can release and let go of the pain and trauma and step into being this amazing person we were born to be, living a life we love.

If you close your eyes and just imagine choosing something different for your life – and just imagine wiping out your past – what do you see? Take a moment. Who do you know whom you think has the life you want, or has what you perceive their life is like? Close your eyes and think about what you would love to create, if you could just let go of all the parts and beliefs that stop you from having it. Just picture that life you are about to create – from the perspective of letting go of all of the trauma – and you can now have wisdom, intuitiveness – from your angels and guides or from your higher, superconscious self – to create whatever it is that you desire.

You just need to choose your perfect end result and live as if you have it all *now!*

You want to be loved? *Be* love! Be loving! Love yourself first!

You want to belong? Self-awareness and self-acceptance are the key. Give yourself permission to feel that you do belong here. Tell yourself that you belong. It is your birthright to belong in this world.

You want to have a sense of self, to be someone who has the right to exist just as you are, and be the highest and most powerful version of yourself? Do it! Be it!

You want to feel that you have a right to feel happy? Guess what? You are entitled to have the right to happiness! You have the right to live the life you want!

When you step into this, you will feel the grief coming through first, which you must release – and that is so important. You have a right to release your pain and seek the help you need. *You have rights!* Adoptees, in my opinion and experience, have come into this world with their rights violated, so this is a big journey for us – let alone allowing ourselves to feel that we have a right to claim back what was stolen from us. To feel we have a right to make our own choices for ourselves and our future is a huge step forward for us all.

I would love for you to give yourself permission to have the right to have whatever it is that you want for yourself – right now. *This is your right!*

To make this clearer for you, I will list some personal rights that I have created, to help you let go of the past and to empower you to live and honour your rights as a human being now. I recommend you write these out and put them on your wall or on your fridge or your mirror and read these every day. This will help to create the powerful shift from 'victim' to 'victorious.' I personally read through these every day, and my life has changed because of it. I am creating new belief systems around my personal rights and so can you!

PERSONAL BILL OF RIGHTS

1. I have the right to be uniquely myself.
2. I have the right to be happy.
3. I have the right to grow and change.
4. I have the right to feel sad, scared, and upset, and to share this with someone who can help me.
5. I have the right to cry and to grieve the pain that I have endured, and to share this with someone who can help me.
6. I have the right to be treated with dignity and respect and love.

7. I have the right to exist as my true self and to belong here as my true self.
8. I have the right to be in a non-abusive environment.
9. I have the right to ask for help when I need it.
10. I have the right to say, 'I don't know.'
11. I have the right to be angry.
12. I have the right to follow my own values, standards, and morals.
13. I have the right to say 'no, I don't want to do that/no, I disagree/no, I am not ready.'
14. I have the right to express all of my feelings – both positive and negative.
15. I have the right to change my mind any time I choose.
16. I have the right to not give excuses or reasons for my behaviour.
17. I have the right to take time out for myself, to give myself space and time.
18. I have the right to live a life of health and vitality.
19. I have the right to be successful and to shine.
20. I have the right to expect honesty, trust, and respect from others.
21. I have the right to make decisions based on my true feelings.
22. I have the right to be uniquely myself and to invest in myself.
23. I have the right to not be responsible for others' feelings or problems.
24. I have the right to make mistakes and to be imperfect.
25. I have the right to feel worthy, good enough/capable

enough/significant enough.
26. I have the right to be playful, cheeky, sexy, and frivolous.
27. I have the right to be healthier and happier than those around me.
28. I have the right to live a life I love.
29. I have the right to be the predominant force in my life, and to make my own decisions.
30. I have the right to live as my true self, my true nature, and in my superpower.
31. I have the right to have more money than I can spend.
32. I have the right to have a body I love.
33. I have the right to go for what I want and take action steps towards achieving it.

Standing by your side,
Coach Charlie X

CHAPTER 19

Snakes and Ladders and Somewhere in the Middle

(Bridgette)

Ouroboros: emblematic serpent of ancient Egypt and Greece represented with its tail in its mouth, continually devouring itself and being reborn from itself. An agnostic and alchemical symbol, ouroboros expresses the unity of all things, material and spiritual, which never disappear but perpetually change form in an eternal cycle of destruction and re-creation.

- Jung

Trauma is a time traveller, an ouroboros that reaches back and devours everything that came before.

– Junot Diaz

I can finally see the patterning of what I now have decided to call the 'Collective Abandonment Syndrome.'

Collective Abandonment Syndrome is an abuse syndrome

initially implemented by the 'other' and which eventually becomes a repetitive action from the 'me' due to a full necessity and integral self-permission state of beingness for survival – to protect oneself from being rejected again. Not just this, but also, from the full self-proclaimed sabotage – which meant that I could never go for what I truly wanted, and which had impacted any future relationship improvements, the ability to have a life I love, and to never be living as my true nature or being the best version of myself.

This Collective Abandonment Syndrome was ruling over me, across the entire board game of my life.

I was cast out of my biological family as a newborn, then again later as an adult, and I needed to protect myself and my son by estranging myself from my adoptive family and biological family. But I had been so focused on self-preservation I couldn't see the forest for the trees anymore. What is worse, I compromised where I shouldn't have. For example, I was so busy preserving my inner child that I wasn't looking out for the adult self at all.

At the end of every exhausting day, all I wanted was to be able to put my love somewhere. I had so much love to give but nobody seemed to want it.

As mentioned, I had reached the point at half a century of age here, and I felt overdue like a lost library book that nobody knew was missing. It was costing me not to let go of the past, but I needed to tidy up a few things. The constant niggling, like the temptation to tear off that loose skin sticking up to attention at the side of the fingernail beds, or a hardened scab – I knew I had to just pick it. I thought the wound and the need for healing would all have gone away by now. As hard as I had tried to distract and dissuade, I couldn't deny to myself that I needed to obtain final closure with a few important people. I had held it off for too long.

In no order of urgency, this meant I had to deal with the following:

a) Potential reconciliation with my birth mother, Jan.

b) Finding my paternal half-sisters.

c) Grieving, forgiving, and healing from so many who had abandoned me, had died or from whom I was still estranged.

* * *

I attended a family constellations workshop for a weekend, interstate. I was one of 100 or so eager students sitting at a table of 10, eyes darting, diverting. I was here to work on my self-acceptance, my forgiveness of family, and family healing. *Now, where was the door again?*

After listening to the twentieth person breaking down on the microphone, sharing their heartfelt grief of not belonging and having some sort of identity crisis, I suddenly felt incredibly inspired. Of course I was comparing.

That day, I decided I was going to reach out to my birth mother, Jan. We hadn't spoken in years after she texted me telling me I didn't 'exist', that she only has two sons, and to please leave her alone. Call me stupid, but I was in a sunny enough mood to override my fear of being hurt again. My superconscious self told me to stop playing small, and to just find a way to ask her if she wanted a new beginning – or, at the very least, to have a more dignified, healing closure. I have had so many non-closures in my life that I figured it was time for one. Plus, I seemed to be coping pretty well with such ruin-ness and debauchery compared to everyone here in the workshop with me. Everyone else's problems seemed easy to deal with, and miniscule compared to what I had been through. What could go wrong?

As I mentioned way back in Chapter 11, I reached out to my birth uncle Tom, Jan's brother, on the first day of this workshop. I asked him if he would please reach out to her on my behalf to see if she might be open to communicating with me again. Tom and his wife, Maude, had always been okay with me, and likewise I, with them, even after what happened at Gala's funeral, where I felt Uncle Tom was using me as the scapegoat. As the only remaining patriarch in the family, he had started sending me Christmas wishes each year after her funeral. He was the one person I figured carried some weight and who could best help forge a connection between his sister and me.

I hadn't heard back from him, and it was now day three of my family constellation conference. I was feeling amped up, floating high on the unlimited possibilities of how wonderful life can be if you believe it to be. Then later that morning, I read the reply that finally came back from Uncle Tom: 'Hi, hope you are well. We do not understand your issues with Jan, and Maude and I do not wish to get involved. All the very best, Tom and Maude.' (No 'Uncle and Aunt' *this* time).

Furiously, I scribbled out their names on the thick red piece of paper that we had each been issued on day one, a 'forgiveness list.' I added them to my already long list of people I needed to forgive today. I had nearly run out of ink and space on that paper, along with my positive, upbeat 'I can do anything because life is so wonderful' mindset. I couldn't deny my irritation and extreme anger at him. It was now burning up the waters of me; I felt the heat of my unworthiness and my insignificance boiling up into my veins, eating my life force up like the snake with its tail, destroying every shiny new belief system I had paid for that weekend.

I felt the hot iron of the branding of abandonment once again, like a birthmark. Adoption really is an invisible birthmark that tortures the soul, and that day, I was reminded of my place in this world – an outcast of insignificance and unworthiness and no new belief system of the opposite seemed to be able to breathe itself into me for a very long time after that.

Down the ladder I fell.

✳ ✳ ✳

It took me around six months later to decompress from my defeat, let alone to feel ready to respond to Uncle Tom.

I met up with my friend Bev, one of my wise women in my tribe, to discuss the matter and to glean some advice. It was a hot summer's afternoon, and more than a breeze was blowing, but still, it was a better option than sitting in a humid café with ceiling fans attempting to relieve the hint of stench of perspiring patrons. I asked the duty manager to ensure Bev was looked after before I could settle into our meeting. She ordered a latte; I ordered another glass of wine.

'Look Bridge, whatever you do next, I would just reach out to see if your Uncle Tom might be willing to reconsider helping you.'

Oh, the faith people have in others. Hopefulness had set into her eyes along with her answer, and whilst I greatly appreciated her advice, her words had clicked me over into understanding the truth of how I was feeling – she had helped me unlock what I w*asn't* prepared to do.

Feeling totally undervalued by my uncle, I was becoming undone, and that was the signal for *Sam* to be unleashed – she wasn't taking any more of this bullshit from this side of the family. She had waited in the shadows long enough.

Like clockwork when in times like these, Sam woke me up in my head around three o'clock that next morning – in a sweat, hair sticking to my forehead, pyjamas drenched, heart pounding and a thirst in need of quenching. My panic attack was the signal that it was time to release the starving maternal bloodhounds inside of me. From harsh lessons finally learned, I knew to choose my words carefully – out of self-respect more than anything. By six that morning, watered and fed with a second Nespresso and Vegemite on toast, in a fresh change of pyjamas, I was more than ready to open the gate and let those heaving dogs out.

This is what my uncle would have read that morning on Facebook messenger – and you know how you know when they've read it:

'It is out of a mix of shock…and respect for myself that I have taken my time to respond to your last message to me. I asked you for help to see if Jan would be open to having a conversation with me, for you to simply just ask her the question. As the patriarch, you are the only person on my maternal side of the family whom I thought I could

trust to help me. But instead, you dismissed me, saying you do not want to get involved. As my uncle, you always have been involved; you are involved by default. But you are doing the same thing you did when I was a baby – once again, by not getting involved.

I am pretty sure this maternal family motto is 'we do not get involved.' You all threw me out as a newborn, instead of fighting to keep me, let alone to ensure my future safety and well-being, and now you are throwing me out again as an adult. You and your parents and your sister have had complete rule and power over my whole life by casting me out and leaving me for dead, to be abused and abandoned in an orphanage or by a family of strangers.

I really don't know how you all can live with yourselves. How could you do that to a baby, let alone a baby of your bloodline? Do you all have no conscience? No fear of consequence? Judging by your response to me, you are obviously protecting your sister. That's fine, but I am now not interested in any living member of this family. I am about to launch my memoir chronicling my entire experience of being adopted out. No stone will be left unturned. Don't worry – you all won't be named, but perhaps you might like to let your sister know?

I can forgive – but I never forget. You can all shut me out, but you can't shut me up. It is now **my** turn to walk away.'

Ahhhhh...the ease of sending back a powerful, life-changing message on Facebook messenger! I blocked all of the maternal family from my Facebook that morning, cousins and all. It was the right thing to do; they had never been interested in my life or the well-being of my son. I closed the door on all of them and hoped to soon be ready to forgive, but I went back to my place in the middle of that Jacob's ladder, because there was still work to do with my goal to find more of my missing family, whom I might not want in my life either – or who may reject me first. It's a risk I seem to be always willing to take in this game of Snakes and Ladders.

I had wanted to find my sisters Liz and Roxy as soon as I found out about them – they were the last two missing members of my family that I knew about – and had yet to finish searching for them. Roxy is three years older than me and Liz is eleven years older. Roxy was impossible to find – there were hardly any clues – so I decided to search for Liz. With her first name and her adoptive last name, a rough location of birthplace and her birth mother's full name, I finally found her after a sporadic five-year search. This time it was on ancestry.com, from a newspaper clip of the death of her adoptive grandfather. From there I contacted each person at the funeral via social media, inquiring about Liz.

My paternal aunt, uncle, and grandparents had known of her. They knew her when she was a baby because my father and Liz's mother were married. My paternal grandmother had kept in touch with her until she was about 17 years of age, but of course, she was kept a secret in general from the rest of the family. My first cousins where vaguely aware of her existence, but only when they were all adults. Out of the three of us girls, Liz was the only one of my father's children that anyone knew about.

Not only were my entire paternal family relying on me to find her a few years back, they also offered me no further or current information of her whereabouts. They simply didn't know. Or maybe one of them did. Oh, *this ladder of mine to climb in this tiresome game of Family Snakes and Ladders!*

Of course, I obviously really wanted to find Liz – not just for

CHAPTER 19

myself, but for my paternal family. I won't lie; my fantasy was to have a big sister who would nurture me and love me in the way that only a big sister could. And now apparently, I had two! Two sisters whom I dreamed would love me in the way I needed to be loved. Whom I could look up to. Whom I could depend upon and who could help me feel 'real', safe, loved, thought about. Someone to say, 'Hey, I've got you kid' and 'It's all going to be okay.' I wanted them to fill the empty sink hole in my body, heart, and soul. And down that snake I slid.

I found Liz, but she wasn't anything I wanted. I was bitten hard, with utter disappointment, and the venom eroded my fantasy of my 'ideal sister' and poisoned my heart towards her. Sad and unwell, Liz had lived a life of unhealthy choices. Mentally fragile. Physically fragile. Unintelligent and seemingly void of emotion, personality, drive, passion, or presence. She was stunted by her inability to get over what I thought were the dumbest of things, like what colour to paint her nails today – meaningless 'stuff.' I would have been able to fulfil my true potential, had I had the life *she* had.

But she managed to lose herself long ago – and she wasn't about to find herself now.

My sister Liz had the life I never had. Her birth mother didn't give her away like mine did – she didn't throw her away as an inconvenience or despise her because she reminded her of our father, Ron. Sure, Liz's mum had married our father, and he cheated on her repeatedly, and she divorced him, leaving her as a single mother raising a baby in the 1960s. Still, *her birth mother kept her*; even though our father never supported her emotionally, financially, or physically. Her birth mother kept her and gave her a good life filled with the gift of a new, loving father, younger half-siblings, grandparents, extended family, friends, the comforts of home, and a very comfortable lifestyle and all of the education and opportunities she desired.

Her birth mother kept her, loved her all of her life, *and* still does. Perhaps I am jealous of her for that. Well of course I bloody am!

One lucky girl is Liz, and yet, she still managed to destroy herself. That's the other stinging point – imagine if she had lived my life? She certainly would not have survived it. I just couldn't feel sorry for how she ended up, considering all of the support and love she had around her. But some of her family say she is schizophrenic; some say she is bipolar. What does Liz say? Not much. We have nothing in common, we look nothing alike, and whilst she is probably a lovely person, I have no time for her. I would not get anything in return, and I don't have anything left in the tank for that.

I do know now that I am not obliged to be there for anyone – to give myself to them – in exchange for nothing. I don't want to people-please, babysit, or to spoon-feed; I've had enough of that. I don't want to 'do' Monday morning phone calls each week. I didn't sign up to this catering role, serving my sister, for the rest of my life, a sentence of sisterly obligation. I am happy to have found one missing sister to help me complete the last few pieces of the jigsaw and to introduce her to my cousins and uncle. And I did.

The fantasies are over the minute you meet your first family in person. It's like any new person you meet – when you meet face to face, you decide whether you actually like them and if they are worthy of your time, energy, and commitment. You weigh up the pros and cons for keeping them in your life or to simply just make up an excuse to walk away.

Well, this time I chose to walk, just like I had done with my maternal family and adoptive family of fuckwits.

Liz and I kept in touch for around a year, but now we have both moved on. I'm really happy that she has met her extended paternal family and can learn more about her paternal grandparents. But I doubt she is really all that interested.

Liz, you are welcome. One thing in this game of 'search and rescue' – I obviously don't do it with the expectation of being thanked. It's a thankless and heart wrenching job.

Such a sad outcome, but at least we've all met her. 'Hey, thanks Bridgette, good one!'

* * *

The real kicker came when I finally found my other big sister, Roxy.

She is *so* much like me. We have the same sense of humour – we even laugh the same way – and we have eerily similar voices and styles of communication, facial and hair features, and more. We chatted over the phone for hours on end, shared pictures, and even arranged for her to visit soon after I found her. But suddenly, she sent a text to me and said that this was all too much for her and she decided that she didn't have room for me or my son in her life.

Huh?

So, out of all the family I grew up with and all the biological family I have found – that is over 40 people – I can only count on one hand whom I am currently in a positive, thriving, healthy relationship with. But remember, my true goal was just to find them – minus any expectation of us liking each other. That was a bonus! (Big love to those family members who are reading my book!)

☀ ☀ ☀

When I am existing in the greatness of my being, I imagine that I am the conduit between our Mother Earth and our Sky Father. I see myself as a warm, vibrant, golden ladder that connects these two extraordinary worlds. In one world, I am physically nourished and protected by a feeling of belonging and realness, rooted into the ground. My wants, needs, and desires are fulfilled each day through my 'Earth Mother.' I can finally have the life I love, and time to relax, nourish myself, and rest.

In the other world, I am spiritually inspired and enlightened, transformed to create my desired reality. I am connected to my superconscious self – trusting completely that I will be protected, guided, and mentored through my 'Sky Father.'

I imagine that I am held in the space between. I can create like an alchemist, yet still be able to rest in the arms of the Mother, meditating and transcending the three-dimensional world deeply and safely. There is no disconnect from the two. If I remember to both ground myself *and* protect myself with light – to stay connected to the universal, creative realms of the superconscious and to sit in the comfort of knowingness that Mother Earth will provide her support and nourishment

– then all is well. At any time, I can consciously choose to believe that the Earth and the sky are my real parents who I can turn to whilst I am on my little sojourn in three-dimensional human form.

This helps me to realign with who I truly am: *a spiritual being on a human journey.* I am up and down along the ladder, receiving everything I need to live a life I love, living between the Earth and the sky.

But of course, there *is* the fact that I am just a mere mortal with massive sabotaging belief systems, and my actual ladder is more like that beastly Jacob's ladder my personal trainer punishes me with at the gym. The higher I attempt to climb, the more I lose my balance, feel nauseous with motion sickness, and become easily fatigued, never reaching the top. The neurological looping repeats itself metaphorically; I can't sustain the energy one requires to move up into my transformation. I am forever cast back down to the earthly realms without a feeling of belonging here, thrown off the edge. Just like the board game, you can suddenly slide down the snake from the random yet repetitive consequence of the simple landing of the dice. *How random is it? Is it all pre-destined? Free will or chance? And who is really casting the dice?*

I've spent more time in the snake pit for these last 50+ years, and I am starting to wonder and really question *why.*

Ouroboros. Snakes. According to Hindu mythology, the head of the snake is called Rahu, and the tail is called Ketu (pronounced 'Cato') – they are known as 'shadow planets' in Vedic astrology. Over a Zoom call, my astrologer conveyed to me that I have resided on Earth in Ketu throughout much of my existence, blindly navigating my way from the tail end, unable to climb up to ride the head of Rahu – instead, I found myself thrashed into unforeseen karmic obstacles and delays. And just like I couldn't see my chosen lifetime of doom, my karma was also doomed to be invisible for the outside world to see, or ever compute, what I was going through internally. I didn't make it obvious either – until I wrote this memoir – so it looked like I had nothing untoward to complain about.

I have spent the last 50 years in my make-believe, futile, helplessness of existence, too afraid to reach for the top and even more afraid of reaching rock bottom, exhausting myself every day to survive somewhere in the middle. Hanging onto the middle of the ladder for fear of falling or rising, I was poisoned from the beginning - in a state of the rebirth of trauma on repeat – returning to the start of my timeline. I have learned that for some of us, we keep proving we can survive, by re-creating events to demonstrate that we can just play the same programming we learnt, from the ages of zero to eight to survive – to justify our existence as an adult. Forever trying our hardest to simply connect to another whilst switched on to survival mode in feelings of mistrust. We quickly over-ride everything to do with trust though, because we just need to connect. Trust is something for somebody else.

Read that last paragraph. Again.

The Experience of Trauma –> Survival –> Abuse from Others to Prove to Self You Can Survive It –> Rinse and Repeat.

Writing part three of my memoir is a most complicated task for me, but it will introduce you to me – the authentic 'unadopted' me – hopefully, it will introduce you to unlimited possibilities.

CHAPTER 19

The old me doesn't like that one little bit – she doesn't know any differently of course...

The new *me*, who was never allowed to be honoured with being identified legally as my first and given name of *Bridgette*, is now finally sitting at the *head* of the snake and riding it full throttle into my future. From writing my memoir, working on forgiveness, retraining as a transformation coach, and studying resource therapy, I was beginning to see clearly through the foggy gaslighting bullshit of my past and attract in the happiness that was stolen from me. I was brainwashed by my adoptive mother and was a victim of psychological, physical, and sexualized abuse. It is now crystal clear to me how inhumanely I was treated as a newborn, as a child, then as an adult right through to discovering in my 50s when I discovered that I was jilted out of my legal inheritance.

I am happy to say that I am no longer ruminating over being disowned by my biological parents and family members, or suffering the trauma of forcing to estrange myself from my adoptive family for my mental wellbeing. I have come to accept that the majority of my adoptive and biological family were just snakes in my board game of life, and that the rolling of the dice wasn't just by chance but was already planned for me by God/The Divine Creator.

I will say though, if God really is the creator of all things, then he really is one twisted, masochistic, sadistic motherfucker. Isn't that right Damian! If I can forgive those that have trespassed against me, then I can forgive God too. And vice versa.

After 50 years, I have now found every member of my family who belong on my newly created and very own tree, and the outward search and rescue for all lost ones is finally over. I can now finally focus on being here just for me, my son, and my loved ones, and for my future generations. I can create a better future now.

Unlike me, when my future grandchildren are old enough to be curious, they will at least now know their family lineage from their father, my son. A lineage which was destined (or not?) to be erased and kept hidden as a secret forever. I am no longer angry about it, or grieving it, but I am writing this book for myself and my future generations, and so that I can finally move forward and have a better future.

I do it in the hope that I can desist from the transfer of my pain onto future relationships, diverting attracting in the same abusers in different disguises, and not attracting in abandoners due to my poor-quality control.

The *ouroboros* is finally at the head of the ladder and staying there as much as she possibly can. At times it still is a fight to not fall into the past patterning and programming to once again destroy herself. But that is completely understandable now.

Coach Charlie:

Forgiveness is the sacred ceremony of goodbye toward those whom you are estranged from, and for closure with those who have cut you out. It is the letting go of disenfranchised grief, and it gifts you with the self-assurance and self-acceptance, to enable you to thrive instead of just survive.

What beliefs do you hold? How do they affect the hold over your values? How do they impact your values? When we start to look at how much we are shifting and changing in our lives, we can't help but do an audit on our values. Inadvertently we inherited our ancestral beliefs, our family bloodlines, our family constellations. But did you know that you can be the first person to break these systems for your future generations? You can be free of these systems and subpersonalities and aspects of seven generations are passed down to you – but you need to get your mindset educated and do the work. And trust me, it isn't for the fainthearted.

No wonder it is such an impossible overwhelming task that you would prefer to leave in the procrastination corner of your life. But you are here to smash through those unwanted boundaries, to shift into uncovering all these parts of yourself, to uncover the true essence of self to reveal your true value systems and true belief systems.

Your simple life plan evolves from here – free of the past – to create a life you love. What does it look like? How would it feel? What would be different in your life?

As you start to review your life and look at such concepts to recode and reinvent your new life, you are changing the structure of your life. What is the old structure and old systems you hold on to? How are they keeping you stuck and not moving forward?

The alchemy is turning the lead of the past into the gold of your future. You pre-send your future from your past so of course it feels like nothing has changed in your old mindset, but the very fact that you are reading this has created the change inside of you by confirming that you were already desiring this change – as this moment has been 'pre-sent' from your past. Trippy stuff, right?

We can now create our new desired reality, based on a new construct of how we want to live. Imagine now, being without your past – release and let go and choose to value love, success, connections, deep trust, honest relationships, inner calm, peace, happiness, joy, acceptance, and forgiveness. Above all else – you choose to value yourself now, above the past loss, shame, and blame.

Your subconscious beliefs *will* fight with you – these are old programs that will show up to prevent you from actioning your goals and will force you to just give up. Answer me this: What is your big dream and purpose here on Earth? Why were you born? How are you going to get to the 'I want'? How do you move out of your current reality into your desired reality?

When you picked up this book, what was your vision or your goal from doing so? What was your big dream? To heal? To gain insight? To feel understood? To feel supported? To be encouraged to also write about your own similar experiences? What is stopping you? What is the next aligned action step to live out your big dream? Without that next step – you will never arrive there. How about choosing the end result of where you want to be, first?

Start with spending time each day meditating on the four core end results that I have covered earlier. Write these on Post-it notes and recite them every morning as if you already have this, feeling what it is like to live in these end results, as that will help you to shift out of old conditioning and into new beginnings:

1. I choose the end result of living a life I love.
2. I choose the end result of health and vitality.
3. I choose the end result of being the predominant cre-

ative force in my life.
4. I choose the end result of living and expressing my true nature and purpose.

We want all of these things, but without healthy value systems, it is nearly impossible to take the first step or any steps afterwards; you need to release the from bungy cord of the neurological looping.

You are a creative spiritual being. Afterall, you created a life to bring you here today to read this! That means you are ready! You are acknowledging the true power of who you are. You *are* the predominant creative force of your life!

Release from the old values that you were conditioned to believe in, and which limited you, and create a new list of values for yourself. You will 'pre-send' these imprints of values to be present in these values and feelings whenever you recite them! You will tap into being bigger than your physical body and just sit in your heart and be connected to all the good that there is. You will hold the power to create whatever you want, stepping into this amazing spiritual creative force, with these true values and valuing yourself. You can now shift and change into living these values – stepping into this power – by reciting and recoding your mindset each day. The more you step into feeling you are being this, the more you become it!

HIGHER SELF VALUES

1. I value my existence and my unfolding true purpose and true nature.
2. I value that I am the alchemist, leaving the past behind and creating a life I love.

3. I value the feelings that are rightfully mine to give me the life I want and to honour who I am.
4. I value my body and all that it does to support my life.
5. I value my incredible capabilities to create everything that I dream is possible.
6. I value that I am a creative spiritual being.
7. I value myself and I love myself and I forgive myself.
8. I value my ability to forgive those who have trespassed against me.
9. I value that I can create a life I love.
10. I value loving and respecting myself.
11. I value deep trust and honesty from myself and from others.
12. I value being highly successful with what I am passionate about.
13. I value my wisdom, my knowledge, and my deep understanding.
14. I value my higher self, self-love, and self-respect.

Author's Note: When we start to take care of all the struggle by facing it, and getting the right help required, by stepping into the ability to let it (person, place, habit, thing) go - we can truly change who we were, into who we potentially are.

Big hugs to you,
Coach Charlie X

CHAPTER 20

Completion

(All in)

I booked a writing retreat in Ubud, Bali in order to complete this manuscript. About a month before my departure, the thought suddenly crossed my mind that there was still one part of my life that wasn't anywhere to be found in my adoption file. I have grown to respect the universal order of 'divine timing,' and it was no coincidence that as I inched closer and closer to finishing my book, I had suddenly run out of time and excuses, for not dealing with this final missing piece of my life's complex puzzle.

I had no idea where I had been living during the first three to six weeks of my life. (I say three to six weeks because I am still not 100% sure how old I was before I was placed. My adoptive mother told me I was six weeks old when I was issued to her, and the agency said I was three-and-a-half weeks. Who the fuck knows?) After cross-checking my files dozens of times, still thinking I may have somehow simply overlooked this, there was no doubt in my mind that I didn't have any information on my whereabouts during that time. I also didn't have any records of who was responsible for looking after me from the time of my birth to the day they handed me over to my adopters.

Was I ready to face this next missing piece of my history? Of course I was – well, I had to be - for my story, for its completion, literally. I wasn't about to compromise the integrity of my book – either for myself or for my lovely readers – because of the fear of the unknown. That had never stopped me before!

I knew I needed to address this missing part of the puzzle of my life for my story to be complete, so I set a call to action for myself and I sent the New Zealand Government 'Oranga Tamariki Ministry for Children' an email to enquire about this period of time.

This was their response:

> Hi Bridgette,
>
> Sorry for the delay in coming back to you. I have spoken to my colleagues, who described that at the time in which you were born there was no specific legal mechanism for babies who were awaiting to be adopted. They spoke of children remaining in the hospital where they were born and some going to the Karitane Hospital.
>
> If you were a State Ward, there would be documentation on record but there was none located.
>
> Many babies were cared for at the maternity hospitals/wards until they were placed with their adoptive parents, and we can only guess which option occurred as there are no specific notes on your adoption records.
>
> Regards,

CHAPTER 20

Adoption Services
Oranga Tamariki
Ministry for Children, New Zealand

'*No legal mechanism for babies who are awaiting to be adopted?*' There you go – you read it straight from the staff at the Ministry for Children! We had no legal representation, no human rights lawyer, no actual human rights. And I *was* labelled a 'Ward of the State' in other documents.

'*…We can only guess which option occurred as there are no specific notes on your adoption records.*' Another example of their misconduct and malpractice. But it wasn't their fault, it was the fault of the legal system. Right? And remember, I am just voicing an opinion.

I thought I would have been strong enough to cope with their answer either way, but I certainly was not prepared for this utterly disrespectful response. I felt crumpled and discarded; insignificant. Devalued and derailed, that my life meant nothing to them then and nothing to them now.

I will never know where I was housed or who attended to me or how my health was. Did I sleep regularly? Did I feed well enough? Was I allergic to anything? How was I developing? This next question haunts me often: Did somebody abuse me in those first three to six weeks? These questions will never be answered, and I will continue to live out the rest of my life without ever knowing the truth of what happened to me.

I know I am not the only one this has happened to in New Zealand during the Forced and Closed Adoption Act of 1955, let alone being subjected to the continued violation of our human rights to this day as an adopted person.

✳ ✳ ✳

The fear of not knowing what had happened to me was a constant gnawing, during the night especially, and it ground me to the core. Worst of all, I was soon going to discover how this situation created another personality part to take control – let's just call her 'Panic Attack' for now. 'Panic Attack' has certainly popped up before, but only a few times as far as I can remember. This just goes to show that when you are the adopted one on the search for your origins, you should watch your step, because each stone of truth may very well send you over the edge and into a newly triggered and yet very old pathological emotion. And time doesn't heal – how can it? We are always having to return to the past for answers that more often than not, can be brutally painful.

Turns out, I really had a whole lot of parts to bring into a more harmonious way of being, ones that were not only continually violated by the 1955 Closed and Forced Adoption Act of New Zealand, but also the parts that were violated by my birth parents, maternal grandparents and by my adoptive family.

Whilst I knew I was writing this book from the secrets finally unlocked by my newly-discovered personality parts, I wanted to not only understand why and how my brain engineered this – before the axons and dendrites fired and wired together – but why, after years of therapy, I was still so dysfunctionally stuck, in comparison to who I was constantly striving to become.

The answers, I knew, likely lay in the hands of a concept called 'ego state therapy.' I first stumbled across this during my training as a magnetic mind coach.

CHAPTER 20

According to the Australian Institute of Clinical Hypnosis and Psychotherapy, this methodology is described as conceptualizing the ego as consisting of parts – or so-called ego states – different neuro-physiological systems that can become activated in certain situations or contexts. Different life experiences and trauma, cause 'parts' to develop through differentiation and dissociation of the self.

Even with this awareness, I was still mystified as to why I had never been able to move away from these parts of myself that were controlling my life. Over the last 35 years, I have tried literally everything I thought would help me. It is a little embarrassing and exhausting to recount. Are you ready for this? OK, here goes. I have invested my time and money into transcendental meditation, hypnosis, cognitive behavioural therapy, inner child therapy, reiki healings, healing touch therapy; auric cleansing, chakra balancing, chanting, akashic record removal, alien implant removal, detoxes, fasting, an alcohol-free lifestyle, a vegan/vegetarian lifestyle, mindfulness, quantum healing, past life therapy, life coaching, counselling, numerology readings, astrology chart readings, self-love affirmations, and meditations, forgiveness work, retreats (oh so many!), oneness blessing ceremonies, sacred water ceremonies, cacao and kava ceremonies, mushrooms, language of light (speaking in tongues) blessings, emotional freedom technique, yoga, biotherapy, art therapy, Egyptian high priestess healings in the King's Chamber in Egypt, Uluru sunrise healings, homeotherapy, naturotherapy, colour healing therapy, chakra dancing, talk therapy...everything except walking on fire! And I know from my best friend that her walk through coals on fire didn't give her the tools she was seeking to make significant changes in her life either.

Desperate as I was, and as frustrated as I was with throwing money around to seemingly pay for these people's mortgages, my research finally led me to 'resource therapy,' the genius work of Dr Gordon Emmerson. It was here that I found my eureka moment. I connected with his teachings semantically and structurally; his acute understanding of the purpose behind the creation of these interesting personality parts of mine resonated with me. I felt seen, heard, and held for the first time. Seriously.

Why? I learned that resource therapy is an empowering psychotherapy based on the understanding that the personality is composed of parts, and the part that presents an issue in therapy is seldom the part that needs change; therefore, therapy is often not as effective as it could be. I felt held because this resonated with me to the bone and because I knew I wasn't crazy or suffering from dissociative identity disorder – according to resource therapy I just had many parts just like everybody else – adopted or not! I felt validated for the first time! Was resource therapy the answer my parts were searching for? I was beginning to think so, yes!

Was I now able to begin the unpacking behind the mystery of their 'emotional states'? Yes. But it is one thing to identify these parts, and another to know where they originated from. I hadn't really explored or played behind the scenes with each state, and I really wanted to work one-on-one with a trained resource therapist. I wanted to identify with each state – in what I learned Dr. Gordon Emmerson would label as a 'pathological' resource state (a part that is emotionally or behaviourally unhealthy) – to finally bring the state into a more cohesive, normal condition. I felt I was truly on the verge of an even deeper up-levelling for the personal transformation that I needed to complete this final chapter of the story of my past – and therefore I would need the right support and the right level of professional supervision to do so safely.

I took a leap of faith, and I decided to go all in on my quest. I signed up to attend a 10-day clinical resource therapy intensive training and counselling supervision course in Ubud, Bali, which happened to coincide with my writing retreat I'd booked during June 2024! *(I can hear what you are thinking, I am psychic remember?)* Yup I invested more time and money into yet another course. But in all fairness, I had already been concerned that I would need a little distraction from the day-to-day grind of just writing, eating, meditating, sipping cocktails, and swimming on my lonesome. (And I do know how ungrateful that sounds!) To be trained up by the president of Resource Therapy International, and founder and CEO of the Resource Therapy Institute Australia, psychologist Philipa Thornton, and her husband, co-founder of the Resource Therapy Institute and psychologist Christian Paulin, learning all about resource therapy for 10 days was a timely and mind-blowingly serendipitous opportunity that I just had to sign up for.

In these short 10 days, I learned more about myself and the parts that needed to change than through all the years and money spent anywhere else. Why? Because resource therapy focused on the parts who had been comfortably hiding behind the parts that would show up for therapy!

The presenting part that turns up for therapy is usually

reporting or complaining about another part of themselves – the part that gets anxious, or the part that cannot stop eating sugary food isn't the part that seeks therapy; it's the part that wants to be calmer or healthier that seeks help. Have you ever thought, 'I should do some exercise,' only to have another part of you say, 'It's been a long day, I should just relax on the couch instead or reward myself at the pub with friends.'

The resource therapist is able to skillfully bring the part of the personality that needs change, up to the surface and into the therapeutic process, to speak with it compassionately and respectfully so that it can be worked with directly. Resource therapy facilitates a quicker, deeper, and longer-lasting change when the right part is understood and addressed properly.

My methodology as a magnetic mind coach focuses the client to step into their desired state of reality with the question, 'What do you want to create?' The resource therapist focuses the client into the purpose of the session by using one simple question at the start: 'So, what is it that you want to change?' A simple, yet powerful question focusing on connecting to the part that wants to change.

Resource therapy focuses on what *isn't working* in one's life right now, and magnetic mind focuses in on what one *wants to have* in their life right now. The two modalities have equal weight in importance, but they can't create the desired result without each other, in my opinion. I have personally tried and tested each modality, and I have discovered that magnetic mindset coaching and conscious creating will NOT be successfully actioned without the client being in the right resource state – just as resource therapy sessions cannot demonstrate 'change' without the client taking the next obvious action step through the new lens of change. The two are the missing parts in and of themselves.

As a magnetic mind coach, I was overstepping the obvious. I wasn't engaging in working with the part of the personality the client wanted to 'change/fix/heal/recode/find' as a new resource part to consciously captain the ship of their life.' And, as a resource therapist, I wasn't engaging in setting up an 'action' to follow up with the new part that had been activated (the part that wanted change), in order for the client to be a conscious creator of such a change.

* * *

At the training course in Bali, I learned that the guardians of the traumatic chapters of my life you have read about and heard from – Sam, Kaiyah, Amy, Georgiana, Bridgette and Coach Charlie – are actually called 'resource states.' These resource states had developed from the parts of my brain (dendrites and axons) that were firing and wiring the repeated feelings of unwanted emotions which in turn were creating unwanted behaviours from the womb to primarily around eight years of age. No doubt they also were strengthened in their fear, confusion, disappointment, and rejection from ongoing repetitive coping skills with recurring feelings I endured as an adult. They were operating as separate parts of the whole of me, and they did a tremendous job in being the reporter of these pivotal events that you have now read about, from my timeline of my lived adoption experiences, consequences, and evaluations. So, in other words, the personality of you is composed of certain parts, and those particular parts are your 'resources'.

You have already met my personality parts, but I learned that each part (aside from Coach Charlie) was actually a 'vaded' pathological state. 'vaded' - means they are not 'emotionally healthy' parts. These parts were created early on to assist me to cope with difficult situations and people. In resource therapy there are four main 'vaded' unwanted emotional states:

1. Vaded in Fear – nightmares/terrors, panic attacks, OCD, fear of something in the past and the thought that it is still real, anxiety, dissociation, addictions, workaholism, and PTSD.
2. Vaded in Rejection – social phobia, the feeling of being unwanted or unlovable or not good enough, the feeling of being an imposter/fake, the seeking of approval, the compulsion to be a people pleaser, and over-competitiveness.
3. Vaded in Disappointment – depression, blame, prolonged and intense feelings of loss, the feeling that life isn't going to plan, lack of energy, and detachedness from life.
4. Vaded in Confusion – guilt, shame, complicated bereavement and endings of relationship breakdowns, existential angst, and rumination over not letting a thought go about a person or event.

These are pathological states, or 'coping skills,' that can be problematic in one of two ways:

Vaded Conscious: These states come into the conscious mind and exhibit their unresolved emotions in the form of anxiety, panic, and/or withdrawal.

Vaded Avoided: These states come into or close to the conscious mind and then are immediately driven from the conscious by a retro avoiding state in the form of a behaviour like OCD, eating disorders, and addictions – basically any behaviours that the resource states do not like and want to stop. This can include anti-social behaviour such as pouting, passive-aggressive behaviour, and personality disorder behaviour.

The process of resource therapy is to bring back ALL states to normality. For example, if the resource state is *vaded in fear*, the normal state one must return to is enjoying being in the conscious awareness and focusing on what is around them, not on a negative feeling. If the resource state is *vaded in rejection* – one must have positive feelings about themselves, enjoy their time in the conscious, and feel like they have a lot to offer. If the resource state is *vaded in disappointment*, to return to the normal state one must enjoy life and celebrate the happiness of the other states. And if the resource state is *vaded in confusion*, one must let the past stay in the past and experience inner peace and stay in the present moment with their focus.

Until all states return to normality, they will act out with 'Retro State Conditions,' (like excessive drinking, addicted to online shopping, eating too much/not eating at all, smoking, sex addictions, gambling, etc.) – which are unwanted behaviours that are also hidden away from our conscious awareness. Our behaviour is our highest form of communication from ourselves into the world around us whether we are conscious of it or not.

Let's play a little game to help you connect the dots. Which of the four vaded states (Vaded in Fear, Rejection, Disappointment or Confusion) are my parts stuck in?

Sam guardian/protector/angry/ruthless/independent/bullish/narcissistic/addictive/abusive part – sometimes takes on the energy of my adoptive mother when I am out of control and drink too much. I act as 'her' to continue punishing myself on her behalf and hurt anyone else who tries to love me.

Vaded in _____

Amy – She is a positive, upbeat cheerleader who ignores feelings, is selfless to the point of dehumanizing her own self-worth and needs to make everyone else feel better and keep them happy.

Vaded in _____

Georgiana – servant/slave/people pleaser, a perfectionist for other's needs. Though she is ruled by her head, she ignores own needs and feelings and can become a chameleon, merging and taking on the energy of somebody she needs to win over – to be praised and adored by them to avoid rejection.

Vaded in _____

Kaiyah – She is a spiritual escape artist. A spiritual gaslighter who bypasses all of her problems with proclamations that the Divine/God/Goddess will work everything out and therefore, she doesn't really need to take responsibility for the mess her life is in. She is too scared to be that grounded in the physical world.

Vaded in _____

Bridgette – The sum of all parts and yet never permitted to exist, Bridgette was forgotten, forced to live in the shadows and smashed into pieces and her identity stolen. Until first we saw her that day in the manila folder. The baby and the mother, the wounded and the healer, the dark and the light, and the lost and the found.

Vaded in _____

If you guessed these parts were 'Vaded in Fear or Rejection,' you are correct. Of course, Bridgette was vaded in all core four – coded up in the womb by the rejection of my birth family and the abandonment at birth, which created fear and confusion. The damage from my adoptive mother created fear, rejection, and confusion too. I now understand that I was also deeply vaded in disappointment, and I hid my depressive state somewhere outside of myself as I wasn't allowed to show sadness, tears, or weakness as a child without my adoptive mother attacking me. I covered that part up in order to protect it.

Now let's do Coach Charlie – Charlie is a life coach, learned and wise. He is the lifeboat, the support, the mentor, the guide, the superconscious coach, the resource therapist, the writer, the reflector, the observer, the generator. He stays grounded in his circle of greatness – which state is he in?

Correct! He is in a *Healthy/Normal Resource State!*

The whole purpose of resource therapy is to bring the vaded states of our childhood wounds into normal, cohesive states now. But just because we are no longer children, that doesn't mean we are no longer affected by developing these similar unwanted emotions and behaviours. Through whichever coping skills we implement after the age of eight and at any time in our adult life, we create a vaded state and usually a retro-avoidant state of unwanted behaviour, which will most likely be more obvious to others because we are usually unaware of it or deny that it is a problem or that we are out of control. But if we are conscious of it, our parts won't like this behaviour at all.

We can also have an incident that suddenly creates a new vaded state or strengthens an existing state that has been dormant in our subconscious mind since the womb and throughout our childhood development. For example, after I received that hideous response from the New Zealand Government's Oranga Tamariki Ministry for Children, wiping their hands clean of their duty of care for me – as a newborn New Zealand citizen –something weird happened.

A day or two later after receiving the email, while I was driving my car in an unfamiliar area on an open road, I had a huge panic attack. I literally couldn't remember which foot I used to brake! I felt like I had disappeared out of the driver's seat and was totally out of control of the car. My wise resource part who remembered how to drive did immediately connect the dots to get me home safe and sound, but I didn't drive anywhere unfamiliar before I left for Bali. I just didn't have the self confidence or assurance that I wouldn't have another panic attack on the open road again.

On day three of the clinical resource therapy course in Bali, I was called up to the front of the room to have a one-on-one session, demonstrating to the class how a somatic memory (how our mind and body can store trauma) can create a vaded state of fear later on in life. I was more than ready to work on this latest part, which I knew had something to do with that letter from the Ministry for Children – and of course, by the abandonment by my mother both before and after she gave birth to me.

When my trainer and supervisor, Philipa, asked me what it was that I wanted to change, I told her that I wanted to change my fear of driving fast in unfamiliar territories. And you guessed

CHAPTER 20

it – the letter from the Ministry for Children triggered a somatic memory of being abandoned and feeling neglected and unsafe in a strange environment. I felt out of control and scared. Knowing the truth of my first three to six weeks of my life was triggering the somatic memory of my birth – my mother wanting me out of her body so fast (speed of the car) and leaving me all alone in a hospital (lost on the roads). When I went into the panic attack, I was a baby crying out for her mother and being sedated to stop my screaming (dissociating from my body in the car when I went into a panic attack on the freeway).

Also, before my session with Philipa, I didn't connect deeply enough into the fact that this vaded state of the fear of driving started 20 or so years ago, around the time when my birth mother decided yet again, that she now no longer wanted me in her life as her adult daughter. It is important to note here, that I had been driving confidently since I obtained my driver's license and bought my first car at the tender age of 16. Right up until around the age of 34, I enjoyed my long, distant drives, driving to unfamiliar places, driving along freeways and at 100 kilometres per hour.

In our session Philipa began a conversation with 'Baby Bridgette,' assuring her that she was safe and protected by the Divine Mother. Through the exercise, she was able to connect all of the dots of where my anxiety and panic started and what age 'Panic Attack' was and who that part was and to give her a voice. Philipa also was able to settle this part into a calm, functioning, relaxed and empowered place - creating a new, healthy resource state.

Apparently, there was not a dry eye in the training room

during my session as my classmates held me in such beautiful compassion and loving energy. I was able to connect to Baby Bridgette, give her the mother part of me that she never had, care for her, nurture her, let her play, and tuck her in safely – allowing her to feel loved, safe and secure. Philipa was also able to connect to the adult mature part that loves to drive. I have been driving back in Australia ever since, and I have felt nothing but confidence driving to new destinations, but I am not yet ready to drive over 100 kilometres yet.

※ ※ ※

I am now qualified to be a resource therapist to help other adoptees like me – quite a phenomenal place I find myself standing in now. My purpose – (to be an author, educator, healer, and therapist, assisting adult adoptees who were not only victims of a forced and closed adoption, but who were also issued into abusive adoptive homes) – had been hidden from me, elusively prompting me to never stay 'there' long enough for my purpose to land, for anything to 'stick.'

Right now, as I sit here planning when to launch this book, all parts of me are united in agreement. We feel a mix of trepidation and excitement, knowing that I have finally exposed the truth of what I once worked so hard at to keep so well hidden. My human redemption journey – one I needed to expose and need to let go of now.

I refuse to waste my life trying to fix or feel responsible for something that I didn't break.

I choose to be a conduit and light between the narrative of

the lie of the history of adoption and the true story of my own lived experience. This is the gift I finally gave to myself and now to you – I hope I have inspired you to do the same.

A few years ago, someone said to me that a story told is a life lived, and once you tell it, you have to let it go. So, I hand it over to you now, with the love and faith that you too may feel inspired to write and share your own story – or to hand mine over to someone who is still silenced.

I also want to take this closing time to publicly address the perpetrators:

To the Government of New Zealand Oranga Tamariki Ministry of Children, the Department of Social Welfare/Social Services, my maternal grandparents, my biological parents, my adopted family, and all those who have inflicted harm upon my body, mind, and soul:

You know who you are. Your actions have caused deep and lasting wounds, but today, I stand before you as a testament to the resilience and perseverance of the human spirit. I have learned to harness the power of words, and through this new strength, I am bringing the truth of the shadows to light.

Your failures to act with integrity and compassion are now laid bare for all to see. The darkness of your deeds can no longer hide in the silence you imposed upon me. By speaking out, I claim my right to justice and demand accountability for the suffering endured.

This is not just my story – this is a call for change, and a demand for the respect and dignity that every human being deserves. The truth will shine through, and it will be heard.

After all, it has just been read and you have all been exposed.

The pain of the past is now a place of reference inside of me, not a place of residence. I encourage you to use the wisdom of your past to navigate the happiness of your future, not its pain. For as we transform, the world transforms.

And now that is all that is left to do.

CONCLUSION

I realize that writing this book is a risk for me on so many levels. There are certain people in this world who may be offended by my story – people in my personal life and people in the adoption community were my initial concern, but then that concern stretched to include people in the scientific community who might be shocked or want to criticize my pseudo-psychological approach and my spiritual and esoteric theories, especially professionals in the field of psychology.

With regards to the adoption community, many may take offense at the way I speak about my adoptive mother, members of my adoptive family, my birth parents, and members of my birth family. They may also take offense to how I refer to myself as an 'adoptee,' or how I use the phrase, 'biological mother.' They may judge me with how I associate my adoption with my spiritual references. Regarding my personal life, many friends, colleagues and family could take offense as to why I have never shared the truth of my past with them, and some will roll their eyes and wonder why I just don't get over my adoption and be grateful for once. Oh, if I had a dime for every time that has been said to me!

But you know what, I have learned that what other people think is none of my business anymore.

I used to be overly concerned about people's opinions, and in the early stages of attempting to write this book (which started many years ago, in fact,) I was caught up with trying to ensure that 'they' would approve of me. Consequently, my writing was censored by my own volition – I lost motivation and eventually my book was shut down. I spent most of my time seeking belonging, connection and acceptance from both my adoptive and birth families, my husband and his family, the adoption community, my psychologists and mentors, work colleagues, clients and my friends. Just to belong and connect became my life's focus instead. It didn't matter about the truth of what had happened to me, or what was true, or anything to do with my feelings at the time. I desperately needed and wanted to establish approval from those closest to me by deliberately *not* speaking about my adoption, as that is what was coded up from my childhood – I had to be silent and perfect and be somebody else to be loved.

I had to pretend to myself and to the world, that my adoption never happened.

And when I finally dipped my first toe in the water, sharing my adoption experiences, I found my concerns were indeed validated by others' reactions. I was judged, gaslit, condemned, unfriended, and discarded and yes, I was told I should get over it and I should be grateful that I was adopted.

But now I have realized, the only way to get over it is to go through it. I also realized that some people are not going to like me no matter who I am, or what I write about.

I could no longer 'people-please' my way out of my soul purpose: to write this book and get it published.

Firstly, I had to learn how to rise above my wounded ego needs for acceptance and approval and just go for it. I had been wasting my energy on keeping myself 'safe, perfect, and silent' for everybody else, and it was wrecking my mental and physical health in so many destructive ways. I was pretending that I was okay about what had happened to me – even creating healing workshops for other adoptees when I was completely in denial of my own suffering.

Only through writing this book have I finally woken up to the true extent of my pain and have realized how important self-awareness and self-healing really is. It also became obvious that my experience and insight could perhaps help someone else like me.

I am no longer interested in denying my pain or hiding my story or being the 'safe, perfect, silenced one.' I am no longer interested in being accepted by pretending to be somebody I am not. I am finally coming to life through my story and, therefore, I am being the person the people closest to me deserve to be finally able to meet.

Whilst writing this was extremely confronting – and eventually, healing – I was encouraged by the hope that my story may inspire you to share your own story of adoption, and to explore your own personality parts. It is my hope as well that it may assist you in understanding what could be going on behind the eyes of anyone you care about who has been adopted.

I am no longer a real nobody or a fake somebody. I am just me.

I stand in the fire of my wounds to light the way for others to see in the dark.

THE END

Thank you for taking the time to read my book! If you enjoyed it, I would greatly appreciate it if you could leave an honest review on Amazon, Goodreads, or any other platform you prefer. Your feedback helps other readers discover books they'll love and makes a big difference. Thank you for your support!

If you would like to keep in touch,
please visit my Facebook profile
(https://www.facebook.com/sherrybridgettehealey)
and follow me.

If you would like to book a free introductory session for yourself or a loved one regarding any of the issues covered in this book related to being an adult adoptee - please visit my website (https://www.thereyouare.life).

RECOMMENDED READING AND RESOURCES

BOOKS:

The Primal Wound: Understanding the Adopted Child by Nancy Verrier

You Don't Look Adopted and To Be Real by Anne Heffron

Being Adopted: The Lifelong Search for Self by David M. Brodzinsky, Marshall D. Schecter, Robin Marantz Henig

Twenty Things Adopted Kids Wish Their Adoptive Parents Knew by Sherrie Eldridge

Lost & Found: The Adoption Experience by Betty Jean Lifton

Healing Tree by Danielle Gaudette

Journey of the Adopted Self by Betty Jean Lifton

Coming Home to Self: The Adopted Child Grows Up by Nancy Verrier

Crazy Bastard: A Memoir of Forced Adoption by Abraham Maddison

All You Can Ever Know by Nicole Chung

Tree of Strangers by Barbara Sumner

The Adoption Constellation: New Ways of Thinking About and Practicing Adoption by Dr. Michael Grande

PODCAST:

Adoptees On: https://www.adopteeson.com/

Jigsaw: https://www.jigsawqueensland.com/adopt-perspective

YOUTUBE:

Paul Sunderland's *Addiction and Discovery*, a lecture on adoption: https://www.youtube.com/watch?v=Y3pX4C-mtiI

Paul Sunderland's *Understanding the Impact of an Early Psychological Wound*, a lecture on relinquishment and adoption: https://www.youtube.com/watch?v=PX2Vm18TYwg

Jeanette Yoffe: https://www.youtube.com/@Jeanette-icallySpeaking

Jennifer McRae, *The Clean Break of Adoption*: https://www.youtube.com/watch?v=6QeZMPQqj3c

FACEBOOK:

Sherry Bridgette Healey: https://www.facebook.com/sherrybridgettehealy. Send me a friend request and join me here, or head to my website www.thereyouare.life and have a consultation with me.

Adopted In Australia: https://www.facebook.com/groups/11911568162

Adoption Sucks: https://www.facebook.com/groups/10484382277

Family Constellations International: https://www.facebook.com/groups/52021062442

Adoptee Rights Action Group: https://www.facebook.com/groups/364375293637544/

Adoptees Speak: https://www.facebook.com/groups/791292877610573

NZ Adoptions 1955 – 1989: https://www.facebook.com/

groups/1647494385532179

Adopted Adults NZ: https://www.facebook.com/groups/625871447891121

Is Adoption Trauma: https://www.facebook.com/IsAdoptionTrauma

Adoption Truth and Transparency Worldwide Information Network: https://www.facebook.com/groups/214366235299424/

SUPPORT SERVICES

Reach out to these support services in the country you are in when required as they can be most helpful in your times of need.

AUSTRALIA:

Beyond Blue: https://www.beyondblue.org.au

Jigsaw Queensland: https://www.jigsawqueensland.com/forced-adoption

LifeLine: https://www.lifeline.org.au

Relationships Australia: https://www.rasa.org.au/support/services/post-adoption-support-services/

Adoptee Rights Australia: https://www.adopteerightsaustralia.org.au

Resource Therapy: https://www.facebook.com/groups/11911568162

NEW ZEALAND:

LifeLine: https://www.lifeline.org.nz/

Health NZ: https://info.health.nz/mental-health/

Adoption NZ: https://www.adoptionnz.com/support

USA:

Adoptees United: https://adopteesunited.org/

American Adoptions: https://www.americanadoptions.com/adoption/adoptee-support-resources

Intercountry Adoptee Voices: https://intercountryadopteevoices.com/post-adoption-support/usa/

UK:

Barnardo's: https://www.barnardos.org.uk/adopt/support-birth-families-adult-adoptees

PAC-UK: https://www.pac-uk.org/our-services/adopted-adults/

Adult Adoptee UK: https://adultadoptee.org.uk/

ACKNOWLEDGEMENTS

To my dear son: Thank you for always checking in, for listening patiently to chapters of my story, and for your unwavering encouragement. Your heart hugs and belief in your somewhat crazy Mumma mean more than words can express. I am profoundly grateful for your patience and for holding space for me to finish this, even when you saw my wounds reopening and wished for it all to stop. It fills my heart with joy to know that your future family will understand the truth of my life through these pages. May my story live on through our descendants. I love you more than words can say.

To my dearest friends: Your willingness to listen, spend time with me, and continuously encourage me has meant the world. Thank you for always being there and supporting me through it all.

To my best friend: Do you really promise that next time, after a few too many glasses of wine, we'll stay on our metaphorical rocket ship? This earthly realm can be a bit of a downer sometimes, huh? I'm so over the moon that we found each other here...again!

To my paternal family, especially my aunt and uncle: You welcomed me in and never kicked me out – this is a first from my family. Obviously, I am so happy to have found such a supporting and welcoming family finally. Unicorn clans do exist!

To my first writing coach, Anjanette Fennell: Seven years ago, you planted the seeds of encouragement that have now grown into this magnificent oak tree. Thank you for believing in me and guiding me when I had no idea where to begin.

To my dear editor and writing coach, Megan Close Zavala: Your unwavering support and accountability made the seemingly impossible suddenly achievable. Without you, this accomplishment would likely have not been possible. Thank you for helping me bring this story to life.

To my superconscious coaches and colleagues and to my resource therapy teachers and colleagues: You have helped me discover my greatness and purpose for the first time. I felt truly held, heard, and seen. Thank you for your profound impact on my journey.

To my inspiring Monday meditation teacher and her wonderful group of meditators: Your compassion and the safe space you provided have been profoundly meaningful. Thank you for holding me with such care and understanding as I shared my writing journey with you all.

To all the brilliant and supportive individuals who took the time to read the manuscript and endorse my book: Thank you for your invaluable feedback and your encouraging words. Your support has been deeply appreciated.

SOURCES

Introduction

Maté, Gabor. *When the Body Says No: The Cost of Hidden Stress.* Vintage Canada, 2003.

Chapter 1

Verrier, Nancy Newton. *The Primal Wound: Understanding the Adopted Child.* Gateway Press, 1993.

Chapter 3

Dolfi, Maria. "Relinquishment Trauma: The Forgotten Trauma." mariedolfi.com, 2022.

Dolfi, Marie. "The Adverse Relinquishment & Adoption Experiences (ARAEs) Assessment Project." *Journal of Adoption & Fostering* 31, no. 4 (2007): 45-5.

Chapter 8

Hellinger, Bert. *Love's Hidden Symmetry: What Makes Love Work in Relationships.* Zeig, Tucker & Theisen Inc, 1998.

Verrier, Nancy Newton. *The Primal Wound: Understanding the Adopted Child.* Gateway Press, 1993.

Chapter 9

Williamson, Marianne. *A Return to Love: Reflections on the Principles of 'A Course in Miracles.'* Harper One, 1992.

Johnson, John C. "Freud and the Early Psychoanalytic Theory of

Adoption." *Journal of Psychoanalytic History* 23, no. 2 (2011): 113-130.

Bowlby, John. *Attachment and Loss: Volume 1: Attachment*. New York: Basic Books, 1969.

Chapter 10

Verrier, Nancy Newton. *The Primal Wound: Understanding the Adopted Child*. Gateway Press, 1993.

Lifton, Betty Jean. *Journey of the Adopted Self: A Quest for Wholeness*. Basic Books, 1994.

Brodzinsky, David M., Marshall D. Schechter, and Robin Marantz Henig. *Being Adopted: The Lifelong Search for Self*. Doubleday, 1992.

Chapter 15

Emmerson, G. (2003) *Ego state therapy*. Crown House Publishing.

Emmerson, G. (2006). *Healthy parts happy self*. [Self-published].

Emmerson, G. (2017). *Resource therapy: The complete guide*. Resource Therapy International.

Chapter 16

Wikipedia: Genetic Sexual Attraction. Wikimedia Foundation, 2023.

Maddison, Abraham. *Crazy Bastard*. Wakefield Press 2023.

Gonyo, Barbara. *I'm His Mother, But He's Not My Son*. Chicago: Atriad Press, 1989.

Westermarck, Edvard. *The History of Human Marriage*. London: Macmillan & Co., 1891.

Oxford English Dictionary. 2011. *Limerence*. Oxford University Press.

Hayes, Nicky. *Foundations of Psychology*. Boston: Cengage Learning, 1994.

Tennov, Dorothy. *Love and Limerence: The Experience of Being in Love*. New York: Stein and Day, 1979.

Gottman Institute. 2018. "The 3 Phases of Love." *Gottman Institute Blog*. Accessed May 5, 2023. https://www.gottman.com/blog/the-3-phases-of-love/.

Wilmott, Lynn, and Evie Bentley. *Exploring Limerence: Reclaim Your Life from the Unhealthy Obsession of Limerence*. London: Routledge, 2017.

McDaniel, Kelly. *Mother Hunger: How Adult Daughters Can Understand and Heal from Lost Nurturance, Protection, and Guidance*. Carlsbad: Hay House, 2021.

McDaniel, Kelly. *Mother Hunger: Surrogate Comfort*. Self-published e-book, 2016.

Chapter 17

Black, Edward. *The Horrifying Medical Roots of Nazi Eugenics*. New York: The Journal of Medical History, 2003.

Hitler, Adolf. *Mein Kampf*. Munich: Franz Eher Nachfolger GmbH, 1925-1926.

Evans, Richard J. *The Coming of the Third Reich*. New York: Penguin Books, 2003.

United States Holocaust Memorial Museum. *Holocaust Encyclopedia*. New Haven: Yale University Press, 2001.

Ploetz, Alfred. *Grundlinien einer Rassenhygiene*. Berlin: Fischer Verlag, 1895.

Galton, Francis. *Inquiries into Human Faculty and Its Development*. London: Macmillan, 1883.

United States Holocaust Memorial Museum. *Brochure for the Lebensborn Program*. Accessed August 17, 2023. https://perspectives.ushmm.org/item/brochure-for-the-lebensborn-program.

Davenport, Charles B. *Heredity in Relation to Eugenics.* New York: Henry Holt and Company, 1911.

Black, Edwin. *War Against the Weak: Eugenics and America's Campaign to Create a Master Race.* New York: Four Walls Eight Windows, 2003.

"Lebensborn Program." *Wikipedia, The Free Encyclopedia.*

Weale, Adrian. *The SS: A New History.* London: Little, Brown, 2010.

Ericsson, Kjersti, and Eva Simonsen, eds. *Children of World War II: The Hidden Enemy Legacy.* Oxford: Berg Publishers, 2005.

Cohen, Nick. "Torment of ABBA Star with a Nazi Father." *The Guardian*, August 22, 2000. Accessed May 5, 2023. https://www.theguardian.com.

Freud, Sigmund. *Mourning and Melancholia.* Vienna: International Psycho-Analytical Press, 1917.

Bowlby, John. *Attachment and Loss: Volume 1: Attachment.* New York: Basic Books, 1969.

Campbell, Helen E. M. R. *Past Forced Adoption Policies and Practices in Australia: It's Time to Make Amends.* Canberra: Australian Government, 2012.

Bowlby, John. *Attachment.* New York: Basic Books, 1969.

Bowlby, John. *Separation: Anxiety and Anger.* New York: Basic Books, 1973.

Bowlby, John. *Loss: Sadness and Depression.* New York: Basic Books, 1980.

West, Ruth L. T. *Past Adoption Experiences.* Melbourne: Australian Institute of Family Studies, 2005.

Australian Institute of Family Studies. *Past Adoption Experiences: National Research Study on the Service Response to Past Adoption Practices.* Melbourne: Australian Institute of Family Studies, 2012.

Legislation - Social Security Amendment Act 1973, No. 117. Wellington: Government of New Zealand, 1973.

Chapter 19

Smith, Alexander P. *The Ouroboros: A Study in the Symbolism of the Serpent Eating Its Own Tail*. New York: Philosophical Library, 1956.

Jung, Carl. *Symbols of Transformation*. London: Routledge, 1956.

Godwin, Joscelyn. *The Alchemical Tradition in the Late Twentieth Century*. Rochester, VT: Inner Traditions, 1991.

Díaz, Junot. *The Brief Wondrous Life of Oscar Wao*. New York: Riverhead Books, 2007.

Chapter 20

Australian Institute of Clinical Hypnotherapy and Psychotherapy. (n.d.). *Ego state therapy*. Accessed May 7, 2023. https://www.aichp.com.au/ego-state-therapy/.

Thornton, P. (n.d.). *Resource therapy intensive training*. Resource Therapy International.

Emmerson, G. (2003). *Ego state therapy*. Crown House Publishing.

Emmerson, G. (2006). *Healthy parts happy self*. [Self-published].

Emmerson, G. (2017). *Resource therapy: The complete guide*. Resource Therapy International.

Sherry Bridgette Healey (birth name 'Bridgette,' adoptive name 'Sherry') is an author, intuitive healer, consultant, facilitator, mindset coach, and resource therapist living in Australia. Sherry helps clients to uncover their identity parts, stepping them into their true potentials and natures to live their lives to the fullest. One of the many victims of the Forced and Closed Adoption Act in New Zealand, Sherry has made it her mission to create global awareness of the violation of our human rights to create a better future and to empower fellow adoptees to heal from the ongoing atrocities of the adoption wounds.

Learn more about Sherry and book in a consultation at www.thereyouare.life and join her on Facebook: www.facebook.com/sherrybridgettehealey.

Printed in Great Britain
by Amazon